A PIECE OF WORK

Five Writers Discuss Their Revisions

A PIECE OF WORK

EDITED BY JAY WOODRUFF

University of Iowa Press
Iowa City

University of Iowa Press, Iowa City 52242

Printed in the United States of America

Design by Richard Hendel

Photo credits: page 7, Jerry Bauer; page 53, Marion Ettlinger; page 99, Lilian Kemp; page 149, Layle Silbert; page 229, Gary Samson

 Printed on acid-free paper.

Library of Congress Cataloging-in-Publication Data

A piece of work: five writers discuss their revisions / edited by Jay Woodruff.

p. cm.

ISBN 0-87745-408-6 (hard), ISBN 0-87745-409-4 (pbk.)

1. American literature—20th century—Criticism, Textual. 2. Authors, American—20th century—Interviews. 3. Authorship. 4. Editing. I. Woodruff, Jay.

PS225.P54 1993 92-39413

810.9'0054—dc20 CIP

97 96 95 94 93 C 5 4 3 2 1

97 96 95 94 93 P 5 4 3 2 1

For Sarah, and Joey, and Sam,

and for my mother, Marcie Woodruff,

who taught me to read

And who, after all these centuries,

can describe the fineness of an autumn

day?

JOHN CHEEVER

"The Brigadier and the Golf Widow"

CONTENTS

ACKNOWLEDGMENTS

I want to thank Tim Disney and Bill Haney for their wonderful help. I am also grateful to the Lyndhurst Foundation for its generous support. Connie Procaccini and the folks at Mulberry Studio in Cambridge, Massachusetts, provided excellent help transcribing audiotapes. Kathleen Manwaring of the special collections office at the Syracuse University Library was generous with her time and suggestions, as was Roland Goodbody of special collections at the University of New Hampshire. I also want to thank Chris Hollern, who works with Robert Coles at Harvard, and Dorothy Catlett, who works with Tess Gallagher. Steve Hill at *Antaeus* and Peter Stine at *Witness* also provided friendly assistance when I needed it.

I am deeply grateful to the writers who agreed to talk with me. The generosity one finds in their work is not limited, I discovered, to their writing.

INTRODUCTION

The debate over whether writing can be taught may not be the most tedious one in the world, but surely it ranks right up there. Most serious writers I've known have only limited interest in such discussions. They're too busy trying to find their way through the poem, story, essay, novel or script gaping up at them from their desktops. Whether or not writing can be taught, this much is for sure: writers with even the most modest ambitions must learn the craft, and they will generally, and gladly, take help wherever they can get it, whether it comes from John Gardner's *Art of Fiction*, E. M. Forster's *Aspects of the Novel*, Rainer Maria Rilke's *Letters to a Young Poet*, Flannery O'Connor's *Mystery and Manners*, Eudora Welty's *One Writer's Beginnings*, a writing class, or some mostly cheesy how-to magazine article.

The best lessons on good writing, of course, are provided by actual first-rate work itself. In order to study precisely how J. D. Salinger believes a story should be written, all anyone has to do is open the pages of *Nine Stories* and start reading. Yet the finished product, especially for young writers, can be daunting, published in all its impressive perfection, seeming to have sprung forth fully formed, like Aphrodite from the foam. Those legends of white-hot inspiration students hear about along the way tend to suggest that great work results from the occasional, random strike of lightning: Samuel Coleridge's dictating "Kubla Khan" from a dream; Ernest Hemingway's completing "The Killers," "Ten Indians," and "Today Is Friday" all in one twenty-four-hour span; Shirley Jackson's mailing "The Lottery" off to the *New Yorker* the same day she wrote it; Jack Kerouac's popping Benzedrine and rigging his typewriter so he could compose *On the Road* in a single sitting.

For young writers stumbling along, trying to keep their agonizing doubts at bay, and struggling to receive what John Cheever described as "an education in economics and love," it is reassuring and instructive to study the privately recorded thoughts of great writers or artists: the letters of Flaubert or Flannery O'Connor or Vincent Van Gogh; the journals and notebooks of Yeats or Chekhov or Virginia Woolf. One of the most illuminating resources available to anyone interested in good writing is the literary interview, the kind that the *Paris Review* pioneered and has popularized for forty years, collected regularly in the *Writers at Work* series. Unlike the journalistic interview, these more generous conversations represent a collaboration with an author, an effort to provide her with every opportunity to express precisely what she wishes to say on the subject of her work and writing life.

I was, in fact, rereading such an interview when the idea for this project occurred to me. "Most writers of my acquaintance," Raymond Carver told the *Akros Review*, "and most writers I know anything about, have been great re-writers. It's instructive and heartening to us all, all of those who want to be writers, to look at the early drafts of the great writers."

This book is intended to provide such an opportunity, a chance to peek over the shoulders of several accomplished writers, to study their drafts and hear them discuss the nuts and bolts of their craft in relation to a particular piece of their work; to follow their descriptions of how they got from initial impulse to final version—the precise moments of illumination, the particular struggles over specific words, sentences, and punctuations. The broad, wide-ranging, traditional literary interview (if it is, indeed, fair to describe a relatively new genre, the literary interview, as traditional) yields tremendously valuable information about a writer's life and work habits. But I hoped that focusing a lengthy discussion on a single piece of work might provide not only a sense of a given writer's general aesthetic but also a greater incidence of the specific examples that enable the reader to see how good writing becomes better.

It's helpful, for example, to come across the kind of dictum John Cheever expressed in his interview with the *Paris Review*: "The first principle of aesthetics is either interest or suspense. You can't expect to communicate with anyone if you're a bore." Yet the young writer struggling to gain some mastery of the craft may benefit even more from the kind of specific example Flannery O'Connor offers in her essay "Writing Short Stories," in which she discusses her great story "Good Country People":

> When I started writing that story, I didn't know there was going to be a Ph.D. with a wooden leg in it. I merely found myself one morning writing a description of two women that I knew something about, and before I realized it, I had equipped one of them with a daughter with a wooden leg. As the story progressed, I brought in the Bible salesman, but I had no idea what I was going to do with him. I didn't know he was going to steal that wooden leg until ten or twelve lines before he did it, but when I found out that this was what was going to happen, I realized that it was inevitable. This is a story that produces a shock for the reader, and I think one reason for this is that it produced a shock for the writer.

Such moments of shock are what Tobias Wolff writes for, and he discusses them during our interview: "I wonder if a writer is able to identify the motion in his mind that suddenly delivers up a possibility. I can't do that in retrospect. Because the mind surprises you. I'll bet that Cheever was surprised by the image of those leaves blowing across the headlights of the car when he was writing 'The Sorrows of Gin.' I'll bet that in the first draft anyway he was taken aback by it. Startled and frightened."

No less an authority on the workings of the mind than psychiatrist Robert Coles concurs (*Conversations with Robert Coles*, University Press of Mississippi, 1992, p. 239): "I would bow to the mystery that Tobias Wolff feels and celebrate that mystery rather than trying to explain it away or explain it even. Remember, Flannery O'Connor said that the task of the fiction writer is to deepen mystery, and then she added this: 'Mystery is a great embarrassment to the modern mind.'"

I approached the five writers who agreed to participate in this project simply because I admire their work. Had I approached five different writers, this would be, I imagine, a different book. I have attempted to offer some variety in genre and style. I encountered an early obstacle when I received this response from Tobias Wolff, the first writer I contacted: "One big problem in my case," he wrote, "is that I never keep rough drafts. As soon as a story is complete I throw away all interim versions." This seemed at first a huge difficulty. But then I decided Wolff's decision *not* to save drafts represented an interesting issue to discuss with him.

Though Wolff saves nothing, he proved wonderfully forthcoming about the development of his story "In the Garden of the North American Martyrs." In contrast, Joyce Carol Oates, the last writer I contacted, appears to save a great deal yet is somewhat reticent about her writing of "Naked." "When I finish a piece of writing," she remarked during our interview, "I try my best to forget the preliminary stages, which involve a good deal of indecision, groping, tension." Some writers, quite obviously, would rather not talk in any great detail about their work. Who can blame them, really? Ultimately, it's the work itself that matters most. Oates's reticence in the interview is compensated for, I hope, by the detailed handwritten and typed preliminary notes included here with her draft material.

What I hope this book reveals is just how much these writers depended on patience and perseverance to find their way through these particular pieces. Each piece required varying amounts of revision, but none came without the kind of effort that calls to mind Donald Hall's ox-cart man, or Joyce Carol Oates's unnamed woman, struggling naked through the dark, trying to find her way home. The interviews and draft material that follow reveal that each of these writers must struggle every time he or she sits down to begin a new piece—sometimes more, sometimes less. Robert Coles stares out his window. Tobias Wolff paces. Tess Gallagher does a few chores. Donald Hall works for an hour or so on one poem, then puts it aside and turns his attention to another.

As students of literature (or even better, as just plain old readers), we tend to fall into the habit of placing what we read into neat categories. "This is a *conventional* story," we note. "This is an *experimental* poem." It's easy to forget that every attempt at writing is an experiment in expression and communication. Whether you're writing a story, a poem, a letter to your Aunt Babby, or a marketing report, you begin with a blank page and the hope that you might succeed in communicating something that will prove significant to another human being. "Over the years," John Steinbeck once commented, "I have written a great many stories, and I still don't know how to go about it except to write it and take my chances. If there is a magic in story writing, and I'm convinced there is, no one has ever been able to reduce it to a recipe that can be passed from one person to another. The formula seems to lie solely in the aching urge of the writer to convey something he feels important to the reader. If the writer has that urge, he may sometimes but by no means always find the way to do it."

In his interview, Donald Hall discussed his concept of "total dispersal": "Only if you empty the well will the water return to the well." Elsewhere, Tess Gallagher talked about the role of intuition in her work: "I grew up in a gambling family, and there was always poker being played somewhere, and that depends on intuition. So I think there's a good current of intuitional knowledge that's kind of embedded in this blood that I run on." Regardless of their idiosyncratic methods, each of these writers seems to rely on what John Gardner referred to as a "divine stubbornness," a persistence that depends upon some peculiar mixture of craft and instinct. Much of the process, however, remains a mystery, a kind of alchemy. If Freud couldn't fathom those qualities of talent and inspiration that enabled Dostoevsky to produce his great work, then I don't know who will.

As Tobias Wolff says,

> The thing you have to remember, that all of us have to remember who are writers, is that in almost every other way in life, time is our enemy. But time is a writer's friend. Because writing happens over time and it gets better over time, with very, very few exceptions. The time that works against you in every other way is working for you in this way. You're seasoning, you're deepening. If you continue to write, and if you ask the best of yourself, and if you're working toward that all the time, it will happen. You don't give up. If you know the sound you want to hear, you'll hit the note eventually.

I interviewed three of these writers—Robert Coles, Tess Gallagher, and Tobias Wolff—in person, tape-recording our discussions, which were then transcribed. I conducted the interviews with Donald Hall and Joyce Carol Oates through the mail. In each case, the writer and I exchanged the interview several times to revise and shape the discussion, cutting here, elaborating there.

I begin each section of the book with brief remarks about the author and the work or works under consideration. The most recent published version of each work follows, and then the interview, with initials indicating my questions and the author's responses. Drafts, notes, and previously published versions of the works follow the interviews in chronological order.

TOBIAS WOLFF

'In the Garden of the North American Martyrs'

"In the Garden of the North American Martyrs" provided the title for Tobias Wolff's first collection of stories (New York: Ecco Press, 1981). Wolff is also the author of another collection, *Back in the World* (Boston: Houghton Mifflin, 1985), and a short novel, *The Barracks Thief* (New York: Ecco Press, 1984), which received the 1985 PEN Faulkner Award and was subsequently reissued as *The Barracks Thief and Selected Stories* (New York: Bantam Books, 1986). In addition, Wolff has edited a contemporary story anthology entitled *Matters of Life and Death* (Green Harbor, Mass.: Wampeter Press, 1983) and a collection of stories by Anton Chekhov, *A Doctor's Visit* (New York: Bantam Books, 1988). Wolff's own stories appear frequently in anthologies. "The Liar" is included in *American Short Story Masterpieces* (New York: Dell, 1987), edited by Raymond Carver and Tom Jenks. A childhood memoir, *This Boy's Life* (New York: Atlantic Monthly Press, 1989), reached several national best-seller lists and has since been adapted into a major motion picture.

Wolff has received numerous grants, including awards from the National Endowment for the Arts and the Guggenheim Memorial Foundation. After taking a degree at Oxford, he studied at Stanford University. He currently lives in Syracuse, New York, where he is professor of English at Syracuse University.

I interviewed Wolff in mid-February of 1991 at his home. We spoke in the attic he's had converted into a large study. I tape-recorded our conversation, and we sent the transcript back and forth several times through the summer of 1991 until we'd edited it into its current form.

Since Wolff does not save any drafts and seems to expunge all records of his writing, it is difficult to ascertain precisely when he wrote "In the Garden of the North American Martyrs." The story first appeared in *Antaeus* (no. 37) in the spring of 1980, so it seems likely that Wolff drafted the story between mid-1978 and mid-1979. After its initial appearance, the story was reprinted in *Prize Stories 1981: The O. Henry Awards* (Garden City, N.Y.: Doubleday). (I have not included this *O. Henry Award* version here because the story was reprinted in that collection precisely as it appeared in *Antaeus*.) The final version of the story reveals that Wolff made numerous subtle revisions to the *Antaeus* version before publishing it in his first book.

In the Garden of the North American Martyrs

When she was young, Mary saw a brilliant and original man lose his job because he had expressed ideas that were offensive to the trustees of the college where they both taught. She shared his views, but did not sign the protest petition. She was, after all, on trial herself—as a teacher, as a woman, as an interpreter of history.

Mary watched herself. Before giving a lecture she wrote it out in full, using the arguments and often the words of other, approved writers, so that she would not by chance say something scandalous. Her own thoughts she kept to herself, and the words for them grew faint as time went on; without quite disappearing they shrank to remote, nervous points, like birds flying away.

When the department turned into a hive of cliques, Mary went about her business and pretended not to know that people hated each other. To avoid seeming bland she let herself become eccentric in harmless ways. She took up bowling, which she learned to love, and founded the Brandon College chapter of a society dedicated to restoring the good name of Richard III. She memorized comedy routines from records and jokes from books; people groaned when she rattled them off, but she did not let that stop her, and after a time the groans became the point of the jokes. They were a kind of tribute to Mary's willingness to expose herself.

In fact no one at the college was safer than Mary, for she was making herself into something institutional, like a custom, or a mascot—part of the college's idea of itself.

Now and then she wondered whether she had been too careful. The things she said and wrote seemed flat to her, pulpy, as though someone else had squeezed the juice out of them. And once, while talking with a senior professor, Mary saw herself reflected in a window: she was leaning toward him and had her head turned so that her ear was right in front of his moving mouth. The sight disgusted her. Years later, when she had to get a hearing aid, Mary suspected that her deafness was a result of always trying to catch everything everyone said.

In the second half of Mary's fifteenth year at Brandon the provost called a meeting of all faculty and students to announce that the college was bankrupt and would not open its gates again. He was every bit as much surprised as they; the report from the trustees had reached his desk only that morning. It seemed that Brandon's financial manager had speculated in some kind of futures and lost everything. The provost wanted to deliver the news in person before it reached the papers. He wept openly and so did the students and teachers, with only a few exceptions—some cynical upperclassmen who claimed to despise the education they had received.

Mary could not rid her mind of the word "speculate." It meant to guess, in terms of money to gamble. How could a man gamble a college? Why would he want to do that, and how could it be that no one stopped him? To Mary, it seemed to belong to another time; she thought of a drunken plantation owner gaming away his slaves.

She applied for jobs and got an offer from a new experimental college in Oregon. It was her only offer so she took it.

The college was in one building. Bells rang all the time, lockers lined the hallways, and at every corner stood a buzzing water fountain. The student newspaper came out twice a month on mimeograph paper which felt wet. The library, which was next to the band room, had no librarian and no books.

The countryside was beautiful, though, and Mary might have enjoyed it if the rain had not caused her so much trouble. There was something wrong with her lungs that the doctors couldn't agree on, and couldn't cure; whatever it was, the dampness made it worse. On rainy days condensation formed in Mary's hearing aid and shorted it out. She began to dread talking with people, never knowing when she would have to take out her control box and slap it against her leg.

It rained nearly every day. When it was not raining it was getting ready to rain, or clearing. The ground glinted under the grass, and the light had a yellow undertone that flared up during storms.

There was water in Mary's basement. Her walls sweated, and she had found toadstools growing behind the refrigerator. She felt as though she were rusting out, like one of those old cars people thereabouts kept in their front yards, on pieces of wood. Mary knew that everyone was dying, but it did seem to her that she was dying faster than most.

She continued to look for another job, without success. Then, in the fall of her third year in Oregon, she got a letter from a woman named Louise who'd once taught at Brandon. Louise had scored a great success with a book on Benedict Arnold and was now on the faculty of a famous college in upstate New York. She said that one of her colleagues would be retiring at the end of the year and asked whether Mary would be interested in the position.

The letter surprised Mary. Louise thought of herself as a great historian and of almost everyone else as useless; Mary had not known that she felt differently about her. Moreover, enthusiasm for other people's causes did not come easily to Louise, who had a way of sucking in her breath when familiar names were mentioned, as though she knew things that friendship kept her from disclosing.

Mary expected nothing, but sent a résumé and copies of her two books. Shortly after that Louise called to say that the search committee, of which she was chairwoman, had decided to grant Mary an interview in early November. "Now don't get your hopes *too* high," Louise said.

"Oh, no," Mary said, but thought: Why shouldn't I hope? They would not go to the bother and expense of bringing her to the college if they weren't serious. And she was certain that the interview would go well. She would make them like her, or at least give them no cause to dislike her.

She read about the area with a strange sense of familiarity, as if the land and its history were already known to her. And when her plane left Portland and climbed easterly into the clouds, Mary felt like she was going home. The feeling stayed with her, growing stronger when they landed. She tried to describe it to Louise as they left the airport at Syracuse and drove toward the college, an hour or so away. "It's like *déjà vu*," she said.

"*Déjà vu* is a hoax," Louise said. "It's just a chemical imbalance of some kind."

"Maybe so," Mary said, "but I still have this sensation."

"Don't get serious on me," Louise said. "That's not your long suit. Just be your funny, wisecracking old self. Tell me now—honestly—how do I look?"

It was night, too dark to see Louise's face well, but in the airport she had seemed gaunt and pale and intense. She reminded Mary of a description in the book she'd been reading, of how Iroquois warriors gave themselves visions by fasting. She had that kind of look about her. But she wouldn't want to hear that. "You look wonderful," Mary said.

"There's a reason," Louise said. "I've taken a lover. My concentration has improved, my energy level is up, and I've lost ten pounds. I'm also getting some color in my cheeks, though that could be the weather. I recommend the experience highly. But you probably disapprove."

Mary didn't know what to say. She said that she was sure Louise knew best, but that didn't seem to be enough. "Marriage is a great institution," she added, "but who wants to live in an institution?"

Louise groaned. "I know you," she said, "and I know that right now you're thinking 'But what about Ted? What about the children?' The fact is, Mary, they aren't taking it well at all. Ted has become a nag." She handed Mary her purse. "Be a good girl and light me a cigarette, will you? I know I told you I quit, but this whole thing has been very hard on me, very hard, and I'm afraid I've started again."

They were in the hills now, heading north on a narrow road. Tall trees arched above them. As they topped a rise Mary saw the forest all around, deep black under the plum-colored sky. There were a few lights and these made the darkness seem even greater.

"Ted has succeeded in completely alienating the children from me," Louise was saying. "There is no reasoning with any of them. In fact, they refuse to discuss the matter at all, which is very ironical because over the years I have tried to instill in them a willingness to see things from the other person's point of view. If they could just *meet* Jonathan I know they would feel differently. But they won't hear of it. Jonathan," she said, "is my lover."

"I see," Mary said, and nodded.

Coming around a curve they caught two deer in the headlights. Their eyes lit up and their hindquarters tensed; Mary could see them trembling as the car went by. "Deer," she said.

"I don't know," Louise said, "I just don't know. I do my best and it never seems to be enough. But that's enough about me—let's talk about you. What did you think of my latest book?" She squawked and beat her palms on the steering wheel. "God, I love that joke," she said. "Seriously, though, what about you? It must have been a real shockeroo when good old Brandon folded."

"It was hard. Things haven't been good but they'll be a lot better if I get this job."

"At least you have work," Louise said. "You should look at it from the bright side."

"I try."

"You seem so gloomy. I hope you're not worrying about the interview, or the class. Worrying won't do you a bit of good. Be happy."

"Class? What class?"

"The class you're supposed to give tomorrow, after the interview. Didn't I tell you? *Mea culpa*, hon, *mea maxima culpa*. I've been uncharacteristically forgetful lately."

"But what will I do?"

"Relax," Louise said. "Just pick a subject and wing it."

"Wing it?"

"You know, open your mouth and see what comes out. Extemporize."

"But I always work from a prepared lecture."

Louise sighed. "All right. I'll tell you what. Last year I wrote an article on the Marshall Plan that I got bored with and never published. You can read that."

Parroting what Louise had written seemed wrong to Mary, at first; then it occurred to her that she had been doing the same kind of thing for many years, and that this was not the time to get scruples. "Thanks," she said. "I appreciate it."

"Here we are," Louise said, and pulled into a circular drive with several cabins grouped around it. In two of the cabins lights were on; smoke drifted straight up from the chimneys. "This is the visitors' center. The college is another two miles thataway." Louise pointed down the road. "I'd invite you to stay at my house, but I'm spending the night with Jonathan and Ted is not good company these days. You would hardly recognize him."

She took Mary's bags from the trunk and carried them up the steps of a darkened cabin. "Look," she said, "they've laid a fire for you. All you have to do is light it." She stood in the middle of the room with her arms crossed and watched as Mary held a match under the kindling. "There," she said. "You'll be snugaroo in no time. I'd love to stay and chew the fat but I can't. You just get a good night's sleep and I'll see you in the morning."

Mary stood in the doorway and waved as Louise pulled out of the drive, spraying gravel. She filled her lungs, to taste the air: it was tart and clear. She could see the stars in their figurations, and the vague streams of light that ran among the stars.

She still felt uneasy about reading Louise's work as her own. It would be her first complete act of plagiarism. It would change her. It would make her less—how much less, she did not know. But what else could she do? She certainly couldn't "wing it." Words might fail her, and then what? Mary had a dread of silence. When she thought of silence she thought of drowning, as if it were a kind of water she could not swim in.

"I want this job," she said, and settled deep into her coat. It was cashmere and Mary had not worn it since moving to Oregon, because people there thought you were pretentious if you had on anything but a Pendleton shirt or, of course, raingear. She rubbed her cheek against the upturned collar and thought of a silver moon shining through bare black branches, a white house with green shutters, red leaves falling in a hard blue sky.

Louise woke her a few hours later. She was sitting on the edge of the bed, pushing at Mary's shoulder and snuffling loudly. When Mary asked her what was wrong she said, "I want your opinion on something. It's very important. Do you think I'm womanly?"

Mary sat up. "Louise, can this wait?"

"No."

"Womanly?"

Louise nodded.

"You are very beautiful," Mary said, "and you know how to present yourself."

Louise stood and paced the room. "That son of a bitch," she said. She came back and stood over Mary. "Let's suppose someone said I have no sense of humor. Would you agree or disagree?"

"In some things you do. I mean, yes, you have a good sense of humor."

"What do you mean, 'in some things'? What kind of things?"

"Well, if you heard that someone had been killed in an unusual way, like by an exploding cigar, you would think that was funny."

Louise laughed.

"That's what I mean," Mary said.

Louise went on laughing. "Oh, Lordy," she said. "Now it's my turn to say something about you." She sat down beside Mary.

"Please," Mary said.

"Just one thing," Louise said.

Mary waited.

"You're trembling," Louise said. "I was just going to say—oh, forget it. Listen, do you mind if I sleep on the couch? I'm all in."

"Go ahead."

"Sure it's okay? You've got a big day tomorrow." She fell back on the sofa and kicked off her shoes. "I was just going to say, you should use some liner on those eyebrows of yours. They sort of disappear and the effect is disconcerting."

Neither of them slept. Louise chain-smoked cigarettes and Mary watched the coals burn down. When it was light enough that they could see each other Louise got up. "I'll send a student for you," she said. "Good luck."

The college looked the way colleges are supposed to look. Roger, the student assigned to show Mary around, explained that it was an exact copy of a college in England, right down to the gargoyles and stained-glass windows. It looked so much like a college that moviemakers sometimes used it as a set. *Andy Hardy Goes to College* had been filmed there, and every fall they had an Andy Hardy Goes to College Day, with raccoon coats and goldfish-swallowing contests.

Above the door of the Founder's Building was a Latin motto which, roughly translated, meant "God helps those who help themselves." As Roger recited the names of illustrious graduates Mary was struck by the extent to which they had taken this precept to heart. They had helped themselves to railroads, mines, armies, states; to empires of finance with outposts all over the world.

Roger took Mary to the chapel and showed her a plaque bearing the names of alumni who had been killed in various wars, all the way back to the Civil War. There were not many names. Here too, apparently, the graduates had helped themselves. "Oh yes," Roger said as they were leaving, "I forgot to tell you. The communion rail comes from some church in Europe where Charlemagne used to go."

They went to the gymnasium, and the three hockey rinks, and the library, where Mary inspected the card catalogue, as though she would turn down the job if they didn't have the right books. "We have a little more time," Roger said as they went outside. "Would you like to see the power plant?"

Mary wanted to keep busy until the last minute, so she agreed.

Roger led her into the depths of the service building, explaining things about the machine, which was the most advanced in the country. "People think the college is really old-fashioned," he said, "but it isn't. They let girls come here now, and some of the teachers are women. In fact, there's a statute that says they have to interview at least one woman for each opening. There it is."

They were standing on an iron catwalk above the biggest

machine Mary had ever beheld. Roger, who was majoring in Earth Sciences, said that it had been built from a design pioneered by a professor in his department. Where before he had been gabby Roger now became reverent. It was clear that for him this machine was the soul of the college, that the purpose of the college was to provide outlets for the machine. Together they leaned against the railing and watched it hum.

Mary arrived at the committee room exactly on time for her interview, but the room was empty. Her two books were on the table, along with a water pitcher and some glasses. She sat down and picked up one of the books. The binding cracked as she opened it. The pages were smooth, clean, unread. Mary turned to the first chapter, which began, "It is generally believed that . . ." How dull, she thought.

Nearly twenty minutes later Louise came in with several men. "Sorry we're late," she said. "We don't have much time so we'd better get started." She introduced Mary to the men, but with one exception the names and faces did not stay together. The exception was Dr. Howells, the department chairman, who had a porous blue nose and terrible teeth.

A shiny-faced man to Dr. Howells's right spoke first. "So," he said, "I understand you once taught at Brandon College."

"It was a shame that Brandon had to close," said a young man with a pipe in his mouth. "There is a place for schools like Brandon." As he talked the pipe wagged up and down.

"Now you're in Oregon," Dr. Howells said. "I've never been there. How do you like it?"

"Not very much," Mary said.

"Is that right?" Dr. Howells leaned toward her. "I thought everyone liked Oregon. I hear it's very green."

"That's true," Mary said.

"I suppose it rains a lot," he said.

"Nearly every day."

"I wouldn't like that," he said, shaking his head. "I like it dry. Of course it snows here, and you have your rain now and then, but it's a *dry* rain. Have you ever been to Utah? There's a state for you. Bryce Canyon. The Mormon Tabernacle Choir."

"Dr. Howells was brought up in Utah," said the young man with the pipe.

"It was a different place altogether in those days," Dr. Howells said. "Mrs. Howells and I have always talked about going back when I retire, but now I'm not so sure."

"We're a little short on time," Louise said.

"And here I've been going on and on," Dr. Howells said. "Before we wind things up, is there anything you want to tell us?"

"Yes. I think you should give me the job." Mary laughed when she said this, but no one laughed back, or even looked at her. They all looked away. Mary understood then that they were not really considering her for the position. She had been brought here to satisfy a rule. She had no hope.

The men gathered their papers and shook hands with Mary and told her how much they were looking forward to her class. "I can't get enough of the Marshall Plan," Dr. Howells said.

"Sorry about that," Louise said when they were alone. "I didn't think it would be so bad. That was a real bitcheroo."

"Tell me something," Mary said. "You already know who you're going to hire, don't you?"

Louise nodded.

"Then why did you bring me here?"

Louise began to explain about the statute and Mary interrupted. "I know all that. But why me? Why did you pick *me*?"

Louise walked to the window. She spoke with her back to Mary. "Things haven't been going very well for old Louise," she said. "I've been unhappy and I thought you might cheer me up. You used to be so funny, and I was sure you would enjoy the trip—it didn't cost you anything, and it's pretty this time of year with the leaves and everything. Mary, you don't know the things my parents did to me. And Ted is no barrel of laughs either. Or Jonathan, the son of a bitch. I deserve some love and friendship but I don't get any." She turned and looked at her watch. "It's almost time for your class. We'd better go."

"I would rather not give it. After all, there's not much point, is there?"

"But you *have* to give it. That's part of the interview." Louise handed Mary a folder. "All you have to do is read this. It isn't much, considering all the money we've laid out to get you here."

Mary followed Louise down the hall to the lecture room. The professors were sitting in the front row with their legs crossed. They smiled and nodded at Mary. Behind them the room was full of students, some of whom had spilled over into the aisles. One of the professors adjusted the microphone to Mary's height, crouching down as he went to the podium and back as though he would prefer not to be seen.

Louise called the room to order. She introduced Mary and gave the subject of the lecture. But Mary had decided to wing it after all. Mary came to the podium unsure of what she would say; sure only that she would rather die than read Louise's article. The sun poured through the stained glass onto the people around her, painting their faces. Thick streams of smoke from the young professor's pipe drifted through a circle of red light at Mary's feet, turning crimson and twisting like flames.

"I wonder how many of you know," she began, "that we are in the Long House, the ancient domain of the Five Nations of the Iroquois."

Two professors looked at each other.

"The Iroquois were without pity," Mary said. "They hunted people down with clubs and arrows and spears and nets, and blowguns made from elder stalks. They tortured their captives, sparing no one, not even the little children. They took scalps and practiced cannibalism and slavery. Because they had no pity they became powerful, so powerful that no other tribe dared to oppose them. They made the other tribes pay tribute, and when they had nothing more to pay the Iroquois attacked them."

Several of the professors began to whisper. Dr. Howells was saying something to Louise, and Louise was shaking her head.

"In one of their raids," Mary said, "they captured two Jesuit priests, Jean de Brébeuf and Gabriel Lalement. They covered Lalement with pitch and set him on fire in front of Brébeuf. When Brébeuf rebuked them they cut off his lips and put a burning iron down his throat. They hung a collar of red-hot hatchets around his neck, and poured boiling water over his head. When he continued to preach to them they cut strips of flesh from his body and ate them before his eyes. While he was still alive they scalped him and cut open his breast and drank his blood. Later, their chief tore out Brébeuf's heart and ate it, but just before he did this Brébeuf spoke to them one last time. He said—"

"That's enough!" yelled Dr. Howells, jumping to his feet.

Louise stopped shaking her head. Her eyes were perfectly round.

Mary had come to the end of her facts. She did not know what Brébeuf had said. Silence rose up around her; just when she thought she would go under and be lost in it she heard someone whistling in the hallway outside, trilling the notes like a bird, like many birds.

"Mend your lives," she said. "You have deceived yourselves in the pride of your hearts, and the strength of your arms. Though you soar aloft like the eagle, though your nest is set among the stars, thence I will bring you down, says the Lord. Turn from power to love. Be kind. Do justice. Walk humbly."

Louise was waving her arms. "Mary!" she shouted.

But Mary had more to say, much more; she waved back at Louise, then turned off her hearing aid so that she would not be distracted again.

INTERVIEW

JW How did this story get started? What was its genesis?

TW Well, there are a few things that I can trace it to. One is a job interview I had several years ago which was not, it turned out, a serious interview. That is, I had been brought across the country in order to fulfill a requirement of the college that so many people be interviewed for each position. And when I found this out it really burned me up. I tried writing the story a couple of times from a personal point of view, my own point of view. This never really took. It sounded whiny, "poor me." After all, I live a rarified life, one that's lucky compared to almost everybody else's. This didn't seem to be the stuff of tragedy.

I'd had the experience of watching my mother struggle and have a harder time of it than she would have had if she were a man. It occurred to me that this was the kind of experience women have a lot more often than men. And once I was able to make that leap, get out of my own case and see the whole question of injustice in a larger way, then this story began to take. I began to feel its possibilities. I went back to it and worked on it for several months. And this is what I came up with. I was ransacking my files here, hoping to find some remnants of that original draft. But I couldn't find it, so I must have thrown it away. Anyway, I put it through many different versions. That's the genesis of the story.

JW How long did you struggle with those first attempts before you put the story aside?

TW I'm a very slow writer. If people knew how hard it was for me they'd think I was crazy to be a writer. I suppose a couple of months, anyway. It usually takes me that long to give up. I'll usually even finish a bad story and then not send it off rather than not finish it, because I'm terrified of developing the habit of giving up on stories as I write them. I've had trouble with even my best stories along the way, and I've been tempted to quit on them. So I know from experience that if I see it through I might end up with a good story. Then again I might not. But it's the only chance I've got to finish the thing. I did finish a story—it just wasn't a story that I liked, that's all. But that took me a couple, three months to write. And then I went back and worked another three months on the version you're reading now.

JW Once you'd made that leap and knew this was going to be in the third person with a female point-of-view character, how much at that point did you know about the story?

TW Well, by no means everything. I was surprised, as I often am in writing a story, by many of the things that came up. For example, the appearance of the Jesuit martyrs in the story was a late thought in the process. You ask, what's the genesis of a story? Almost everything a writer is doing at a given time can be part of the genesis of a story. I was reading Parkman's wonderful book, *The Jesuits in North America*, and I was riveted by his description of the martyrdom of Brébeuf and Lalement. I dreamt about it a couple of nights. It exerted itself on the story I was writing in a strange way, because it helped me to see that much of what the story was about had to do with power. It illuminated that for me. There are so many forces at play in the writing of a story. Take "The Dead," Joyce's story. Why did he write that story in the first place? Because somebody scolded him about *Dubliners*, told him he'd left out something essential to the people of Dublin, their great sense of hospitality. And he agreed. He went back and he wrote, I think, the greatest thing he ever wrote. Somebody said something that illuminated his own work for him.

When I made the peculiar juxtaposition that allowed the Jesuits to spill into the story, I knew that there was something right and even necessary about it. I wrote this story thirteen or fourteen years ago now, and it's hard to recover all the stages of its evolution because I don't keep rough drafts.

JW Why don't you keep drafts?

TW They embarrass me, to tell you the truth. Many writers seem to have a tremendous confidence in their futures and a certain assumption that generations to come are going to be interested in what they've written at every stage. I guess I really don't have that feeling. I only want people to see my work at its very best. I don't even let my wife look at things I'm writing until I'm done with them, or at least until I've brought them as far as I can. I come very slowly to the ends of my stories, and the work I do to get there is rough. It's often very false. It's awkward. It's not interesting to me. It might be interesting, I suppose, to somebody who wanted to see just how dramatic a difference revision can make to a hopeless writer, to give everyone else hope. But I think part of my reluctance is that people would think I was crazy, really, to be a writer, if they could see my early drafts and see how hard it is for me to get from one place to another.

JW Do you get terribly discouraged?

TW Less and less so because I know now that it will finally work out. It used to be much harder for me because it seems such a strange way to write. And I knew that other people weren't writing that way. I thought there must be something wrong with me. But now I've learned that this is the way I write.

And I can't imagine doing anything else. I love finishing a good story. Or finishing what I think is a good book. No feeling can compare. And then it's all been worth it. But it's hard as it goes, sometimes. Once I get a first draft down, once I really know where I'm going and what the story is about, and what I'm trying to do, then a kind of playfulness enters in to my writing that I absolutely live for. It's getting that first draft out that's very, very hard for me.

JW Do you ever get a draft out and get stuck with it? Like not know—

TW How to crack it?

JW Yeah.

TW Once in a while that happens to me. It does happen sometimes. And then I just throw the story away. I'll fool with it for a while and then throw it away. Once in a while I'll finish something that I like but don't really think is a serious story. That happened to me last year. I'm going to let the story be published, but I'm probably not going to include it in a collection. I think it's a funny story, and it's an odd story. I like it. But in the end it really doesn't really earn its keep for me, so I probably won't collect it.

JW So you have a good number of uncollected stories?

TW Oh yes, I have enough uncollected stories to make a couple of collections, probably. At least one. But I won't collect them. Now and then I'll go back and reread them, wondering if I was just being too hard on myself. And I'll say no, I wasn't.

JW It must be a difficult position to negotiate. I mean to be at a point in your writing life where you could, I would assume, get a story published just about anywhere you want.

TW I wish.

JW Am I completely naive about that? I would assume that most magazines would be very happy to publish your work.

TW I've been very lucky. But there's a lot of competition. Don't forget, Saul Bellow had won the Nobel Prize before he was ever able to place a story in the *New Yorker*. "The Silver Dish" was the first story he ever had in the *New Yorker*. Magazines are run by editors with tastes of their own. And that's the way it ought to be. What other way could it be? Some editors seem hospitable to my fiction; others don't. It isn't a question, though, of my being able to finish a story and send it out and be sure of selling it, because that really isn't the case. I've got a story right now I really like that I'm sending to quarterlies, because I know I can't place it with large-circulation magazines because of the things that go on in it. André Dubus has an essay on being a writer, in which he says that there's a moment when something happens in a story he's writing, something untoward or violent, and he thinks to himself, Well, there goes the *New Yorker*. And the moment he has that thought, a wonderful sense of release and freedom comes over him—that it is no longer even possible to think about responding to some editor's taste. He's beyond the pale already and it gives him freedom. And I think that's exactly where you start becoming interesting as a writer, when you give up trying to second-guess some editor somewhere into taking a story, which you can never count on anyway. It doesn't do to try to figure it out. You just write the best you can and hope that somebody out there is going to hear you.

I know that Ray Carver's stories were submitted to the *New Yorker* for years before they began to publish them. And I know that some of his best stories were rejected by the *New Yorker* before they began to take his stories. Why? I'm not attributing corruption to them just because he got well known in the interim. I honestly think that at some point they began to like his stories, though they hadn't liked the others. But why? Where's the line that was crossed there? I don't see it. So it's a very whimsical business. You become especially aware of it as a short story writer. Novelists will characteristically work for three or four years before they have something to send out. But story writers have something to send out every few months, so they're much more aware of the caprice of response. Also, when you publish a collection of stories and the reviews start coming in, one reviewer says this is a wonderful collection and the story that's obviously the best story in here is such and such. And if only such stories as, and then he names the obviously worst one, would live up to this level . . . blah-blah-blah. Then you get another review which names a completely different set of stories as the obviously best ones and the obviously worst ones. And you suddenly realize that what Edmond Wilson said is true—"No two readers read the same book." In the end you have to be the arbiter of your fiction, the judge of your fiction, the harshest judge of your fiction, as you are your own best reader. Who else is there in the end that you have to please? I have an acquaintance who is a very successful novelist commercially. I happen to know that she hates her own work. She's an absolutely miserable person, a really unhappy woman. And she's defensive. She talks a lot about how much money she makes and all this. She's clearly made miserable by her feelings about her own work. I know another woman who is also very commercially successful whose stuff is crap. But she doesn't believe that her stuff is crap, and she's quite happy. If you're not pleasing yourself, you haven't pleased anybody important.

JW And you probably will never feel any satisfaction.

TW Let's hope not. That's the myth that sustains me.

JW Getting back to "In the Garden of the North American Martyrs": that was not the first story that you wrote in this collection.

TW No, by no means. The first published story in there came out in '76. That is the story called "Smokers." Actually, there's another story in here that predates it, called "Face to Face." That was written in '73 or so, though it wasn't actually published until '78.

JW Do you always have to be sure you've found the right first sentence in order to find the rest of a story?

TW I simply need a place to begin. Later on, when I revise, I often think of a better first line, especially, of course, if I've decided to change point of view, as I did in this story. Once in a while I'm lucky enough to find the right first sentence in the very beginning. For example, the tone I struck in the first line of "The Poor Are Always with Us" was right and helped me find the rest of the story. I also liked the first sentence I wrote for "The Rich Brother." But that doesn't always happen. I try to be as open to chance as possible when I'm writing. If I have things too firmly in mind I lose a certain fluidity and ability to be surprised, which is very important to me. In this story I realized I needed to begin with the image of this woman making herself a completely accommodated creature.

JW What particular passages gave you special trouble? Do you recall any in the story?

TW Her speech, at the end. I didn't know how far to go with it. To some extent it bursts the bounds of traditional realistic fiction. The voice becomes prophetic. In fact, I think some of those passages are from the Psalms and the Prophets. Jeremiah is the source of a couple of lines. They're all jumbled together in my mind, but they came out, I think, coherently. But she's definitely speaking in a heightened voice there. It isn't a realistic story of the kind, say, in *Dubliners*. And the decision whether to allow that to happen in the story was a tough one to make because it then became a different kind of story—a parable, almost, rather than the kind of story I think of myself as writing.

JW That ending seems to work very well on a realistic level, though. I guess partly that might be because she's at a podium giving a lecture to an audience.

TW It lends itself to that, it does. I tried to hold it as close as I could to the possible. I didn't want to lose the story's authority by becoming just clever, or facile.

JW John Gardner talks about psychic distance, something I've never felt completely confident that I understood. But this story starts from a fairly distant point of view and sort of zooms in quite seamlessly. And it was only on rereading it several times that I could identify the moment when the perspective becomes more intimate. I think this happens with the arrival of Louise's letter. That's where the dialogue begins. I was wondering whether this was something that had given you a lot of trouble—achieving that sort of fluidity.

TW Sure. It's hard to know when to give up that omniscience. The problem is that if you don't give it up at certain moments, you compromise the story. You get in the way of the character. Your presence in the story is too . . . how can I put it, *consoling*: Well, things can't go wrong because the master of ceremonies is here, right? You've got to fade at certain points. And obviously the problem is knowing just when to do it. Because there certainly is an unapologetically omniscient voice in the beginning, a voice that's different from hers, when we hear things from her point of view. The temptation was to continue to exercise that throughout the story, and here and there I did. I allow myself comments and explanations that are not exactly in her register, in her voice. But my aim was to hand the story over to her.

JW Did you know much about Louise when you started this version of the story?

TW By the time I got this far along, in this draft, yes, of course I did. But I had to explore her. And the way I explore my characters is by writing them. I'm not very good at sitting down and thinking a whole story out before I write it. I don't seem to have that gift. I really have to sit down and write the story out, and write my way into the story, and just keep going at it again and again and again, sinking farther and farther into it just by spending more time with it. In that way I get to know the characters. The main character was very, very different in different drafts.

JW In what ways?

TW Well, in one draft I had her niece living with her, who'd had to leave home because she was pregnant. So there was an additional onus on Mary and a necessity to work. But that felt cluttered. It was another character to develop, another situation. Once I made the decision to allow the prophetic voice to enter the story, I thought it should have the cleanness of line that a parable has, that it shouldn't have those jagged edges and little tributaries that I'm somehow quite willing and happy to have in a more realistic short story.

JW There seems to be such a fine line between those slightly tangential moments that add a real texture and verisimilitude, and more unrelated asides that can get you sidetracked. I'm thinking of the moment with the deer, when Mary and Louise are in the car. Aside from its immediate vividness, that moment has clear symbolic resonance. But it's not a moment that would have occurred to everybody to include. You then even emphasize the moment by having Mary say "Deer," which adds the slight irony and humor of the double entendre. Was that something that came to you in an earlier draft or something you added later?

TW That was something that came to me as I wrote my way into the story. I was imagining myself going along the road, and the sense of the old country asserted itself in the great wilderness that underlies the veneer we live in. That percolated up from a later sense of the story. So that wasn't in an earlier draft, no. I know what you mean. There's a passage in a John Cheever story that I really love, "The Sorrows of Gin," when a man is driving to get his runaway daughter at the railway station, and a flurry of leaves blows across his headlight. Why that breaks my heart, that image, it's hard to say, but it does. And it's not anything you can thematically explain. You could make an argument for it, but really I think it's irreducible. The image works on the nerves more than in the mind. It's a wonderful moment, Cheever at his very best, I think.

JW In "The Brigadier and the Golf Widow" there's that wonderful line, "Who, after all these centuries, can describe the fineness of an autumn day?"

TW He tries again and again.

JW And his descriptions get more and more amazing every time. There's another moment like that at the very end of your story, when Mary realizes she doesn't know what Brébeuf's last words were. And the silence of her audience is beginning to well up, a silence we already know she equates with water and drowning. At that moment she hears someone "whistling in the hallway outside, trilling the notes like a bird, like many birds." That line recalls the beautiful image at the very beginning, at the end of the second paragraph about her thoughts that she kept to herself: "and the words for them grew faint as time went on; without quite disappearing they shrank to remote nervous points, like birds flying away." That relates both to the wilderness theme and also her struggle to reemerge. Was that something that you were aware of right away?

TW It's an image. Language, especially the language which she speaks at the end, her own language, is freedom, is flight. It's why I use the image of birds there. It's song too.

JW Was that something that you wrote and then discovered, the connection with the image at the beginning? Or did you have to work that in later?

TW I'm not exactly sure which came first, whether the image at the end came and then I went back to the beginning and found a way of preparing for it, or the other way. I have a feeling, though, that the image at the beginning was antecedent to the one at the end. That that was a right, natural way to describe someone's language deserting them. Then it was a natural thing to pick it up again at the end.

I wish you could have talked to me when I was writing the final drafts, because then you would know everything about the story. I'd been living with it for four or five months, thinking about it day and night. And I knew literally why every pause was there. I had a reason for it. Now I have to go back and second-guess myself, which is one of the problems with not keeping drafts.

JW At what point did the ending become clear to you? At what point did you start to get a sense where things might be leading, that there might be this sort of prophetic moment at the end? Did you have a strong sense of direction early on as you were writing it?

TW That ending became possible through my reading the Parkman book. I wonder if a writer is able to identify the motion in his mind that suddenly delivers up a possibility. I can't do that in retrospect. Because the mind surprises you. I'll bet that Cheever was surprised by the image of those leaves blowing across the headlights of the car when he was writing "The Sorrows of Gin." I'll bet that in the first draft anyway he was taken aback by it. Startled and frightened. I know that when I had the idea of doing what I did in this story, I was surprised by it. Obviously that couldn't have come to me if I hadn't been reading that book, and even had a couple of dreams about it. But beyond saying that, who knows? The mind works even when we're not aware of it working or thinking of it working. Certainly when I'm up here "writing," what I'm really doing much of the time is walking around. I walk a lot. I don't even know what I'm doing half the time up here. But something is happening.

JW There's a lot of pacing space up here.

TW Friends of mine come up and say, "Why don't you have a desk in the middle of the room or something like that, or a bed? Why don't you fill this room up?" But what I've always wanted was a place to walk. I just walk back and forth and back and forth.

JW No window to look out while you're sitting at your desk?

TW No, absolutely not. That's death for me. I cannot have a window near my desk. I had an acquaintance in Massachusetts who had a bank of windows looking out on the ocean. I don't know how he ever got a day's work done. He didn't actually get a day's work done.

JW Those moments of surprise that occur when you're writing: are those moments the things that really sustain you?

TW Yes, they are. That's what I live for. They sustain me even if I don't have very many of them. I live with the expectation that I will have more, the faith that I will have more. What I could predict I will do when I sit down to write is not what I want to end up with. I want to end up with what surprises me along the way, what jumps out at me from the potential of my work and not from what I've already realized about it before I've even started. If I'm simply writing down what I already know, it is of no earthly interest to me. And not only that, everyone else will know it anyway. Simply obvious stuff. I'm not subtle. When I sit down to write, I discover things that I have, for one reason or another, not admitted, not seen, not reflected on sufficiently. And those are the things that I live for in other people's fiction as well as my own.

JW At one point in this story, you offer this description of Louise: "Enthusiasm for other people's causes did not come easily to Louise, who had a way of sucking in her breath when familiar names were mentioned, as though she knew things that friendship kept her from disclosing." This strikes me as a good example of what we're talking about.

TW That's an important moment for me in the story because in writing that sentence I came to know something about that character. I didn't start off knowing that about Louise. I discovered it by writing that sentence. You know, language leads you to these discoveries. Until you start practicing the language of the story, start hearing the music of the story, you can't learn what the story has to tell you. That's why it's so important for me to learn from the writing. Writing is not just a process of getting out what I've already thought, what's already in my head. Though it can be for very good writers exactly that. A writer of my acquaintance had a blackboard that ran all around his office, and he would keep detailed notes on the blackboard of everything that was going to happen in the novel he was writing. That worked for him; it wouldn't work for me.

JW These pivotal moments, these moments of surprise that you talk about happening in your stories: do most of them occur in revision, as opposed to the first draft where you're just trying to get the skeleton down?

TW Well, it's hard to assign an order to these things, especially now. When I used to work in longhand, it would almost always be in subsequent drafts those things would come to me. Now that I work on a computer like almost everybody else I know, it's hard to say which draft is which because I'm always going back. I don't have stacks of paper. It's an ideal machine for me because all the drafts are killed. The word dies as soon as it becomes obsolete. I don't even have to throw it in the trash can anymore. But yes, revision is a very imaginatively active time for me. I have a hard time letting go of stories because I enjoy revising so much.

JW Does it seem almost artificial to you to even distinguish between drafts?

TW At this point it does. I used to have discrete drafts. I had a first and a second and a third and a fourth and a fifth. Now it's impossible to identify different drafts because it's all one, with this new machine we've got.

The truth is, I wouldn't keep drafts anyway. Part of that, I guess, is just wanting to—what would be an explanation? I tend to have effaced a lot of things about my past. I've only recently begun to write about my past. Maybe it's a symptom of that desire to appear in some ideal mode right in the present, as if I'd sprung there, full-blown. I think that has something to do with why I don't keep drafts. If I write something good, I'd like the impression to be that it arrived by magic rather than struggle.

JW Why does it make me think of the boy in *This Boy's Life* creating his transcripts and letters of recommendation?

TW Right. He's creating a fictional, ideal boy, isn't he?

JW At what point did you know that Louise had to be a scholar, a Benedict Arnold scholar?

TW That was one of those little flashes. I remember writing it. I was getting on toward the end of the story. I had never mentioned what her scholarship was. And I thought that would be perfect. She would have written the book on Benedict Arnold.

JW I guess this is an example of what my English teachers would have called foreshadowing, but at its best: you sense it's a fact without realizing its full significance. I only noticed it when I was rereading.

TW Right. You don't know what's going to happen when you first come across it, so it has no meaning then. It's a neutral fact, except that it can color your sense of her a little bit, without your quite knowing it.

JW A similar moment occurs when Louise says to Mary on the phone "Now don't get your hopes *too* high."

TW Exactly. It all means something. You just don't know what it means at the time.

JW In retrospect, the reader can also appreciate the cumulative significance of

Mary's physical problems, too—the hearing aid, the lung disorder, and maybe especially the disappearing eyebrows. Have you ever sensed that any of your academic colleagues have been offended by this story?

TW Oddly enough they seem to like it. None of them seem to think that this applies to them.

JW They just *know* jerks.

TW Sure, it's somebody else. It's had the unfortunate effect that I get stuck on a lot of search committees because they think I'll be clean and won't do that kind of thing, which is true. I invented a rather demonic search for the sake of the story. I certainly know that things like that happen, but I've always been impressed with the fairness of the people I work with.

JW You meet both good people and jerks in any line of work.

TW You do, absolutely. I just teach in the fall now, and I have been for the last five years. I'm not quite so immersed in the life of the department as I was for the two or three years before. But I've noticed that during tenure cases, even people who have been at odds ideologically with other people in the department don't use that against them when they're up for tenure and promotion. They try to figure out what it is they're really trying to do and call it that way. It's always impressed me, the fundamental fairness of the people here. But I understand that's not true everywhere.

JW One particular line in the story captures perfectly a kind of pompous fatuousness—during the interview, when Dr. Howells is ruminating on precipitation and says "But it's a *dry* rain."

TW Well, that's the kind of thing you only hear in interviews, isn't it?

JW How do names come to you?

TW I fool around a lot with names. Names are important. It's obvious, I suppose. But often I'll read a story and not be comfortable with it. An unease will come over me, and I won't be able to identify it. And then I'll realize, well, this character has the wrong name.

JW Is that reading your story or someone else's?

TW Someone else's. But that happens to me in the beginning of my own stories. I won't be able to write about the character until I get the right name.

JW And is it just sort of hit or miss?

TW I keep fooling around with it until I find the name.

JW Did these names change at all?

TW Oh yeah. I fooled around with them.

JW Do you remember what some of the names were for Mary?

TW I don't remember what the names were, I'm sorry. It's hard to recover all the processes I went through in writing this story.

JW How come the Marshall Plan?

TW That was a misstep, I think, because an Arnold Scholar wouldn't have been writing about the Marshall Plan in the first place.

JW Maybe that's why she didn't do anything with this particular paper—tried something new without success. I like that line, "I can't get enough of the Marshall Plan," because you can't tell for sure whether Dr. Howells is being snide or sincere.

TW Right. I think that line had a lot to do with it. I think I actually once heard somebody say that, and it went into my bank.

JW What about the title of the story? Was that from the Parkman book?

TW No. There's a church up in northern Vermont called the Church of the North American Martyrs. A writer named Roger Weingarten, a poet, had a book of poems called *Ethan Benjamin Bolt* published in the late '70s. And there's a line in there which goes, "Near the garden of the North American Martyrs." I was writing the story at the time and it just lashed out at me, so I asked him if I could use it. There's no way I could quote it as an epigraph because it had nothing to do with what I was writing about. He wasn't writing about any of these things. I asked him if I could use that phrase as the title of the book, and he was pleased to have me do that.

JW Do you have a hard time with titles?

TW I have a hard time with titles in that it takes me a while to get them. They're a very important part of the story, so I work pretty hard at getting them. Just as an example, these are all possible titles for a piece I'm working on right now [showing a page-length list]. I'm always writing things down as they come to me. Almost all of these are absolutely terrible. But one of these days I'll write one down and it won't be.

JW In reading this story as it first appeared in *Antaeus* and then later in the O. Henry anthology, I did notice a few changes. The O. Henry version is exactly the same as the *Antaeus* version, and the changes between this draft and the final one that appeared in your first collection are all relatively minor. Here, for example: "on wet mimeographed paper" becomes "on mimeographed paper which felt wet." Or: "No library and no books to speak of," and in the later version you got rid of the "to speak of."

TW That was a grotesque emendation, wasn't it? It was no books to speak of . . . if it has no books, how can it possibly be a library, right? It's a comical, grotesque change. Why I changed the other, I don't remember. I think for the sake of accuracy. And also, there's something in the sentence, the sound of the sentence that I like: "on mimeographed paper which felt wet." That sentence duplicates for me the sensation of picking one of those newsletters up—the delayed reaction you have when you pick it up and it feels wet. That's what I wanted to catch in that sentence. Why did I change the other one though?

JW I wonder if maybe you were thinking that this attributed to Mary an element of superiority or snobbishness that you didn't like?

TW Could be. It might well have been the reason. It does do that a little.

JW Because it does sound almost a little like Louise.

TW Being a little superior about the books in there. No *real* books.

JW And this suggests that this school, perhaps, is not long for this world.

TW No, it isn't. They haven't even stocked their library yet.

JW And then the comma after . . .

TW I always mess around with commas. After Benedict Arnold is it?

JW Yes.

TW I don't know why. I have these fits when I don't like commas at all, and I take them all out of everything. But I don't like comma-ridden prose. Jim Harrison's prose has a lot of velocity and power and he hardly uses commas at all.

JW This was an interesting one: from "expense of bringing me" to "expense of bringing her." A subtle shift in point of view.

TW Yeah, I like that better.

JW Then, a little farther down the page, you changed "as if" to "like."

TW Technically, of course, this is the more grammatical way but I preferred the colloquial here.

JW Most of the revisions of the *Antaeus* version are, if not minor, quite subtle. Do you regard these changes mostly as tinkerings?

TW Yes. Tinkerings.

JW Here's another change you made: in the early version "sonofabitch" is run together.

TW I put it all together? I think that's the way she would have said it. She'd run it together.

JW And when Mary's waiting for the interview to begin, you just changed the time to twenty minutes from the original half hour.

TW I'll tell you something else I would change here. This woman would never have written two books. She would have written maybe one book. And that's the way I read it now, when I read it out loud. She never would have gotten another book out.

JW And you changed "attacks" to "raids."

TW I'm endlessly fooling with words. Every time I sit down to write, I go through just about everything I've written up to that point. It takes me hours just to get where I can start writing for the day, because I'm fooling around with words all the time. I just reread with great pleasure, this book of Phillip Roth's, *The Ghost Writer.* Zuckerman goes to visit Lonoff, the famous writer. And Lonoff is this old sourpuss who talks about going up to his study and monkeying around with words and taking them out and putting them in and changing around the order and so on. This is this great writer's life. I felt such a sense of dismal recognition.

JW Reading it ["In the Garden of the North American Martyrs"] again the other day, did you see anything else you'd change now?

TW Not really. The kind of stories I mostly prefer to read these days are not of this kind, to tell you the truth. It has a lot of symbolic machinery, this story. It has an almost mathematical logic. It leads very purposefully to where it's going. It has a very clear ending, almost a triumphal ending. It's a well-made story. It's written with a great deal of irony. And those are all things that I'm not particularly interested in doing myself right now. I prefer to write a story that doesn't have any obvious symbolic machinery, that is essentially unironic. The voice that tells it might be, but the conception is not. And a story in which the ending is not quite so clean and well pronounced as in this story.

JW It sounds like you're describing the distinction between this story and, say, "Sanity."

TW That's a possible example.

JW How come?

TW I don't know. It's because I don't have the certainties about things that I think I had then. I have a more tentative feeling about what I know, about what goes on between people. This is a story whose truth is a very abstract truth, it seems to me. It's about power. It's about manipulation. But I pushed the characters to a certain grotesquerie of conception. And now I'm a little more interested, at least for the purposes of my stories, in nuances of relationships between people, and "Sanity" is a good example because that's also a story about power. It's about a girl trying to take the upper hand for her own protection. But the plot is less pronounced.

JW But in this collection there are stories that have less emphatic endings.

TW There are stories more of the other kind in this collection.

JW "Smokers," I think, ends on sort of a more open note.

TW "Smokers" is more in that line.

JW Now, did you submit this ["In the Garden," *Antaeus* version]? Did you submit the earlier drafts before you hit on the final one?

TW No. I knew they weren't right. I knew they weren't right.

JW Did you submit it any place other than *Antaeus*?

TW No, I didn't. How did it happen? I sent it there and Dan Halpern called me up about two weeks later. Said how much he loved the story and asked me if I had any others. In fact, I had two other stories that I hadn't even sent out. I sent them to him, and he took those stories too. It was an incredible break for me. I was living in Arizona at the time, and it was a very encouraging thing for me to have that happen. The same as with Michael Curtis publishing that story "Smokers" in the *Atlantic* a couple of years before. In terms of the publication times, it would have been almost four years before, because he published that in '76 and these stories didn't come out until '80. I had a long period where I didn't have anything published at all. But you don't want to be thinking about that. And God knows, you don't ever want to think about how old you are, not for any reason.

JW So you think it took you a total of four or five months to get that story out?

TW That's right.

JW How many drafts would you guess?

TW Oh boy, that story ate up drafts. Eight or nine drafts for that story before the last *t* was crossed.

JW How did you decide to place this where you did in the collection?

TW I was thinking about that the other day because I was looking for it. I couldn't find it. It made me laugh, because I remember I gave a lot of thought to placing these stories in the collection. Each one of them had a great reason for being where it was. Now I couldn't even find it. We think these things are so damn important at the time. And here I am, the author of the collection, and I have no idea where to look for the story. I will go on doing that with my next collection. I will always do it. But the fact of the matter is, when I sit down to read a collection, I skip around, even though I know that the poor son of a bitch who wrote the collection did the same thing I did.

I just got William Trevor's collection *Family Sins* the other day. I skipped around looking for the short ones to read first to see if I liked them, and then I read a couple of the longer ones here and there. I always look for stories whose titles I like. And I tend to read those before stories whose titles seem bland to me, or conventional. So readers are constantly confounding the purposes of writers in organizing their work. A novel is obviously different. Nobody can do that with a novel.

JW One of my favorites in this collection is "Hunters in the Snow." That's another story that tests some of the sort of traditional conventions.

TW Does it?

JW I think it does.

TW Not formally it doesn't.

JW No, because it's very well made.

TW It's a "well-made" story, true.

JW The whole business about the dog, that's very carefully constructed.

TW Exactly.

JW What I mean is that this realistic narrative begins to spiral into the surreal. These guys driving off in the wrong direction with their buddy bleeding to death in the bed of the pickup. I've often wondered if, on one level at least, this story wasn't intended to lampoon the sort of gushy, confessional mentality that's been so prevalent in recent years.

TW The language they speak is very much that language. That story has been made into a couple of little movies, three of them actually. People keep making it into these half-hour movies. It's very easy to adapt. They take the dialogue directly. And they've all made them with the hope of selling them to PBS, but it's such an ugly little story that they won't show it. I can see why they do it. It's got a good strong narrative line, and the dialogue is funny in a way that the characters who speak it aren't aware of. I like that story. That's one of my favorite stories still.

JW Does your reading change while you're working?

TW Yes, it does. When I'm in hot pursuit of my own work, I tend to read history and biography and canonical, classic fiction by inimitable writers like Dickens and Tolstoy. Right now I'm reading Turgenev's *Sportsman's Sketches*.

JW Inimitable so you won't be tempted?

TW Absolutely. At these times I try to stay away from contemporary writers. I read them in the lulls, when I'm in a valley between writing periods. I do, in fact, keep up pretty well with contemporary American fiction. But sometimes I need to stand back from it. By reading the older fiction I'm setting myself up in relationship to their standards rather than those of my contemporaries. That's as much of an explanation as I can make for it.

JW Do you think about that a lot—critical reputation or historical significance—or do you try not to think about it?

TW No, I don't think about it much. That way lies madness. I can remember thinking, If I ever get a story published—just one—I'll be happy. And I haven't ever lost that sense of excitement at having a story taken somewhere, or even finishing a story that I like a lot. I never, ever thought that

I'd be able to have the kind of life that I've been able to have as a writer. It's been an amazing kind of surprise and blessing to me. The rest, as Eliot said, is not our business, it really isn't.

The thing you have to remember, that all of us have to remember who are writers, is that in almost every other way in life, time is our enemy. But time is a writer's friend. Writing happens over time and it gets better over time, with very, very few exceptions. The time that works against you in every other way is working for you in this way. You're seasoning, you're deepening. If you continue to write, and if you ask the best of yourself, and if you're working toward that all the time, it will happen. You don't give up. If you know the sound you want to hear, you'll hit the note eventually.

JW In one of his interviews, Carver talked about how heartening it is for any struggling writer to look at the early drafts of great writers.

TW I certainly agree that it is heartening. I enjoy reading the first drafts of other writers. And it's certainly neurotic of me not to want to share mine. I had file cabinets full of things. Not just rough drafts, but stories I had finished that I thought, well, it seems bad to me now but someday it might seem better. When we moved here, I did a real purging. Just emptied it out. It felt great. Carrying out to the garbage can things that I worked months on, years on. A very strange feeling. In what other profession can you do that?

JW In your introduction to the Chekhov collection you edited [*A Doctor's Visit* (New York: Bantam Books, 1988)], you discuss the sense of proximity and unpredictability in Chekhov. I think of those as being two hallmarks of your work. In "The Missing Person," for example, you never expect when you start the story that it's going to lead—

TW To the odd places it leads to.

JW Yes. I wondered whether what you'd written in reference to Chekhov is equally important to you in your own work.

TW Yes. I was rereading that introduction the other day. And I was amused at myself, as I would have been if someone else had written it, as assigning to Chekhov virtues that really are virtues that I would hope for myself. Do you know what I mean? I'm not saying it's a self-serving introduction so much as one that expresses my own hopes as a story writer. I look at him and maybe what I'm seeing are a lot of my own hopes realized. I guess I'm praising him for the things that I value. And I'm probably not mentioning things that other people would. For example, I don't talk much about his wonderful characterizations, which are of a different kind than interests me. He works a little more from type than I like to. Russian literature abounds in character types. He does that too. In his best stories he particularizes more, like Gurov in "Lady with Pet Dog." Anyway, that is something about his stories that I like—that they are very immediate. Do you like Chekhov's stories?

JW Yes, but I'm always uncertain about translations. One version is titled "Lady with Pet Dog," another "Lady with Lap Dog." Or take the story "Enemies," which is included in your anthology, *A Doctor's Visit*. I've seen several different translations of that story. Sometimes it's titled "Two Tragedies." The very first paragraph changes dramatically from one translation to another. The first line of one indicates the events are taking place at ten in the morning, and of the others, ten at night. One translator describes the mother giving way to "the first paroxysm of despair," while the next describes her yielding to "the ecstasy of despair." Those kinds of inconsistencies make me nervous, make me wonder how much actual Chekhov I'm getting.

TW I've read a lot of different translations, too. I think the Constance Garnett translations—they took a beating from Nabokov and from Edmund Wilson and from other people—are the best translations available in English. They might not be the most *accurate*. I understand they're not. But Ronald Hingley, who is accurate, has such a dead ear. Ann Dunnigan has some very, very fine translations, as good as Garnett's. "At Sea" and "In Exile" in *A Doctor's Visit* are both by Ann Dunnigan.

JW Now you also mention his dissatisfaction with "The Steppe" for being too episodic and loose-knit. And I wonder also if that's something that you're suspicious of in general.

TW "The Steppe" is not pointed the way his later fiction is. It's like Turgenev in *A Sportsman's Sketches*. You can see very clearly the antecedent of "The Steppe" there, where you've got the young fellow wandering around the province and recording his observations. But you don't have a strong sense of how this is affecting him. What's his stake in what he's reporting here? He's simply the eye; he's the camera of the story. What Chekhov developed so beautifully in his later fiction is the suggestion that the narrator of the story cannot escape the consequences of the story he's telling, that if he does, it's not a story. It's an anecdote, it's a tale, or something else. It's the same with Joyce. In "Araby," for example, the narrator is implicated in his story. The narrator is changed by his story. He realizes his folly as he's standing in the empty gallery. That isn't there in Turgenev, and it's not there in some of the early Chekhov.

JW In your introduction to another anthology you've edited, *Matters of Life and Death*, you describe the stories that you chose as speaking to us "without flippancy about things that matter." I thought maybe that summed up succinctly your ultimate criterion for a good story.

TW We all know that some things matter and other things don't matter. And it's bullshit to pretend otherwise. That's what the best fiction really does. It requires that our attention be on matters of importance. Those stories in that anthology are about things that were of urgency to the writers. Not necessarily because they're autobiographical. How could Stanley Elkin's story be autobiographical? But it is clearly a cry about something that is deeply disturbing to him in the makeup of this universe. He wrote a continuation of that particular piece called "The Living End" about a dead man conscious in his grave. It's an amazing, nightmarish work, surreal and at the same time absolutely believable, the way a dream is when you're caught in it. I can only imagine that Elkin is writing about what it's like to be caught in a body that doesn't work anymore. It's a vital spirit, his is. And he's found a way of writing about his situation that isn't autobiographical in the traditional sense but has a spiritually autobiographical truth. You don't have to know that about him to appreciate the work. But I can't help noticing it. I think that's why Poe wrote so much about people being buried alive and walled up in tombs before they're dead, that kind of thing. He had a sense of being different, an outsider in this culture and place, as he was, and ostracized. I think he had a personal sense of being buried alive. And he was writing out of his sense of alienation and being the only living thing in a musty tomb, which was how his society appeared to him. This nightmare feeling gets transmuted into those horrible images in his fiction.

JW Sometimes it seems such a fine line between flippancy and the kind of vitality that can really make a story breathe. I wonder if you have a hard time walking that line?

TW I do, at times. When I was a kid, one of the ways I got by was as a cutup, a class clown. Being a wise guy, making people laugh. I can do it. I can make the lines. But fiction isn't a collection of funny lines, or even quotable lines. One of the things about Ray Carver's work, for example, is I can think of very few lines to quote. That tells you something of the power of his work. Everything should be subordinated to the integrity of the story, to its larger, ultimate purposes. And so people like me have to learn to make their sense of humor, such as it is, larger.

In the Garden of the North American Martyrs

When she was young, Mary saw a brilliant and original man lose his job because he had expressed ideas that were offensive to the trustees of the college where they both taught. She shared his views, but did not sign the protest petition. She was, after all, on trial herself—as a teacher, as a woman, as an interpreter of history.

Mary watched herself. Before giving a lecture she wrote it out in full, using the arguments and often the words of other, approved writers, so that she would not by chance say something scandalous. Her own thoughts she kept to herself, and the words for them grew faint as time went on; without quite disappearing they shrank to remote, nervous points, like birds flying away.

When the department turned into a hive of cliques, Mary went about her business and pretended not to know that people hated each other. To avoid seeming bland she let herself become eccentric in harmless ways. She took up bowling, which she learned to love, and founded the Brandon College chapter of a society dedicated to restoring the good name of Richard III. She memorized comedy routines from records and jokes from books; people groaned when she rattled them off, but she did not let that stop her, and after a time the groans became the point of the jokes. They were a kind of tribute to Mary's willingness to expose herself.

In fact no one at the college was safer than Mary, for she was making herself into something institutional, like a custom, or a mascot—part of the college's idea of itself.

Now and then she wondered whether she had been too careful. The things she said and wrote seemed flat to her, pulpy, as though someone else had squeezed the juice out of them. And once, while talking with a senior professor, Mary saw herself reflected in a window: she was leaning toward him and had her head turned so that her ear was right in front of his moving mouth. The sight disgusted her. Years later, when she had to get a hearing aid, Mary suspected that her deafness was a result of always trying to catch everything everyone said.

In the second half of Mary's fifteenth year at Brandon the provost called a meeting of all faculty and students, to announce that the college was bankrupt and would not open its gates again. He was every bit as much surprised as they; the report from the trustees had reached his desk only that morning. It seemed that Brandon's financial manager had speculated in some kind of futures and lost everything. The provost wanted to deliver the news in person before it reached the papers. He wept openly and so did the students and teachers, with only a few exceptions—some cynical upperclassmen who claimed to despise the education they had received.

Mary could not rid her mind of the word "speculate." It meant to guess, in terms of money to gamble. How could a man gamble a college? Why would he want to do that, and how could it be that no one stopped him? To Mary, it seemed to belong to another time; she thought of a drunken plantation owner gaming away his slaves.

She applied for jobs and got an offer from a new experimental college in Oregon. It was her only offer so she took it.

The college was in one building. Bells rang all the time, lockers lined the hallways, and at every corner stood a buzzing water fountain. The student newspaper came out twice a month on wet mimeograph paper. The library, which was next to the band room, had no librarian and no books to speak of.

The countryside was beautiful, though, and Mary might have enjoyed it if the rain had not caused her so much trouble. There was something wrong with her lungs that the doctors couldn't agree on, and couldn't cure; whatever it was, the dampness made it worse. On rainy days condensation formed in Mary's hearing aid and shorted it out. She began to dread talking with people, never knowing when she would have to take out her control box and slap it against her leg.

It rained nearly every day. When it was not raining it was getting ready to rain, or clearing. The ground glinted under the grass, and the light had a yellow undertone that flared up during storms.

There was water in Mary's basement. Her walls sweated, and she had found toadstools growing behind the refrigerator. She felt as though she were rusting out, like one of those old cars people thereabouts kept in their front yards, on pieces of wood. Mary knew that everyone was dying, but it did seem to her that she was dying faster than most.

She continued to look for another job, without success. Then, in the fall of her third year in Oregon, she got a letter from a woman named Louise who'd once taught at Brandon. Louise had scored a great success with a book on Benedict Arnold, and was now on the faculty of a famous college in upstate New York. She said that one of her colleagues would be retiring at the end of the year, and asked whether Mary would be interested in the position.

The letter surprised Mary. Louise thought of herself as a great historian and of almost everyone else as useless; Mary had not known that she felt differently about her. Moreover, enthusiasm for other people's causes did not come easily to Louise, who had a way of sucking in her breath when familiar names were mentioned, as though she knew things that friendship kept her from disclosing.

Mary expected nothing, but sent a resume and copies of her two books. Shortly after that Louise called to say that the search committee, of which she was chairwoman, had decided to grant Mary an interview in early November. "Now don't get your hopes *too* high," said Louise.

"Oh, no," said Mary, but thought: Why shouldn't I hope? They would not go to the bother and expense of bringing me to the college if they weren't serious. And she was certain that the interview would go well. She would make them like her, or at least give them no cause to dislike her.

She read about the area with a strange sense of familiarity, as if the land and its history were already known to her. And when her plane left Portland and climbed easterly into the clouds, Mary felt as if she were going home. The feeling stayed with her, growing stronger when they landed. She tried to describe it to Louise as they left the airport at Syracuse and drove toward the college, an hour or so away. "It's like déjà vu," she said.

"Déjà vu is a hoax," said Louise. "It's just a chemical imbalance of some kind."

"Maybe so," said Mary, "but I still have this sensation."

"Don't get serious on me," said Louise. "That's not your long suit. Just be your funny, wisecracking old self. Tell me now—honestly—how do I look?"

It was night, too dark to see Louise's face well, but in the airport she had seemed gaunt and pale and intense. She reminded Mary of a description in the book she'd been reading, of how Iroquois warriors gave themselves visions by fasting. She had that kind of look about her. But she wouldn't want to hear that. "You look wonderful," said Mary.

"There's a reason," said Louise. "I've taken a lover. My concentration has improved, my energy level is up, and I've lost ten pounds. I'm also getting some color in my cheeks, though that could be the weather. I recommend the experience highly. But you probably disapprove."

Mary didn't know what to say. She said that she was sure Louise knew best, but that didn't seem to be enough. "Marriage is a great institution," she added, "but who wants to live in an institution?"

Louise groaned. "I know you," she said, "and I know that right now you're thinking 'But what about Ted? What about the children?' The fact is, Mary, they aren't taking it well at all. Ted has become a nag." She handed Mary her purse. "Be a good girl and light me a cigarette, will you? I know I told you I quit, but this whole thing has been very hard on me, very hard, and I'm afraid I've started again."

They were in the hills now, heading north on a narrow road. Tall trees arched above them. As they topped a rise Mary saw the forest all around, deep black under the plum-colored sky. There were a few lights and these made the darkness seem even greater.

"Ted has succeeded in completely alienating the children from me," Louise was saying. "There is no reasoning with any of them. In fact, they refuse to discuss the matter at all, which is very ironical because over the years I have tried to instill in them a willingness to see things from the other person's point of view. If they could just *meet* Jonathan I know they would feel differently. But they won't hear of it. Jonathan," she said, "is my lover."

"I see," said Mary, and nodded.

Coming around a curve they caught two deer in the headlights. Their eyes lit up and their hindquarters tensed; Mary could see them shaking as the car went by. "Deer," she said.

"I don't know," said Louise, "I just don't know. I do my best and it never seems to be enough. But that's enough about me—let's talk about you. What did you think of my latest book?" She squawked and beat her palms on the steering wheel. "God, I love that joke," she said. "Seriously, though, what about you? It must have been a real shockeroo when good old Brandon folded."

"It was hard. Things haven't been good but they'll be a lot better if I get this job."

"At least you have work," said Louise. "You should look at it from the bright side."

"I try."

"You seem so gloomy. I hope you're not worrying about the interview, or the class. Worrying won't do you a bit of good. Be happy."

"Class? What class?"

"The class you're supposed to give tomorrow, after the interview. Didn't I tell you? *Mea culpa*, hon, *mea maxima culpa*. I've been uncharacteristically forgetful lately."

"But what will I do?"

"Relax," said Louise. "Just pick a subject and wing it."

"Wing it?"

"You know, open your mouth and see what comes out. Extemporize."

"But I always work from a prepared lecture."

Louise sighed. "All right. I'll tell you what. Last year I wrote an article on the Marshall Plan that I got bored with and never published. You can read that."

Parroting what Louise had written seemed wrong to Mary, at first; then it occurred to her that she had been doing the same kind of thing for many years, and that this was not the time to get scruples. "Thanks," she said. "I appreciate it."

"Here we are," said Louise, and pulled into a circular drive with several cabins grouped around it. In two of the cabins lights were on; smoke drifted straight up from the chimneys. "This is the visitors' center. The college is another two miles thataway." Louise pointed down the road. "I'd invite you to stay at my house, but I'm spending the night with Jonathan and Ted is not good company these days. You would hardly recognize him."

She took Mary's bags from the trunk and carried them up the steps of a darkened cabin. "Look," she said, "they've laid a fire for you. All you have to do is light it." She stood in the middle of the room with her arms crossed and watched as Mary held a match under the kindling. "There," she said. "You'll be snugaroo in no time. I'd love to stay and chew the fat but I can't. You just get a good night's sleep and I'll see you in the morning."

Mary stood in the doorway and waved as Louise pulled out of the drive, spraying gravel. She filled her lungs, to taste the air: it was tart and clear. She could see the stars in their figurations, and the vague streams of light that ran among the stars.

She still felt uneasy about reading Louise's work as her own. It would be her first complete act of plagiarism. It would change her. It would make her less—how much less, she did not know. But what else could she do? She certainly couldn't 'wing it.' Words might fail her, and then what? Mary had a dread of silence. When she thought of silence she thought of drowning, as if it were a kind of water she could not swim in.

"I want this job," she said, and settled deep into her coat. It was cashmere and Mary had not worn it since moving to Oregon, because people there thought you were pretentious if you had on anything but a Pendleton shirt or, of course, raingear. She rubbed her cheek against the upturned collar and thought of a silver moon shining through bare black branches, a white house with green shutters, red leaves falling in a hard blue sky.

Louise woke her a few hours later. She was sitting on the edge of the bed, pushing at Mary's shoulder and snuffling loudly. When Mary asked her what was wrong she said, "I want your opinion on something. It's very important. Do you think I'm womanly?"

Mary sat up. "Louise, can this wait?"

"No."

"Womanly?"

Louise nodded.

"You are very beautiful," said Mary, "and you know how to present yourself."

Louise stood and paced the room. "That sonofabitch," she said. She came back and stood over Mary. "Let's suppose someone said I have no sense of humor. Would you agree or disagree?"

"In some things you do. I mean, yes, you have a good sense of humor."

"What do you mean, 'in some things'? What kind of things?"

"Well, if you heard that someone had been killed in an unusual way, like by an exploding cigar, you would think that was funny."

Louise laughed.

"That's what I mean," said Mary.

Louise went on laughing. "Oh, Lordy," she said. "Now it's my turn to say something about you." She sat down beside Mary.

"Please," said Mary.

"Just one thing," said Louise.

Mary waited.

"You're trembling," said Louise. "I was just going to say—oh, forget it. Listen, do you mind if I sleep on the couch. I'm all in."

"Go ahead."

"Sure it's okay? You've got a big day tomorrow." She fell back on the sofa and kicked off her shoes. "I was just going to say, you should use some liner on those eyebrows of yours. They sort of disappear and the effect is disconcerting."

Neither of them slept. Louise chain-smoked cigarettes and Mary watched the coals burn down. When it was light enough that they could see each other Louise got up. "I'll send a student for you," she said. "Good luck."

The college looked the way colleges are supposed to look. Roger, the student assigned to show Mary around, explained that it was an exact copy of a college in England, right down to the gargoyles and stained-glass windows. It looked so much like a college that moviemakers sometimes used it as a set. *Andy Hardy Goes to College* had been filmed there, and every fall they had an Andy Hardy Goes to College Day, with raccoon coats and goldfish-swallowing contests.

Above the door of the Founder's Building was a Latin motto which, roughly translated, meant "God helps those who help themselves." As Roger recited the names of illustrious graduates Mary was struck by the extent to which they had taken this precept to heart. They had helped themselves to railroads, mines, armies, states; to empires of finance with outposts all over the world.

Roger took Mary to the chapel and showed her a plaque bearing the names of alumni who had been killed in various wars, all the way back to the Civil War. There were not many names. Here too, apparently, the graduates had helped themselves. "Oh yes," said Roger as they were leaving, "I forgot to tell you. The communion rail comes from some church in Europe where Charlemagne used to go."

They went to the gymnasium, and the three hockey rinks, and the library, where Mary inspected the card catalogue, as though she would turn down the job if they didn't have the right books. "We have a little more time," said Roger as they went outside. "Would you like to see the power plant?"

Mary wanted to keep busy until the last minute, so she agreed.

Roger led her into the depths of the service building, explaining things about the machine, which was the most advanced in the country. "People think the college is really old-fashioned," he said, "but it isn't.

They let girls come here now, and some of the teachers are women. In fact, there's a statute that says they have to interview at least one woman for each opening. There it is."

They were standing on an iron catwalk above the biggest machine Mary had ever beheld. Roger, who was majoring in Earth Sciences, said that it had been built from a design pioneered by a professor in his department. Where before he had been gabby, Roger now became reverent. It was clear that to him, this machine was the soul of the college, that indeed the purpose of the college was to provide outlets for the machine. Together they leaned against the railing and watched it hum.

Mary arrived at the committee room exactly on time for her interview, but it was empty. Her two books were on the table, along with a water pitcher and some glasses. She sat down and picked up one of the books. The binding cracked as she opened it. The pages were smooth, clean, unread. Mary turned to the first chapter, which began "It is generally believed that . . ." How dull, she thought.

Nearly half an hour later Louise came in with several men. "Sorry we're late," she said. "We don't have much time so we'd better get started." She introduced Mary to the men but with one exception the names and faces did not stay together. The exception was Dr. Howells, the department chairman, who had a porous blue nose and terrible teeth.

A shiny-faced man to Dr. Howells' right spoke first. "So," he said, "I understand you once taught at Brandon College."

"It was a shame that Brandon had to close," said a young man with a pipe in his mouth. "There is a place for schools like Brandon." As he talked the pipe wagged up and down.

"Now you're in Oregon," said Dr. Howells. "I've never been there. How do you like it?"

"Not very much," said Mary.

"Is that right?" Dr. Howells leaned toward her. "I thought everyone liked Oregon. I hear it's very green."

"That's true," said Mary.

"I suppose it rains a lot," he said.

"Nearly every day."

"I wouldn't like that," he said, shaking his head. "I like it dry. Of course it snows here, and you have your rain now and then, but it's a *dry* rain. Have you ever been to Utah? There's a state for you. Bryce Canyon. The Mormon Tabernacle Choir."

"Dr. Howells was brought up in Utah," said the young man with the pipe.

"It was a different place altogether in those days," said Dr. Howells. "Mrs. Howells and I have always talked about going back when I retire, but now I'm not so sure."

"We're a little short on time," said Louise.

"And here I've been going on and on," said Dr. Howells. "Before we wind things up, is there anything you want to tell us?"

"Yes. I think you should give me the job." Mary laughed when she said this, but no one laughed back, or even looked at her. They all looked away. Mary understood then that they were not really considering her for the position. She had been brought here to satisfy a rule. She had no hope.

The men gathered their papers and shook hands with Mary and told her how much they were looking forward to her class. "I can't get enough of the Marshall Plan," said Dr. Howells.

"Sorry about that," said Louise when they were alone. "I didn't think it would be so bad. That was a real bitcheroo."

"Tell me something," said Mary. "You already know who you're going to hire, don't you?"

Louise nodded.

"Then why did you bring me here?" Louise began to explain about the statute and Mary interrupted. "I know all that. Buy why me? Why did you pick *me*?"

Louise walked to the window. She spoke with her back to Mary. "Things haven't been going very well for old Louise," she said. "I've been unhappy and I thought you might cheer me up. You used to be so funny, and I was sure you would enjoy the trip—it didn't cost you anything, and it's pretty this time of year with the leaves and everything. Mary, you don't know the things my parents did to me. And Ted is no barrel of laughs either. Or Jonathan, the sonofabitch. I deserve some love and friendship but I don't get any." She turned and looked at her watch. "It's almost time for your class. We'd better go."

"I would rather not give it. After all, there's not much point, is there?"

"But you *have* to give it. That's part of the interview." Louise handed Mary a folder. "All you have to do is read this. It isn't much, considering all the money we've laid out to get you here."

Mary followed Louise down the hall to the lecture room. The professors were sitting in the front row with their legs crossed. They smiled and nodded at Mary. Behind them the room was full of students, some of whom had spilled over into the aisles. One of the professors adjusted the microphone to Mary's height, crouching down as he went to the podium and back as though he would prefer not to be seen.

Louise called the room to order. She introduced Mary and gave the subject of the lecture, not knowing that Mary had decided to wing it after all. Mary came to the podium unsure of what she would say; sure only that she would rather die than read Louise's article. The sun poured through the stained glass onto the people around her, painting their faces. Thick streams of smoke from the young professor's pipe drifted through a circle of red light at Mary's feet, turning crimson and twisting like flames.

"I wonder how many of you know," she began, "that we are in the Long House, the ancient domain of the Five Nations of the Iroquois."

Two professors looked at each other.

"The Iroquois were without pity," said Mary. "They hunted people down with clubs and arrows and spears and nets, and blowguns made from elder stalks. They tortured their captives, sparing no one, not even the little children. They took scalps and practiced cannibalism and slavery. Because they had no pity they became powerful, so powerful that no other tribe dared to oppose them. They made the other tribes pay tribute, and when they had nothing more to pay, the Iroquois attacked them."

Several of the professors began to whisper. Dr. Howells was saying something to Louise, and Louise was shaking her head.

"In one of their attacks," said Mary, "they captured two Jesuit priests, Jean de Brébeuf and Gabriel Lalement. They covered Lalement with pitch and set him on fire in front of Brébeuf. When Brébeuf rebuked them they cut off his lips and put a burning iron down his throat. They hung a collar of red-hot hatchets around his neck, and poured boiling water over his head. When he continued to preach to them they cut strips of flesh from his body and ate them before his eyes. While he was still alive they scalped him and cut open his breast and drank his blood. Later, their chief tore out Brébeuf's heart and ate it, but just before he did this Brébeuf spoke to them one last time. He said—"

"That's enough!" yelled Dr. Howells, jumping to his feet.

Louise stopped shaking her head. Her eyes were perfectly round.

Mary had come to the end of her facts. She did not know what Brébeuf had said. Silence rose up around her; just when she thought she would go under and be lost in it she heard someone whistling in the hallway outside, trilling the notes like a bird, like many birds.

"Mend your lives," she said. "You have deceived yourselves in the pride of your hearts, and the strength of your arms. Though you soar aloft like the eagle, though your nest is set among the stars, thence I will bring you down, says the Lord. Turn from power to love. Be kind. Do justice. Walk humbly."

Louise was waving her arms. "Mary!" she shouted.

But Mary had more to say, much more; she waved back at Louise, then turned off her hearing aid so that she would not be distracted again.

TESS GALLAGHER

'Red Poppy,' 'Two of Anything,' 'Black Pudding'

The three poems that form the basis of my conversation with Tess Gallagher are all included in her volume *Moon Crossing Bridge* (St. Paul: Graywolf Press, 1992). Gallagher is the author of five other volumes of poetry and a book of essays entitled *A Concert of Tenses* (Ann Arbor: University of Michigan Press, 1986). She has also contributed introductions to several works: *Carver Country* (New York: Scribners, 1990); Raymond Carver's final book of poetry, *A New Path to the Waterfall* (New York: Atlantic Monthly Press, 1989); and a book of Carver's uncollected work, *No Heroics, Please* (New York: Vintage, 1992). The title story of her collection of short fiction, *The Lover of Horses* (New York: Harper and Row, 1986; reissued in 1991 by Graywolf Press), appeared in *American Short Story Masterpieces* (New York: Dell, 1987).

Formerly professor of English at Syracuse University, Gallagher more recently has held the Lois Mackey Chair at Beloit College. She has received numerous awards, including grants from the National Endowment for the Arts, the Maxine Cushing Gray Award, and a Guggenheim fellowship. She lives now in the town where she grew up, Port Angeles, Washington, and I met with her there in late June 1991. We spoke first in the house she shared briefly with her husband, Raymond Carver, and then continued our conversation at Sky House, the home she had built for herself in the early 1980s, overlooking the Pacific Strait of Juan de Fuca. I tape-recorded our conversation, and we sent the transcript back and forth numerous times through the fall of 1991.

"Red Poppy" first appeared in the *New Yorker* (October 2, 1989) and "Two of Anything" in the *American Poetry Review* (21, no. 1 [January/February 1992]). "Black Pudding" was first published in *A Book of Women Poets from Antiquity to Now*, edited by Aliki Barnstone and Willis Barnstone (New York: Schocken Books, 1992). Gallagher began drafting the poems in January 1989 and continued working on them up until the publication of *Moon Crossing Bridge* in early 1992. "Red Poppy" and "Black Pudding" were begun in the home she shared with Raymond Carver, while "Two of Anything" first occurred to her as she sat in her upstairs bedroom at Sky House, gazing out the large window at a boat passing through the strait.

The material gathered here includes the original handwritten drafts Gallagher composed in her journals, subsequent typed drafts, and copies of the poems as they first appeared in the periodicals and the anthology. The final versions are taken from *Moon Crossing Bridge*, Gallagher's sixth volume of poetry.

Red Poppy

That linkage of warnings sent a tremor through June
as if to prepare October in the hardest apples.
One week in late July we held hands
through the bars of his hospital bed. Our sleep
made a canopy over us and it seemed I heard
its durable roaring in the companion sleep
of what must have been our Bedouin god, and now
when the poppy lets go I know it is to lay bare
his thickly seeded black coach
at the pinnacle of dying.

My shaggy ponies heard the shallow snapping of silk
but grazed on down the hillside, their prayer flags
tearing at the void – what we
stared into, its cool flux
of blue and white. How just shaking at flies
they sprinkled the air with the soft unconscious praise
of bells braided into their manes. My life

simplified to "for him" and his thinned like an injection
wearing off so the real gave way to
the more-than-real, each moment's carmine
abundance, furl of reddest petals
lifted from the stalk and no hint of the black
hussar's hat at the center. By then his breathing stopped
so gradually I had to brush lips to know
an ending. Tasting then that plush of scarlet
which is the last of warmth, kissless kiss
he would have given. Mine to extend a lover's right past its radius,
to give and also most needfully, my gallant hussar,
to bend and take.

Two of Anything

What silk-thin difference is there
if I stay to dream or go.
Kyoko Selden

That small tug, which at first seems
all on its own in the strait,
can eventually be seen to pull two barges, each
twice its size, because water
understands everything and all
day says "pass, pass by." I propose
a plan and we discuss it. I'm afraid I'll never
be happy again. "Bring me
a glass of water," he says. "Someone, you know,
has to stay here and take care of things."
Two ducks fly by. I take
a few sips from his glass. Outside it's
deep blue morning, almost purple
it's so glad to be cheating
the sleepers of its willful drifting, the tangled
blue of night and the blue premonition
that will dissolve and carry
it. Two boys vicious with news fling
the morning paper house to house
down the hill. Two horses out of childhood I loved,
Daisy and Colonel Boy, are hitched
to the wagon. I hear the cold extravagance of
tiny bells welded into their harness straps.
Iron wheels under us over snow
for miles through the walnut groves. The two
pearled hair combs he gave me
make a chilly mouth on the sill. I look up and out
over water at the horizon – no, two
horizons. One reached and entered with him, and so

is under me, and the other
far enough away to be the dead mate of this one.
Between them, lively passage of boats, none
empty. That’s fascinating,
I said to the poet, let me add one. I thought
there was more water in this glass.
I guess not, one of us said.

Black Pudding

Even then I knew it was the old unanswerable form of beauty
as pain, like coming onto a pair of herons
near the river mouth at dawn. Beauty as when the body
is a dumb stick before the moment – yet goes on,
gazes until memory prepares a quick untidy room
with unpredictable visiting hours.
So I brought you there, you who didn't belong, thinking to outsave
memory by tearing the sacred from

its alcove. I let you see us, arms helplessly tender,
holding each other all night on that awkward couch
because our life was ending. Again and again
retelling our love between gusts of weeping.
Did I let you overhear those gray-blue dyings?
Or as I think now, like a Mongol tribesman did I stop the horse
on its desert march, take the meal of blood

from its bowed neck to be heated. This then is my black pudding
only the stalwart know to eat. How I climbed
like a damp child waking from nightmare to find
the parents intimate and still awake.
And with natural animal gladness, rubbed my face
into the scald of their cheeks, tasting salt
of the unsayable – but, like a rescuer who comes too late, too
fervently marked with duty, was unable to fathom

what their danger and passage had been for. Except
as you know now, to glimpse is intrusion enough,

and when there is nothing else to sustain, blood will be thickened
with fire. Not a pretty dish.
But something taken from the good and cherished beast on loan to us,
muscled over in spirit and strong enough to carry us
as far as it can, there being advantage
to this meagerness, unsavoriness that rations itself
and reminds us to respect even its bitter portion.
Don't ask me now why I'm walking my horse.

JW You write your poems first in longhand, in your notebooks?

TG When I'm at Sky House I do. At a certain point, I really like to get cold with the poems and distance myself from my handwriting. The intimate form of the poem is in the handwritten draft. At Sky House, there's just a typewriter. So I then take it out of the notebook, type it on a typewriter, and then I bring it over to my office and the computer in the afternoon. After working all morning I may have a typed version by one PM. I'll write revisions by hand on that typescript. Then I'll transfer those changes to the computer copy. Then I'll work again, hand-drafting onto the computer copy. I don't make changes directly. I like that period of considering. I have two pens that I like to write with. I've had them for years. They're Mont Blancs. I had very bad handwriting, and I found that using a fountain pen improved my handwriting. It had really to do with the flow and the rhythm. And I couldn't get that right with a ballpoint. I didn't have the proper instrument.

JW When did you start using the journals?

TG I've always used those, ever since Theodore Roethke's class. He required that we keep a notebook, so I have been using these, well, since that class with him in 1963 at University of Washington. I've used different kinds of notebooks. Some of them have been more journal-like. I buy them because I like the color or the size. None of them are lined. I like a blank page.

I like to do my drafting in something that's bound, in a bound notebook, because then it's less likely to be lost. When I first met Ray [Carver], he wasn't keeping drafts at all. And I had been keeping them all along, mainly because of advice I got from Mark Strand. He was my teacher in 1970 at the University of Washington, and he was selling his papers at that time, and he said that these were very valuable documents. He said, "Tess, you should start saving your drafts." And I was so impressed that he thought I should save my drafts! So I really began to be more careful about it after that. And then when Ray and I started living together in '79, I told him not to throw away his drafts and I fished them out of the wastebasket. All of those drafts exist because of something Mark Strand said to me in 1970.

This journal, for example, was kept on a trip to Rio, to Brazil. Often a notebook will be half-empty, and I'll go back and make different kinds of notes in the back of it. [Reading] "Mrs. Webster, letting us taste her death before it happens. So she sticks around to see how everyone is acting. How

X makes himself her protector from her friends and exacts balm, protects the life she wants to lose. Is it his doing that she is still alive, when she wanted to die? He is the interpreter."

You know, it's these little ways in which you try to figure out who someone is, and what they're doing, and why they're doing it. Also I include a lot of just odd things from my reading. I used to read the notebooks of writers in those days when Roethke was trying to get us to keep notebooks, trying to figure out what was supposed to go in there. So I read Camus's notebooks and Leonardo da Vinci's notebooks, when they came out in paperback. A notebook can mark your passage. I can tell by the address on this one that this was used in the time I was first living with Ray in El Paso. And I was writing essays then.

Oh, here's "Kisses with Threats Inside," and I might use that in my *Portable Kisses* book. Now you see how valuable a notebook is? Here's a poem that just never got typed up. And I'm going to type that up and see if it will fit in this book. This book, *Portable Kisses,* was published first in the limited edition of 1978 that I showed you. But the poems were written ahead of that. So that's a lot of years to be kind of working on that book.

JW How often do you go back through the journals?

TG Not often enough. But usually when I'm putting a book together, I will go back through to see if there's anything that might enhance the present work. And also, to look for epigraphs, because I have saved little tidbits from my reading.

Now, here's a business card. Ralph Yarborough, attorney at law. Why am I keeping that? Oh, I know why I kept that! He's the one who was responsible for my getting to go to college, because he started the National Defense Fund Loans, and these gave about $500 as a grant to young people starting college. I was seventeen years old and didn't have any money to go to college. The $500 made the difference between my going or not. I met Senator Yarborough somewhere in the Midwest—yes, Lake Forest, Illinois. He had also put through "black lung" legislation that enabled coal miners to get compensation. So I haven't lost him, he's taped into my notebook. I got to thank him in person for helping me get to college.

I read a lot from art books because some of my main relationships have been with artists, the most significant ones being with Alfredo Arreguin, and Susan Lytle. Alfredo was my friend when I was seventeen in Seattle, and so we've had a mutually influential relationship over thirty-one years.

Here I've been reading from Chagall. [Reading] "Chagall himself lays particular stress on the problem of the three lancet window. He calls it 'the wounded window' and compares it to 'a man who limps or has a crooked stance due to one leg being much shorter than the other.' The composition had to justify this external defective order, so to say from within, and yet achieve a balance."

This observation seems really to talk about the whole way in which one works as a writer with the raw material that comes, doesn't it? The composition has to justify its "external defective order." So to say from within, and yet achieve a balance. I never know what use they're going to be, these jottings, you know. I'm just attracted to them at the moment.

JW Do you ever come across poems in the old journals that embarrass you?

TG Not really. I just realize that we start out in these very awkward ways, and we do look a little stupid as we draft, and that's all right. We're not gods, you know, where something comes fully formed. And it's very good for one's humility to look back and realize that it's a complete state of chaos out of which that work begins. And it looks that way too, when you see these early drafts. As you reapproach the material, you gradually get clarity. You make those judgments which form the work. How can you be embarrassed about chaos? I mean, it's just a part of life. And it's a very good part of life, too, chaos. It's not just a menace. You have to be willing to go into the chaos to bring back the beauties.

I feel from poem to poem that I don't know if I can do it. It's a very unwieldy kind of art, writing poetry, because you do these sort of sprints of intense work. And then on the other side you're completely lost again. It's as if you haven't written at all! And you have to begin again. Like an imbecile.

JW When you're really on one of those sprints how do you work? You've mentioned writing by hand in the morning, typing and revising in the afternoons.

TG Yes, I will write the poem into this notebook, and I will do that in the morning. I didn't always work this way. When I was young, I would use any old scrap of time. Now I'm fussy. I want to use the top of my day, the time when my energy is at its best. And so I won't let anything come into my mornings when I'm planning to write. And so I get up early and I begin to move into the mood of the writing, usually with a little reading, and I unplug the telephones and just work.

JW What kind of reading, usually?

TG Well, at my other house, Sky House, there are books everywhere. I'm omnivorous. I'll have all kinds of different books around. Some nonfiction, a lot of poetry, novels, just whatever has come my way. And I read many books at the same time. Just dip in and out of them. And one of the things

I notice myself doing as I come to draft a poem is realizing that the motion for the poem is drawn to what I've been reading. In a certain sense it doesn't matter what language I pick up as I write. Reading some other bits of language will stimulate what is already at work in me. I can make use of almost anything that comes to me during these periods. It's probably one of those "beta" states—near trance, very slowed down. And there's a good sense of my having access to everything.

JW Do you always feel like you're working on many different poems at once, too?

TG No, I work one poem at a time.

JW Through the drafts? You just take it through until it's done?

TG Yes. I really bulldog a poem down. I just stay with it. And usually a poem will be done in a sitting. I'll carry it through the whole day. The process will go the whole day, getting it onto the typewriter then onto the computer, then working again by hand, and it could be the next day before it really has settled down.

The early poems in *Moon Crossing Bridge* were very dense, and they demanded a lot more in the way of revision than some of these ones for *Portable Kisses*. There has been a marvelous kind of ease in that book. In *Moon Crossing Bridge* it was almost like I had to reform language to be able to say the kinds of things I had to say in that book of mourning for Ray.

JW How much of this new ease do you think has to do with the poetry, and how much of it has to do with you? Or is it one and the same?

TG The density of the language had totally to do with me and my life, and those particular feelings I was having, and trying to find an approach to that subject matter, that state of being I was in, having lost the love of my life, and trying to find a way to relate to him through the poetry. Trying also to just stay alive. They were poems that were written in real desperation and necessity. They're high voltage poems. I didn't write them unless I felt them. They aren't out of the "hobby zone," you know. There is heart's blood in those poems.

So naturally there was a lot of intensity in the act of drafting them. Maybe we should talk about "Red Poppy" so we have an actual poem in front of us.

As you notice here, at the beginning [draft 1], I keep starting over. You can tell that I write incantationally, because I'm trying to get the rhythm going, and get the tone set, and that will then lead me into the material. The sound often precedes the meaning, the sound of what the experience is.

I wrote it in here, in front of the fireplace, on that little couch, that little maroon couch.

I remember the things which generated it, which preceded it. A friend of mine in Montreal had sent me an O'Keeffe postcard of this red poppy, and I had looked at that and thought how vibrant, how searingly red-orange it was. And then I had also been reading Peter Matthiessen's *The Snow Leopard*. After Ray died, my best friend from grade school, Molly Radke, gave me that, and I kept it by my bedside and read from it almost every night, a kind of spiritual companion. So there are some images in the poem from that.

Let's see how much remains: "That web of sorrows caught to her garden / in silvery filaments charged with light, / her grandmother's sequined brooch." I don't continue that, I don't feel I'm on it. So then I write, "That linkage of sorrows sent a tremor in June / so the garden, more simplified and quiet." And then, "That linkage of sorrows sent a tremor in June / and we grew more simplified and quiet / like the final black bead weighing the silvery filament."

Okay, then I start again: "That linkage of sorrows sent a tremor in June / just as the garden was taking off." Oh, I don't like that line at all—you *hear* how wrong it is. "That linkage of warnings sent a tremor through June / as if to prepare the apples for dropping in October." Then I crossed out "in October" and "less suddenly in October / as if to prepare the hardest apples for dropping less suddenly." Then there's a bunch of stuff scribbled down here at the bottom.

"It was only inflection / I am scarlet through and through / to no one ending, tasting that plush of scarlet through / and through." See, a later part of the poem is starting to come—I'm writing it down. "I heard your hearing then, that last and clinging / sense, like an underwater bridge meant to tame." Then I start completely over again! "That linkage of warnings sent a tremor through June." It's exciting. I've hit it. I've got the first line.

JW And the second one pretty much, too.

TG "As if to prepare October in the hardest apples." It's right now, isn't it?

JW It seems like you really had to push to get that second line.

TG And the whole thing about the "dropping more tenderly" had to go. Okay, then, "One week / in late July I held his hand, tending those nights / through the bars of his hospital bed. Our sleep / made a canopy." Then I start over again: "One week in late July we held hands like holding hearts / through the bars in his hospital bed." Well, I eventually gave up the "holding hearts." I think one of my readers, Harold Schweizer, said it verged on sentimental. I'm not so sure, but the physicality of it, if you read it literally, made me decide he was right, so I took it out.

JW What's guiding you at this stage of the writing? Is it primarily your ear?

TG My ear, quite a lot. You know, Roethke had great respect for the individual line, and I learned that from him. Music came first. If you got the music right, the meaning often followed or began to evolve. Meaning doesn't precede music. And what I'm doing in the drafting is trying to get the music and the meaning to come together. And sometimes I use music to lead myself, but you have to be careful with that, because it can drag you into saying false and uninteresting things, you know?

So it's really a combination. I'm trying to see the images, the unfolding, and trying to be in it. I'm working on an actual scene, I'm using an actual scene that happened. I did indeed sit by a hospital bed. I did hold hands all night with Ray. And so for the poem to begin successfully, I have to make the reader attend, also.

But you see, the first line has nothing to do with being in a place. It is emotional and—I don't know how you would characterize this movement, "that linkage of warnings sent a tremor"—you don't know what it means—"that linkage of warnings sent a tremor through June, / as if to prepare October in the hardest apples." All you know is that it tantalizes you, and it has a kind of severity about it. It has poise and bearing and a sense of the passage of time.

You feel like a calamity is coming, and that you are looking back with the writer over the terrain of a real severity which has affected the person's life. And yet now they're in possession of the whole story, and they're going to tell you some of that story.

Let's see. "Our Bedouin sleep made a canopy"—see where I've crossed out here?—"in the companion sleep of Bedouin god [of *a* Bedouin god], and now / when the poppy lets go"—"now when the poppy *breaks*," it had said—"I know it is to lay bare / a gratefulness." Now that went—"a gratefulness" had to go. Too limp. Too sappy. "More than that, thickly seeded black coach / at the pinnacle, at the moment of dying." See, I took out "moment." "Pinnacle" is a much better word.

"My shaggy ponies / the stubble where you face it is grazed in a flex of white and blue / the little prayer flags snapping." Now, this last image I got from Peter Matthiessen, when he was going to one of those Tibetan monasteries in *The Snow Leopard*, and he mentions the snapping of prayer flags. And what I did was to transpose that image and put it onto the ponies. *My* shaggy ponies.

JW In the original draft, you don't seem concerned at all about stanza breaks.

TG No.

JW And you don't seem in your early drafts to be overly concerned about lining strategies either.

TG No, but my line breaks are pretty close. But you see, the stanzas won't be as they are in the draft.

JW Your first instinct for a line break often seems to wind up the final one.

TG I grew up in a gambling family, and there was always poker being played somewhere, and that depends on intuition. So I think there's a good current of intuitional knowledge that's kind of embedded in this blood that I run on.

JW Trusting your hunches.

TG And also the daring, the sense of venturing. And of strategy.

"The clatter of hooves so the horseman could / pass over, but over to what?" Okay, well that didn't even seem part of the poem. It must have been just some sideshow that happened while I was working!

JW That looks almost like a note to yourself at that point. "But over to what—question mark." It reminds me of the note you made to yourself in one corner of the first draft of "Two of Anything."

TG Yes, right, where I'm just questioning the poem. "By then *his* breathing"—see, I'd had "your" and that was direct. The "your" made me able to be *with* Ray more. And I was directing it *to* him and then I removed it—"By then his breathing"—and I took out the "had"—"his breathing stopped / so gradually I had to brush lips"—I took off "with you" to make the meaning wider and the movement more concise. "I had to brush lips / to know an ending, tasting then that plush of scarlet / which is the last of warmth *and sears the heart of aftershock*." Now that last phrase didn't work at all. Then I start to go into incantation again, until I wrote "kissless kiss," which I circled, feeling I had made some new formulation. A little farther down, I hit upon the hussar image, which was coming from the poppy, from that vision—looking down on the poppy, that shaggy black head inside the poppy.

After that, it was a question of being able to make myself, as the speaker, take that initiative of the last kiss.

JW Where did this appear?

TG In the *New Yorker*. It was published not too long after Ray died. But the new version has not been seen. The final version will be in the book, the one in which I took out "like holding hearts." I think that's the only change.

I loved getting the sound in, those bells that were braided into the manes of the horses. I used to braid things into my horse's mane. And I could really make those ponies palpable for myself and for the readers with those little bells.

In the early drafting, things will not be as condensed. I will usually, in the refining, find a way to move more quickly, because it's more elegant, and it's more memorable, more affecting. Somebody who's stumbling all over something doesn't convince you. What you're trying to do in the drafting is to find a way that is so compelling and convincing that it carries you, first of all, so the reader will come with you.

JW Sometimes in the very initial draft things appear in the same line or very close together, then later wind up much more separated, in different stanzas even. It's as if you don't want to use up all your thunder all at once, or as if sometimes important realizations occur simultaneously and then need independent development. Are all the poems in *Moon Crossing Bridge* about what you've been going through in the last couple of years?

TG Yes, the last two and a half years. Well, last three years. "Red Poppy" was written a few months after Ray died. He died August 2, 1988, and I wrote this poem in January, right around the start of the year.

JW One of the most striking aspects of your poetry is its playfulness and humor, and I wonder what—

TG Where'd that go, what's happened to that?

JW How do you capitalize on those impulses in a more elegiac poetry?

TG I think the playfulness is much more evident in *Portable Kisses*. But it's fine to just play the oboe. You don't always need the xylophone. This material I was living through with *Moon Crossing Bridge* was extremely demanding, emotionally and psychically, and I didn't think to myself, Well, they're going to think you're an awfully droll character who has only one note. I didn't worry about that at all, because I realize that this book is of a kind, and its material demands something I may never have to face again, let's hope.

JW What you're saying reminds me a lot of something you said in the 1979 interview with Jeannie Thompson that appeared in *Ironwood*: "People ask quite a lot of a poet these days. They seem to want every poem to be an orchestra, when sometimes you wanted only to hear a sad melody played on the flute." It's good to be reminded that a single piece can't accomplish everything at once.

TG No. It has to be in its material as strongly as it can be and find the language for that. I don't think there is any humor in this poem, really. There's a kind of felicity of life, though, in it. This is obviously a voice which I think you would say is responsive to sound and form and texture and is alive in its way of observing. Able to enter experiences on terms that are original, I think. To enter emotional spaces on terms that are original. Actually, that's quite a lot. There's wit in the way in which the language is used.

JW I sense a departure in these poems from the kinds of endings you've created in the past. I'm wondering what your feeling is about that.

TG This poem, "Red Poppy," is breaking boundaries. It's crossing the threshold of a taboo in that kiss which the speaker takes. Yet this moment has happened in lives many, many times. And I suppose the poem is trying to endow this occasion with rights. To give it dignity and import. That's how I came to that ending. I have to be the lover, *and* the beloved, in that kiss. I say "kissless kiss / he *would have* given," and then "my gallant hussar, / to bend and take." The hussar is really a very active, daring figure. And yet here, he can't move. And also, he's one with death. And that's the hussar, too. So he's a complicated form. And I have to admit to myself that this ending represents not just a giving but also a taking. There's an illicitness in the act. I think you feel that, coming into the ending. That word "take" *is* kind of a violence. It's not only tender. It's mixed. And it has a kind of stolen quality about it.

JW The endings of these latest poems have a much different resonance than a lot of your earlier ones.

TG When you say they're different, what do you mean? What do you feel? Can you define that a little bit? Because I haven't talked with anybody about the poems, so I don't really know how you're defining difference.

JW In a lot of your earlier poems, the endings were often surprising in a certain way, sometimes almost launching you off in a slightly unexpected kind of direction.

TG Yes, sort of askew! A turn that undoes everything that the poem has set up, or seems to undo it.

JW Or at least challenges it.

TG Challenges it, yes.

JW That, I think, reveals a fundamental playfulness or humor in your poetry, the final twist that often exists in your poems. The poems that we've been talking about, of course, seem to end differently.

The endings of these poems have a certain kind of finality and authority that is no less resonant but somehow distinct from many of the previous ones.

TG It's more insistent, maybe, and it's embedded in the sense of trying to bring the material into consequence. I may be insisting more on consequence—about which there's been a kind of unspoken embarrassment in contemporary poetry.

JW Do you still feel in these new poems that you've basically been working in two distinct forms? You've talked before about the moment-bound lyric verses and the more narrative, prose kind of poem. You seem to be finding a new way to merge these two impulses.

TG Yes, it's much more merged. The narrative has to serve the lyric impulse more now, it seems.

JW I wonder if that's the fundamental distinction between the poet and the prose writer: whether the narrative serves the lyric, or vice versa.

TG For a fiction writer, the lyrical movements would *have* to serve the story, the narrative. Well, that's what Ray would have said, probably. Although his stories are so much a kind of poetry, much closer to poetry than the writings of many short story writers. In many of these *Moon Crossing Bridge* poems, narrative is subdued, submerged. You don't know exactly the relationships. So you have to be more speculatively invested in the raw emotion itself.

JW Is this the most significant distinction between the poems you're writing now and the poems you were writing fifteen years ago?

TG I think that I used to hit mystery every now and again, but now the mystery is empowering the voice more steadily. And I'm not afraid to be as oblique as I am. Also, I now realize that it's not important where those things I say came from. Where it came from is not as important as how I'm going to *give* that, and the strength of the feeling involved. There are certain poems in *Amplitude*, like the horse poems—"Gray Eyes" is a good example—where there's a very mysterious tone in the poems. And you don't know why things are said the way they're said, or even what the narrative is doing, exactly.

When Ray was alive, I was held a little bit more to his tenaciousness for another kind of linear clarity. And in these poems, since his death especially, I am not held to that. I'm allowing myself my little alcoves and cul-de-sacs.

JW What was the kind of clarity he encouraged?

TG He wanted complete narrative clarity. If you're not going to have narrative carriage in the poem, you can't half-suggest that you're letting somebody know something. You have to subdue narrative to the degree that it isn't a question—you have to subdue it to the point that the reader has to read the poem in an entirely different way, not to unravel the whodunits of the poem. Although they should probably be able to go back and do that, in some sense of the word. Even in the more submerged way I'm working here.

JW Do you think it's possible to look at your career as a process of trying to find a way to reconcile that lyrical, moment-bound type of poetry with the narrative?

TG Yes, I would say that has been part of my struggle. I think from narrative I got "reach," from writing those longer narrative poems. I got a kind of stamina. I got that from my short stories, too. And I sort of worked out that need to diffuse, to almost lame my intensity. I had that need for a while. Just to see what happens to the intensity if I go against it even, if I hurt it a little, you know? I got over that, because such narrative just ultimately wasn't as satisfying. And it didn't work for the material I had in *Moon Crossing Bridge*. The only thing that would work for this material was something that had lyric intensity. The other was just too frail and discursive a method to carry the feeling.

JW Are you suspicious of discursiveness?

TG Right now I have a real hunger for conciseness. For song, because song lifts us, and I think I need badly to be lifted at the moment. I'm tired of figuring things out, I guess. So many of the most important things can't be figured out. They just have to be lived through with investment of being and attitude and fortitude and attentive lostness. They can't be wriggled out of with thinking.

I think that's what the lyric poet does—brings us back bedrock to what we're feeling. There's a poem in here that won't be in the book because it's coming out in *Life*'s compendium entitled, auspiciously, *The Meaning of Life*! It deals exactly with that. It's called "To Whom Can I Open My Heart?"

To Whom Can I Open My Heart?
I step outside to get a clear view
of this night's first stars, but something
urgent and full of an ancient, inexplicable pain
is aloft in the darkness of the hemlocks.
Again and again it makes its shrill cry of panic
that is a plea and a question.
One bird after dark. What has befallen
its nest, its wing, its sun?
So little to tell. Not even the word "tomorrow"
is world enough to offer myself
hearing it.

Yes. I would give a lot for that kind of message. It's a lot more valuable to me than all amount of discursiveness.

JW We've talked about humor and we've talked about musicality and endings. Another thing that I've noticed in your work is the hyphenated word. I'm interested in how that relates to your sense of the music in language. And I'm wondering—

TG How did I come to that?

JW Yes.

TG It was just that sense that you can make a whole other construct by making that little bridge to the two or three words. I studied German when I was very young, and I was impressed with the way the German language just jams several words together to make one word, and I think it possibly came out of my having learned German when I was sixteen. Can you find an example of where I did that?

JW Here, in "Legend with Sea Breeze," you use "pseudo-park."

TG It also makes the tempo move a little faster. Listen to that: "pseudo-park."

JW Here's one, from "Black Pudding": "lost-Eden-way."

TG You know, I loved that, but nobody else liked it. So it came out of that poem, unfortunately.

JW Here, in "Strange Thanksgiving": "moon-bright windows."

TG It seems a way of amplifying, doesn't it? The hyphen really *insists*. It conjoins the two words so there's a bit more fixity. It's not like I'm allowing an ambiguity there. I really hitch up the wagon, you know.

Bill Knott uses hyphens, and I may have gotten some of that off Bill. In this poem, "Another Visit from the Love Inspector," I use "nostalgia-police." Now, Bill could probably do something like that. It's "baton-twirling display." It just sort of jazzes things up; it really affects the tempo. And there's a kind of snap to it. "And if I Babe-Ruth it out of this life"; "our jointly implausible, our once-and-for-spacious descent." If you took out the hyphens, you would say [emphasizing slower pace] "our once and for spacious descent." But this way you have to accelerate: "our once-and-for-spacious descent." So *descent* comes down a lot harder. And there's a kind of swooping quality to this, "our *Once*-and-for-*spacious* descent." It comes all in a motion, in a kind of a wave.

Well, I do that in conversation, too. I'll hyphenate things sometimes when talking. Especially when I'm just with my pals, sitting around. I think we've hit on some of the reasons.

JW Why don't we talk about "Two of Anything."

TG Let's start with that little note I made to myself at the end of the original draft. "There is no one. But how do I know? If lie down, I lie down." I'm just musing there. The most interesting things about this poem, it seems to me, happen as I come into the conclusion of it, where it's obviously a conversation going on between two people and it starts outside, in the outer world, the small tugboat that's being watched, and then the intimacy of this exchange going on between the two people. In the final version, you'll notice there's an epigraph from Kyoko Selden, which I added as I was putting the book together, which says, "What silk-thin difference is there if I stay to dream or go."

It's a very devastating kind of line. But really, that's what's going on here. How do I live if my love is gone? That's the whole narrative of the poem, really. The narrator is with the loved one, just doing very simple things, these really Zen-like things. Then the narrator says something really far-reaching, like "I'm afraid I'll never be happy again." Then the other voice says, "'Bring me / a glass of water,' he says. 'Someone, you know, / has to stay here and take care of things.'"

The change for me comes where I'm saying, "Between them, lively passage of boats, none / of them empty." You have these two horizons, and the boats passing, and that's a rather uplifting kind of idea, yes, that they're none of them empty. They're all under direction, and because of that they will arrive at destinations. And so this really ironic voice comes in and says "that's fascinating, I said to the poet, let me add one." One that's empty! And then, going back to the exchange again, "I thought there was more water in this glass. / I guess not, one of us said." And the two are brought together, you don't have a "he" and a "she" anymore. And the horizons have come together then, in the poem.

But the *authentic* coming together was facilitated by that ironic move, which then says, all right, this poem is a construct. I *know* it's a construct. I've put all this in this particular order. With the emphasis attending. And that emptiness—you know, the fact that water runs out. It's gone. The poem ends, kind of abjectly, but very, very quietly, and at the same time, there's an equanimity which seems a kind of balance. You feel, yes, the ending has come; there's no water in the glass. It runs out. Life runs out. It's just . . . that's what it comes down to, finally.

JW Am I wrong in feeling that that's sort of the tone at the end of a lot of these poems from *Moon Crossing Bridge*?

TG I refuse to deliver the reader into anything except what I feel is true at that moment. I'm not Hollywooding at all. I'm writing it as hard as it is, as hard as I can bear it.

JW What can you tell me about the origins of "Two of Anything"?

TG Well, the writing started right here at Sky House. I wrote a lot of these poems perched up there on that big high bed, looking out at the Strait of Juan de Fuca. And Ray wrote all of *Where Water Comes Together with Other Water* at Sky House, and he wrote a good deal of *Ultramarine* in this house as well. He came out here by himself, from Syracuse. You can always get something from the environment here. Every day tugboats pass, pulling logs through the strait. They're attached to the logs by thick wire cables. You'll see the tugboat way out ahead long before you see the load of logs. So that's what I'm indicating metaphorically in that beginning, that it's hard to tell what something really can do, you know, just by looking at it. "That small tug boat which at first seems / all on its own in the strait / can eventually be seen to pull two barges, each / twice its size and is able to / because water / understands everything and all / day says, 'pass, pass by.'"

JW As you look at this poem on the page, you immediately see a dense column on the left that doesn't exist on the right.

TG Yes, the right is that coupling, see? That's a sign that inside there is this meeting, this intimate exchange. And on the left, that's the barge. I mean that's the tugboat *pulling* the log barge in the poem!

JW This visual effect seems emblematic of what a lot of these poems are about.

TG A density with these little spaces of clarity, yes.

JW And loss, too. The whole, here on the left, yielding to the fragmented, here on the right.

TG Yes. This space quiets it down, you know. Puts some silence into it. And I always look at a poem to see about resting the eye, or to try to rest the eye.

JW Is that one of the reasons why this poem doesn't have stanza breaks?

TG Well, I think that has to do with the continuity of time and motion in the poem. Even though it moves around, I mean it goes backwards and forwards in time. From childhood to the present. And beyond, to the death being faced.

Well, of course, breaking the "frame" of the poem as I did with that ending we were talking about before is really a kind of deconstructionist thing, I suppose. Breaking the illusion of "poem" as enclosure. And breaking the crucible of The Poet. *And* insisting on honesty to the point that you're willing to ruin the illusion. Poems are in love with their own hypnotic intonements. And they have to be, in order to "spell" the reader. But if you *can* break that spell and send the reader interestingly back into a spell *inside* the spell—you know, that seems worth trying. And that's what this poem tries to do.

JW "That small tug boat, which at first"—so this was written almost like just a paragraph, isn't it?

TG Yes.

JW And you changed "because of a thing called water" to "because water understands everything and all / day says 'pass, pass by.'"

TG That's much better. That's making it more dramatic.

JW You added, "I propose"—

TG "I propose a plan and we discuss it."

JW And "I'm afraid I'll never / be happy again. 'Bring me / a glass of water,' he says."

TG Yes, I added all of that. It took longer to establish the exchange. The original was too abrupt.

JW Now, why in "Red Poppy" did it seem you couldn't get past that first page until you had those first two lines, while here you were able to keep going all the way through before going back to make these significant revisions. Does your approach just vary from poem to poem?

TG Yes, it just depends on whether I'm in the voice. I think here I was very much still in the voice, so this, you see, could be added. I hit my note right off the start: "That small tug boat which at first seems / all on its own in the strait / can eventually be seen to pull two barges, each / twice its size." I mean, I'm *in* it. So it doesn't matter if I leave something out, kind of in the middle there. I can go back and supply that later. But if I don't have those initial lines right, then I'm going to be quite in trouble. I have to get those beginning lines down.

JW Would you have been saying this out loud before you wrote?

TG At a certain point, I read things out loud, yes.

JW Are you ever pacing around, saying the first line, trying to get it right, or do you sit quietly until it comes?

TG No. I'm very attentive on those first lines. It's very good to leave a poem later on if you get kind of out of it, if you get stuck a bit. Then it's good to distract yourself, to go get a cup of coffee or let up in some little way. Then you have to resituate, and that's sometimes refreshing.

I do move around sometimes in working on the poem, but it'll just be to different parts of the house. So many things happen to me when I am not thinking about the poem, and things will begin to occur to me in some domestic activity, like washing the dishes or emptying the wastebaskets.

See here, I added this: "I take a few sips from his glass." Just look at some of the dumb things I did. "Those poems are all too long and"—isn't that funny? Look at what I crossed out—"Those poems are all too long and"—it must be some comment I'm making to myself! And "in which we are both extinguished, and one / I reached and entered with him and so is / under me, and one that seems far enough away / to empty those white boats"—"to empty my heart of one love"—"to be the dead mate of this one."

See how many silly, "off" moves I make? But I'm good at correcting.

Why don't we talk about "Black Pudding"? I read a lot about horses, and the central material for this came from reading about Kha-Khan, who was like Genghis Khan, and the Mongol hordes, the way they used their horses. They were very resilient as horsemen and warriors, able to conquer, because they needed very little. And nothing was wasted.

Their transport was also their nourishment. They could seem to retreat and then turn around and be right back on top of the people they were trying to vanquish with a vengeance, because they would take blood from the horse, and that would be their nourishment. They could get out into desert areas, escaping or pursuing, and be able to live there. So it seemed to me a wonderful metaphor for the real problem of how you do sustain yourself on the kind of spiritual journey I was making in this book. And I think I say somewhere that it's "unsavory rations." I mean, these are unsavory rations, but they're *my* rations, you know. That's what I'm given to survive with.

And I like how I get rid of the specifics of Kha-Khan. You see I have him in this version [draft 1]. So that the poem becomes more metaphorical.

JW Did you have "Mongol tribesmen" in this one, or is that what you replaced him with?

TG No, I just have Kha-Khan. So I substituted Mongol tribesmen. I take it out of the imperial and make it more the peasant. The narrative of the poem is the speaker's having revealed a very intimate moment to someone, and then having them not understand or accept it. Then trying to retreat, to go back and protect that unfortunate misuse of confidence after the fact. And that's the premise. The poem was originally entitled "Mistake of Telling." Sometimes you tell something very intimate to someone, thinking this person will share that and will really understand, and perhaps that you will be able to fix, to remember this in a particular way by making it a part of their consciousness as you tell them. But sometimes they don't accept it—they in fact think it's terrible. Not terrible, but they just can't enter that space at all with you. And furthermore, they may even be critical of you.

All of this narrative is left out of the poem. It only exists in this line [draft 2]: "So I brought you there, you who didn't belong, thinking to outsave / even memory by tearing the sacred from / its alcove." Well, this is something that should never have been told to anybody. And I thought, it's so special, I will even violate it! I mean, isn't this awful? It's terrible!

So as I wrote I began to understand what I had done and why—I began in this really rancid feeling. But here's the poem which hopefully delivers meaning beyond that.

This person that the confidence was offered to wasn't able to handle it, and thought this scene was terribly sentimental, and too much to have to witness.

It's not very elegant, the way I had phrased it before. And I'm emphasizing the relationship between the other person and myself.

JW You changed "broken and weeping" to "in that blurted way between gusts of weeping."

TG Yes, that's so much better! "Gusts of weeping" is great. I'd started to write "gusts of *feeling*," I think. But "gusts of weeping" is much better. More honest. More exact.

JW "Weeping" is vivid, active. The sound and feel of the word—"weeping"—is gusty.

TG Gusts of feeling—feeling glances off of it. Feeling is too amorphous. Feeling can be anything. "Take from its bowed neck"—did I have "bowed neck"? Yes. I like that! That I added "bowed" to "take from its neck": "take from its bowed neck," that makes you see the neck. And it's as if the blood is forced more into the neck. Okay, and then it says "to be heated," okay, and then: "This, then, is my black pudding"—and then the poem makes an incredible shift right there. Just an incredible shift.

JW From "how I climbed like a damp child." Now this is my big chance to try to talk about your stanza breaks. Wouldn't this be the obvious place to break, at "how I climbed like a damp child"?

TG Maybe. Sure.

JW You don't break it there because that's too obvious and predictable? And it doesn't emphasize the contrast as much if it's run together like this? The contrast is striking.

TG Yes, I want to say it belongs there, whether you think it does or not. So I keep it together. And this is a kind of pudding, "how I climbed / like a damp child waking from nightmare to find / the parents intimate and still awake." This is another kind of twosome again. This is a scene, that witnessing of the parents, and not understanding what has happened to them.

JW Now these are eight-line stanzas, except the last one's a ten-line stanza. That's not a conventional form.

TG No, I just discovered it as I worked with the poem. The ends of the stanzas run on, they're not end-stopped, so that you're pulled from one stanza into the next by its not being completed.

JW Your lines seem mostly iambic.

TG It's pretty iambic, yes.

JW Now this looks, in the handwritten first draft, as if it were written quickly.

TG Yes.

JW And so you're not even thinking about stanzas at that point.

TG No.

JW So at what point do you begin thinking about stanzas? When you type it?

TG Yes. That's the only time I ever start worrying, is when I start typing. Then I start counting. I look at the first stanza and see where its motion ends. Then I count, checking to see whether the natural breaks reveal any pattern.

JW Do you often discover that there is sort of an instinctive pattern?

TG In this one there was. I like the way this poem ends, this "Black Pudding." That, "Don't ask me now why I'm walking my horse." That sense that it's because you're taking your nourishment from that spirit-beast. You have to respect it, you have to understand that it can't always carry you, and not expect everything from it. And especially if you're eating from it! If it's your meal, you can't also use it for transportation all the time. You have to take things slowly. You have to walk alongside it. And it's the way in which I phrased it, "Don't ask me now why I'm walking my horse," that's also pushing—pushing back. It's as if you will again be misunderstood. Mourning is a time of being misunderstood, and of being asked silly questions.

JW And that ending is more along the lines of—

TG Earlier work. Yes, it is. It's a kind of flaunt, it's bracing, a challenge. It's more the Spanish, it's *duende*. It's like the Spanish dancer when she throws her head back, that way of throwing the shoulder—stomping! Two quick little mean stomps! I believe in temper! How boring it would be if we were all just sort of blandly even and threw no sparks, if we never had any quick rejoinders!

JW Do editors query you a lot about line endings, lining strategies, or stanza strategies?

TG Not now. The only person I ever talk with about lines is Stephen Dobyns. He seems to have very exact feelings about how lines should be broken. But I believe it's very individual, one's way of breaking lines, and it has to be arrived at in an individual way in individual poems, even. I do tend to break mine toward states of emotional suspension. And in such a way that you want to know, what's the next word?

If I say, "Even then I knew it was the old unanswerable form of beauty," then break the line before "as pain," that really modifies and sweeps back over "unanswerable form of beauty."

My mode has just been exploratory. That's the one thing that I have always wanted to do—to see what hasn't been done, what I haven't done, and to be as unexpected with myself and with the reader as I can. Because then the poem will be alive. To evade the reader's expectation I have to evade my own, first of all. So there is this self-mockery that accompanies some of the work.

I heard something that was said about Emily Dickinson in a television documentary. I forget who said it, but the comment was to the effect that she almost wasn't writing poetry, in the sense that she was writing directly out of her soul. I understood that so well. In *Moon Crossing Bridge*, I didn't even think of poetry. I just wrote. Same with the later poems in *Portable Kisses*. Of course, I've been writing poetry, but I feel like I'm writing more urgently than I've ever written before. Life-and-death writing. Tending the soul-bridge of the poems.

days[t]r

Red Poppy

That web of sorrows caught to her garden
~~like a~~
~~in strings of charged with~~
in silvery filaments charged with light,
her grandmother's sequined brocade

Red Poppy

That linkage of sorrows sent a tremor in June
~~and the~~ so ~~the~~ garden, more simplified and quiet,

That linkage of sorrows sent a tremor in June
~~and the garden more simplified and quiet~~
like the final black bead ~~stopping~~ weighting the silvery filament
~~like the final black bead~~

~~if~~
That linkage of sorrows sent a tremor in June
~~just as the garden was taking off.~~

That linkage of warnings sent a tremor through June
as if to prepare the apples for dropping
~~in October.~~ in October.
less suddenly
as if to prepare the hardest apples for dropping
~~into the~~
less suddenly

It was only inflection

I am scarlet through and through
to know an ending, tasting ~~you~~ that plush of scarlet through
and through. & heard you leaving them, that last and clinging
sense, like ~~a bridge~~ an underwater bridge meant to tame

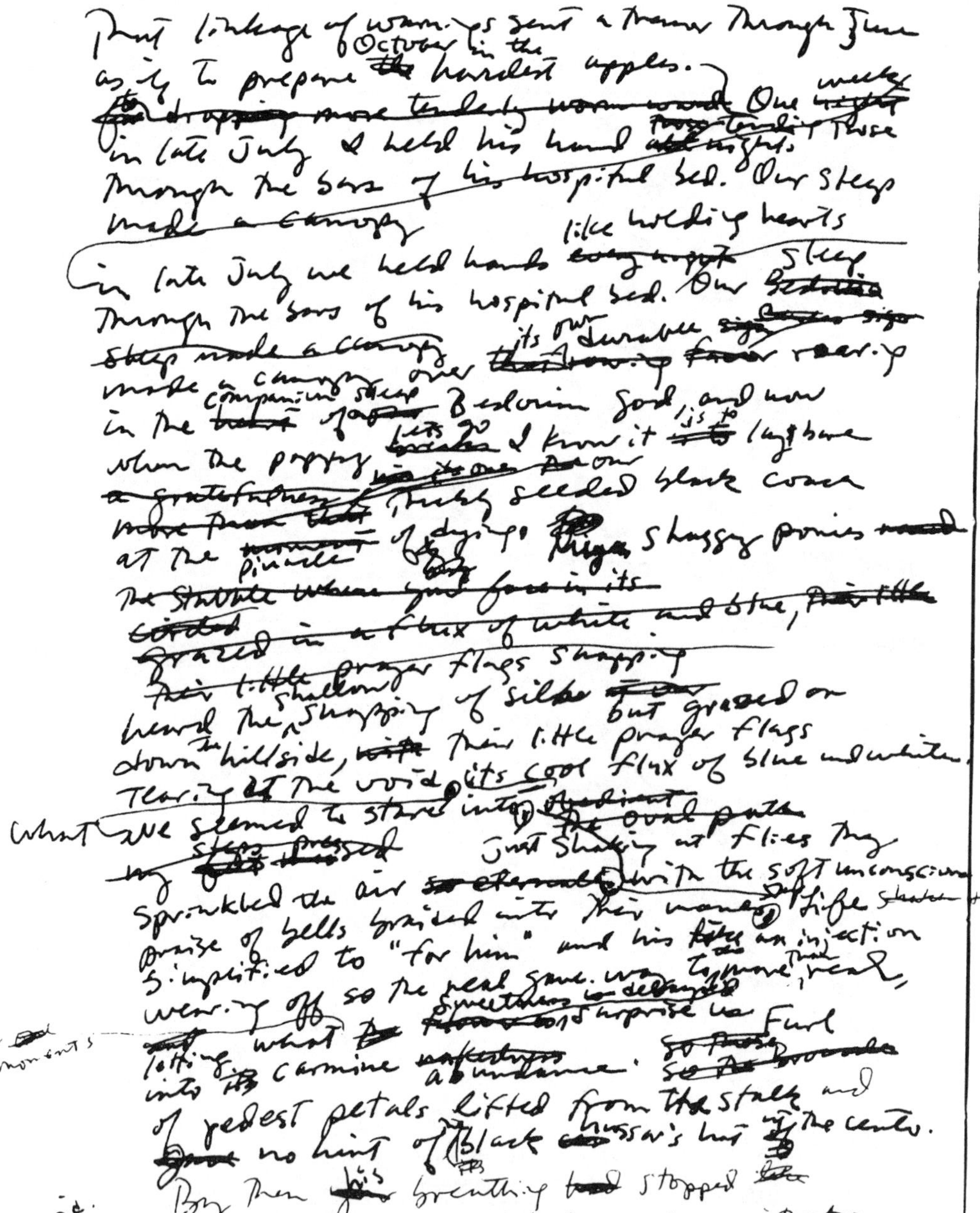
That linkage of warnings sent a tremor through June
as if to prepare October in the hardest apples.
for dropping more tenderly warm wood. One weeks night
in late July I held his hand all nights through those
through the bars of his hospital bed. Our sleeps
made a canopy   like holding hearts
in late July we held hands every night. Sleep
through the bars of his hospital bed. Our [illegible]
sleep made a canopy its own durable sign [illegible]
made a canopy over that rowing forever roaring
in the [illegible] companion sleep Bedouin god, and now
when the poppy lets go I know it is to laugh here
a gratefulness, thickly seeded black coach
more than that [illegible] on
at the pinnacle of dying, shaggy ponies [illegible]
The stubble where [illegible] face in its
circled in a flux of white and blue, [illegible]
grazed prayer flags snapping
their little shallow
heard the snapping of silks but grazed on
down the hillside, their little prayer flags
tearing at the void, its cool flux of blue and white.
What we seemed to stare into the oval path
[illegible] steps pressed   just shaking at flies they
sprinkled the air so eternally with the soft unconscious
praise of bells braided into their manes. Life shaken
simplified to "for him" and his life an injection
wearing off so the real game was to move the real,
what sweetness to surprise us. Furl
letting carmine abundance. So these
into its carmine abundance.
of reddest petals lifted from the stalk and
no hint of black hussar's hat in the center.
By then his breathing had stopped
gradually I had to brush lips with
a moments
void.

~~the clatter of the horsemen's hors~~

~~The clatter of hooves start~~

The clatter of hooves so the horsemen could
pass over, but over to what?

To know an ending, taste your that plush of scarlet
which is the last of warmth. ~~and sears the heart~~ ~~but the start~~
~~of aftershock~~
which is the last of warmth. ~~So dazzling friend~~
which is the last of warmth ~~into an underwater bridge~~ (Kissless kiss)
in which only one of us

→ which is the last of warmth, ~~the kiss~~ he would have
given ~~one~~ gave me as I extended ~~the~~ ~~the radius~~
a ~~the~~ ~~urgent~~ love's right ~~to give~~ ~~and the~~ past its radius
~~also to take~~

to give / send — also most needfully to take.

also most needfully, ~~in the life after death~~,
to take.

~~also~~ also most needfully, my kisser, most tenderly, ~~for you~~
~~to take~~
for both our worlds, to take.

to give, / send — also most needfully, my kisser, most tenderly
in ~~the first~~ ~~love~~ ~~of my new life, to take~~. ~~Shoulder~~ Communed

To send and take.

Red Poppy

That linkage of warnings sent a tremor through June
as if to prepare October in the hardest apples.
One week in late July we held hands like holding hearts
through the bars of his hospital bed. Our sleep
made a canopy over us and it seemed I heard
its durable roaring in the companion sleep
of what must have been our Bedouin god, and now
when the poppy lets go I know it is to lay bare
his thickly seeded black coach
at the pinnacle of dying.

My shaggy ponies heard the shallow snapping of silk
but grazed on down the hillside, their prayer flags
tearing at the void--what we
stared into, its cool flux
of blue and white. How just shaking at flies
they sprinkled the air with the soft unconscious praise
of bells braided into their manes. My life

simplified to "for him" and his thinned like an injection
wearing off so the real gave way to
the more-than-real, each moment's carmine
abundance, furl of reddest petals
lifted from the stalk and no hint of the black
hussar's hat at the center. By then his breathing stopped
so gradually I had to brush lips to know
an ending. Tasting then that plush of scarlet
which is the last of warmth, kissless kiss
he would have given. Mine to extend a lover's right past its radius,
to give and also most needfully, my gallant hussar,
to bend and take.

Red Poppy

That linkage of warnings sent a tremor through June
as if to prepare October in the hardest apples.
One week in late July we held hands
through the bars of his hospital bed. Our sleep
made a canopy over us and it seemed I heard
its durable roaring in the companion sleep
of what must have been our Bedouin god, and now
when the poppy lets go I know it is to lay bare
his thickly seeded black coach
at the pinnacle of dying.

My shaggy ponies heard the shallow snapping of silk
but grazed on down the hillside, their prayer flags
tearing at the void--what we
stared into, its cool flux
of blue and white. How just shaking at flies
they sprinkled the air with the soft unconscious praise
of bells braided into their manes. My life

simplified to "for him" and his thinned like an injection
wearing off so the real gave way to
the more-than-real, each moment's carmine
abundance, furl of reddest petals
lifted from the stalk and no hint of the black
hussar's hat at the center. By then his breathing stopped
so gradually I had to brush lips to know
an ending. Tasting then that plush of scarlet
which is the last of warmth, kissless kiss
he would have given. Mine to extend a lover's right past its radius,
to give and also most needfully, my gallant hussar,
to bend and take.

RED POPPY

That linkage of warnings sent a tremor through June
as if to prepare October in the hardest apples.
One week in late July we held hands like holding hearts
through the bars of his hospital bed. Our sleep
made a canopy over us and it seemed I heard
its durable roaring in the companion sleep
of what must have been our Bedouin god, and now
when the poppy lets go I know it is to lay bare
his thickly seeded black coach
at the pinnacle of dying.

My shaggy ponies heard the shallow snapping of silk
but grazed on down the hillside, their little prayer flags
tearing at the void—what we
stared into, its cool flux
of blue and white. How just shaking at flies
they sprinkled the air with the soft unconscious praise
of bells braided into their manes. My life

simplified to "for him," and his thinned like an injection
wearing off so the real gave way to
the more than real, each moment's carmine
abundance, furl of reddest petals
lifted from the stalk and no hint of the black
hussar's hat at the center. By then his breathing stopped
so gradually I had to brush lips to know
an ending. Tasting then that plush of scarlet
which is the last of warmth, kissless kiss
he would have given. Mine to extend a lover's right past its radius,
to give and also most needfully, my gallant hussar,
to bend and take.

—Tess Gallagher

• •

eventually Two of Anything and is able

~~[illegible]~~ That small tug boat which at first
seems all on its own in the strait
can be seen to pull two barges, each
twice its size because of a thing called
water. "Someone has to ~~take~~ stay here and
take care of things," he said. Two ducks
fly by. It's the deep blue of morning
as it cheats the sleepers, the blue made up
of the blue of night and the blue of
dawn. The two boys are vicious with news,
flinging the morning paper house to house
down the hill. Two horses out of
childhood, Daisy and Kernel Boy are hitched
to the wagon. Iron wheels.

I take a few
Sips from his glass.

to be the dead mate of this one. Between
them, lively passage of boats, none
of them empty. That's fascinating, I said
to the poet, let me add one—there used to be
~~to be~~ water in this glass.

and is able because water understands
everything and all day says, "pass," "passby".
I propose a plan and we discuss it. I'm afraid
I'll never be happy again. "Bring me
a glass of water," he says. "Someone, you know,
has to stay here and take care of things."
Two ducks fly by. Outside it's the deep blue of
morning that is almost purple it is so glad
to be cheating the sleepers of its willful the blue
drifting, the fingers blue made up of night and ~~slice of premonition. It on~~
premonition that will dissolve and carry it. Two
boys jiggling with news are flinging the morning
paper house to house down the hill. Two
horses out of childhood I loved, Daisy and
Kernal Bozy, ~~who~~ and hitched to the wagon.
I hear the cold extravagance of tiny bells
beaded into their harness straps. Iron wheels
under us over snow for miles through the walnut
groves. The two ~~scents~~ pearled hair combs he gave me
make a chilly mouth on the sill. ~~those poems~~ I look up
~~are all too long and~~ ~~horizon~~ ~~over the water~~ no, two horizons one
on water ~~and out at the [illegible]~~
~~whose body is water~~ ~~extinguished and one~~
~~we~~ in which we are ~~[illegible]~~ entered with him and ~~one~~ so is
I reached and ~~[illegible]~~ with him and one that seems far enough
under me, and one that seems far enough away
~~to empty the boat white boats~~
~~to empty my~~ ~~those~~ ~~heart of one love~~
~~that~~ To be the dead mate of this one. Between
them, lovely passage of boats, none
of them empty. ~~There is no one~~ ~~But how do I know?~~
~~If I lie down~~ ~~I lie down~~

Two of Anything

That small tug boat which at first seems
all on its own in the strait
can eventually be seen to pull two barges, each
twice its size and is able
because water understands everything and all
day says "pass, pass by". I propose
a plan and we discuss it. I'm afraid I'll never
be happy again. "Bring me
a glass of water," he says. "Someone, you know,
has to stay here and take care of things."
Two ducks fly by. I take
a few sips from his glass. Outside it's
the deep blue of morning that is almost purple
it is so glad to be cheating
the sleepers of its willful drifting, the tangled
blue made up of night and the blue premonition
that will dissolve and carry
it. Two boys vicious with news are flinging
the morning paper house to house
down the hill. Two horses out of childhood I loved,
Daisy and Colonel Boy, are hitched
to the wagon. I hear the cold extravagance of
tiny bells welded into their harness straps.
Iron wheels under us over snow
for miles through the walnut groves. The two
pearled hair combs he gave me
make a chilly mouth on the sill. I look up and out
over water at the horizon--no, two
horizons. One I reached and entered with him and so
is under me, and one that seems
far enough away to be the dead mate of this one.
Between them, lively passage of boats, none
of them empty. That's fascinating,
I said to the poet, let me add one. I thought
there was more water in this glass.
I guess not, one of us said.

Two of Anything

That small tug boat which at first seems
all on its own in the strait
can eventually be seen to pull two barges, each
twice its size and is able to
because water understands everything and all
day says "pass, pass by". I propose
a plan and we discuss it. I'm afraid I'll never
be happy again. Bring me
a glass of water," he says. "Someone, you know,
has to stay here and take care of things."
Two ducks fly by. I take
a few sips from his glass. Outside it's
the deep blue of morning that is almost purple
it is so glad to be cheating
the sleepers of its willful drifting, the tangled
blue made up of night and the blue premonition
that will dissolve and carry
it. Two boys vicious with news are flinging
the morning paper house to house
down the hill. Two horses out of childhood I loved,
Daisy and Colonel Boy, are hitched
to the wagon. I hear the cold extravagance of
tiny bells welded into their harness straps.
Iron wheels under us over snow
for miles through the walnut groves. The two
pearled hair combs he gave me
make a chilly mouth on the sill. I look up and out
over water at the horizon--no, two
horizons. One I reached and entered with him and so
is under me, and one that seems
far enough away to be the dead mate of this one.
Between them, lively passage of boats, none
of them empty. That's fascinating,
I said to the poet, let me add one. I thought
there was more water in this glass.
I guess not, one of us said.

Two of Anything

<u>What silk-thin difference is there
if I stay to dream or go.</u>
Kyoko Selden

That small tug which at first seems
all on its own in the strait
can eventually be seen to pull two barges, each
twice its size, because water
understands everything and all
day says "pass, pass by." I propose
a plan and we discuss it. I'm afraid I'll never
be happy again. "Bring me
a glass of water," he says. "Someone, you know,
has to stay here and take care of things."
Two ducks fly by. I take
a few sips from his glass. Outside it's
deep blue morning, almost purple
it's so glad to be cheating
the sleepers of its willful drifting, the tangled
blue of night and the blue premonition
that will dissolve and carry
it. Two boys vicious with news fling
the morning paper house to house
down the hill. Two horses out of childhood I loved,
Daisy and Colonel Boy, are hitched
to the wagon. I hear the cold extravagance of
tiny bells welded into their harness straps.
Iron wheels under us over snow
for miles through the walnut groves. The two
pearled hair combs he gave me
make a chilly mouth on the sill. I look up and out
over water at the horizon--no, two
horizons. One reached and entered with him, and so
is under me, and the other
far enough away to be the dead mate of this one.
Between them, lively passage of boats, none
empty. That's fascinating,

I said to the poet, let me add one. I thought
there was more water in this glass.
I guess not, one of us said.

Two Of Anything

What silk-thin difference is there
if I stay to dream or go.

Kyoko Selden

That small tug, which at first seems
all on its own in the strait,
can eventually be seen to pull two barges, each
twice its size, because water
understands everything and all
day says "pass, pass by." I propose
a plan and we discuss it. I'm afraid I'll never
be happy again. "Bring me
a glass of water," he says. "Someone, you know,
has to stay here and take care of things."
Two ducks fly by. I take
a few sips from his glass. Outside it's
the deep blue of morning that is almost purple
it is so glad to be cheating
the sleepers of its willful drifting, the tangled
blue made up of night and the blue premonition
that will dissolve and carry
it. Two boys vicious with news are flinging
the morning paper house to house
down the hill. Two horses out of childhood I loved,
Daisy and Colonel Boy, are hitched
to the wagon. I hear the cold extravagance of
tiny bells welded into their harness straps.
Iron wheels under us over snow
for miles through the walnut groves. The two
pearled hair combs he gave me
make a chilly mouth on the sill. I look up and out
over water at the horizon—no, two
horizons. One I reached and entered with him and so
is under me, and one that seems
far enough away to be the dead mate of this one.
Between them, lively passage of boats, none
of them empty. That's fascinating,
I said to the poet, let me add one. I thought
there was more water in this glass.
I guess not, one of us said.

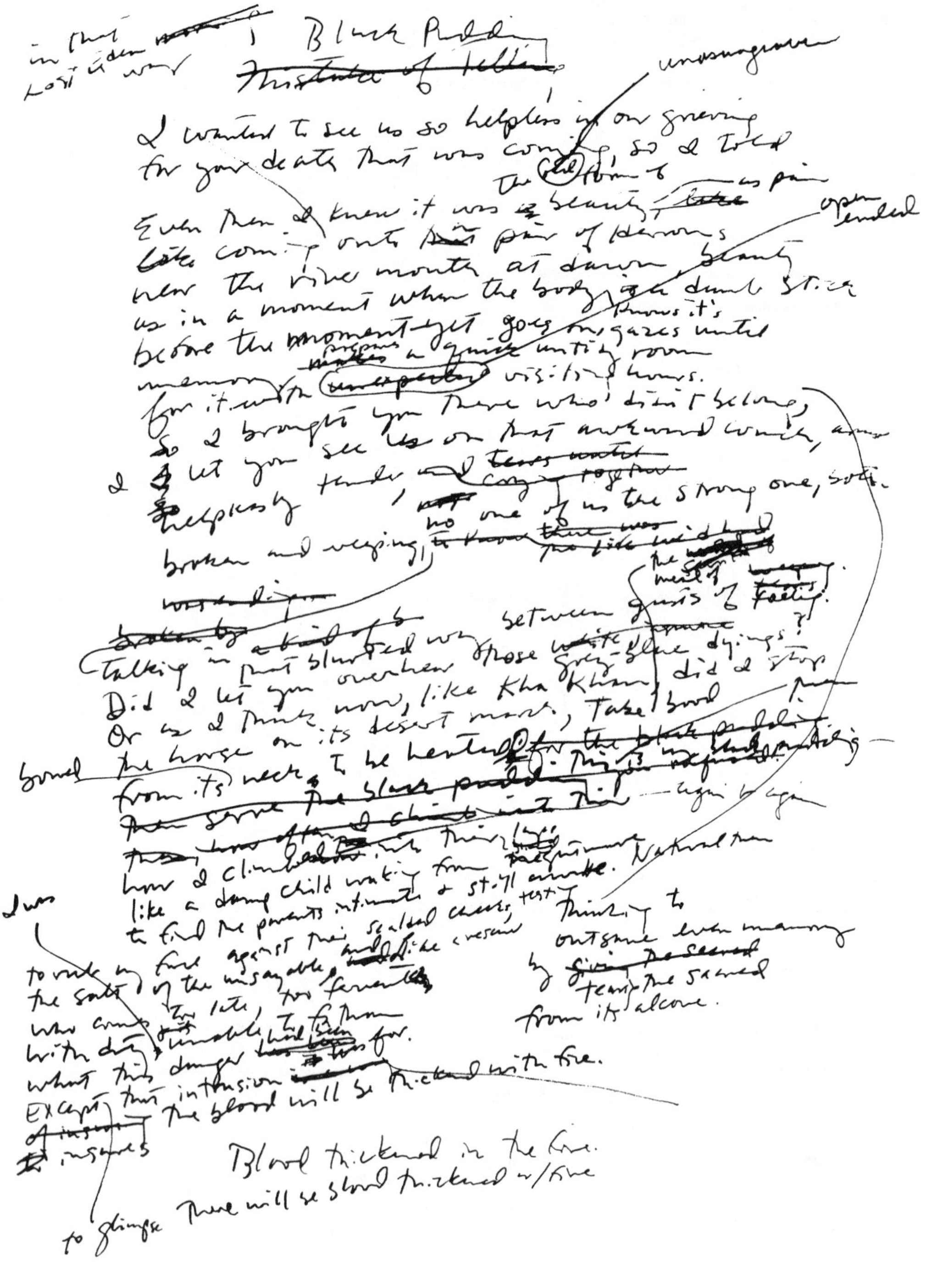

Black Pudding

I wanted to see us so helpless in our grieving
for your death that was coming, so I told
Even then I knew it was beauty,
coming onto a pair of herons
near the river mouth at dawn. Beauty
us in a moment when the body [illegible] dumb stick
before the moment yet goes on, gazes until
[illegible] visiting hours.
for it [illegible] those who didn't belong,
So I brought you there on that awkward couch,
I let you see us [illegible] tender, and
helplessly [illegible] no one of us the strong one,
broken and weeping [illegible]
Talking in that slurred way those grey-blue dyings?
Did I let you overhear [illegible] did I stop
Or as I think now, like Kubla Khan, take
the horse on its desert march [illegible]
from its neck to be heated [illegible]
how I climb [illegible] waiting [illegible]
like a damp child [illegible]
to find the parents [illegible] sealed cases,
Thinking to
outgrow [illegible]
from its alcove.
[illegible] with fire.
Except this intrusion [illegible] the blood will be thickened with fire.

Blood thickened in the fire.
to glimpse There will be blood thickened w/ fire

Black Pudding

Even then I knew it was the old unaswerable form of beauty
as pain, like coming, in that lost-Eden-way, onto a pair of herons
near the river mouth at dawn. Beauty as when the body
is a dumb stick before the moment--yet goes on,
gazes until memory prepares a quick untidy room
with unpredictable visiting hours.
So I brought you there, you who didn't belong, thinking to outsave
even memory by tearing the sacred from

its alcove. I let you see us, arms helplessly tender,
holding each other all night on that awkward couch
because our life was ending. And we fell again and again
into each other like spring water secretly in the wood, murmuring,
retelling our love in that blurted way between gusts of weeping.
Did I let you overhear those grey-blue dyings?
Or as I think now, like a Mongol tribesman, did I stop the horse
on its desert march, take the meal of blood

from its bowed neck to be heated. This then is my black pudding
only the stalwart know to eat. How I climbed
like a damp child waking from nightmare to find
the parents intimate and still awake.
And with natural animal gladness did rub my face against
the scald of their cheeks, tasting the salt
of the unsayable--but, like a rescuer who comes too late, too
fervently marked with duty, was unable to fathom

what their danger and passage had been for. Except
as you know now, even to glimpse this scene is intrusion enough
to insure that when there is nothing else to sustain, blood will be
thickened with fire. Not a pretty dish.
But something taken from the good and cherished beast on loan to us

(no stanza beak)

who is muscled over in spirit and just strong enough to carry us
only as far as it can, there being advantage
to this meagerness, an unsavoriness that rations itself
and reminds us to respect even its bitter portion.
Don't ask me now why I'm walking my horse.

Black Pudding

Even then I knew it was the old unanswerable form of beauty
as pain, like coming onto a pair of herons
near the river mouth at dawn. Beauty as when the body
is a dumb stick before the moment--yet goes on,
gazes until memory prepares a quick untidy room
with unpredictable visiting hours.
So I brought you there, you who didn't belong, thinking to outsave
memory by tearing the sacred from

its alcove. I let you see us, arms helplessly tender,
holding each other all night on that awkward couch
because our life was ending. Again and again
retelling our love between gusts of weeping.
Did I let you overhear those grey-blue dyings?
Or as I think now, like a Mongol tribesman, did I stop the horse
on its desert march, take the meal of blood

from its bowed neck to be heated. This then is my black pudding
only the stalwart know to eat. How I climbed
like a damp child waking from nightmare to find
the parents intimate and still awake.
And with natural animal gladness, rubbed my face
into the scald of their cheeks, tasting salt
of the unsayable--but, like a rescuer who comes too late, too
fervently marked with duty, was unable to fathom

what their danger and passage had been for. Except
as you know now, to glimpse is intrusion enough,
and when there is nothing else to sustain, blood will be thickened
with fire. Not a pretty dish.
But something taken from the good and cherished beast on loan to us,
muscled over in spirit and strong enough to carry us

(no stanza beak)

as far as it can, there being advantage
to this meagerness, unsavoriness that rations itself
and reminds us to respect even its bitter portion.
Don't ask me now why I'm walking my horse.

Black Pudding

Even then I knew it was the old unanswerable form of beauty
as pain, like coming, in that lost-Eden-way, onto a pair of herons
near the river mouth at dawn. Beauty as when the body
is a dumb stick before the moment—yet goes on,
gazes until memory prepares a quick untidy room
with unpredictable visiting hours.
So I brought you there, you who didn't belong, thinking to outsave
even memory by tearing the sacred from

its alcove. I let you see us, arms helplessly tender,
holding each other all night on that awkward couch
because our life was ending. And we fell again and again
into each other like spring water secretly in the wood, murmuring,
retelling our love in that blurted way between gusts of weeping.
Did I let you overhear those grey-blue dyings?
Or as I think now, like a Mongol tribesman, did I stop the horse
on its desert march, take the meal of blood

from its bowed neck to be heated. This then is my black pudding
only the stalwart know to eat. How I climbed
like a damp child waking from nightmare to find
the parents intimate and still awake.
And with natural animal gladness did rub my face against
the scald of their cheeks, tasting the salt
of the unsayable—but, like a rescuer who comes too late, too
fervently marked with duty, was unable to fathom

what their danger and passage had been for. Except
as you know now, even to glimpse this scene is intrusion enough
to insure that when there is nothing else to sustain, blood will be
thickened with fire. Not a pretty dish.
But something taken from the good and cherished beast on loan to
us
who is muscled over in spirit and just strong enough to carry us
only as far as it can, there being advantage
to this meagerness, an unsavoriness that rations itself
and reminds us to respect even its bitter portion.
Don't ask me now why I'm walking my horse.

ROBERT COLES

'Don't Worry, Dad'

Robert Coles is a physician, a child psychiatrist trained in pediatrics and psychoanalysis. The author of some sixty books, he received the Pulitzer Prize in 1973 for two of the five volumes in his *Children of Crisis* series (Boston: Atlantic–Little, Brown, 1967, 1972, 1978). Three additional volumes make up *The Inner Lives of Children* series: *The Moral Life of Children* (Boston: Atlantic Monthly Press, 1986), *The Political Life of Children* (Boston: Atlantic Monthly Press, 1986), and *The Spiritual Life of Children* (Boston: Houghton Mifflin, 1990). Coles's writing has appeared frequently in the *Atlantic*, the *New Republic*, the *New Yorker*, the *New England Journal of Medicine*, the *New York Review of Books*, *Daedalus*, and many other periodicals. The recipient of many awards and honors, Coles was a member of the first group of MacArthur Fellows in 1981.

Coles is professor of psychiatry and medical humanities at Harvard University. He lives with his wife, Jane Hallowell Coles, in the old Concord farmhouse where they raised their three sons, Bob, Daniel, and Michael. I met with Coles at his home in early August 1991, tape-recorded our conversation, and then followed the same editing procedure I've described previously, namely, sending the transcript back and forth several times over a period of months.

Coles drafted "Don't Worry, Dad" at the desk in his Concord study one morning in the spring of 1985. This handwritten draft was then typed by an assistant for subsequent revision. The essay first appeared in *New Oxford Review*

(March 1986) and was later included in a collection of Coles's *New Oxford Review* columns, *Harvard Diary* (New York: Crossroads/Continuum, 1988), which received the Best Spiritual Book of 1988 award from the Catholic Press Association. The essay underwent no revision between its initial publication and its appearance in the collection, so I have chosen to reprint "Don't Worry, Dad" as it appeared finally in *Harvard Diary*. Other materials included here are Coles's original, handwritten draft and the typed copy with his handwritten revisions.

Don't Worry, Dad

The three boys are gone, I say to myself. The boys are no longer boys, I remind myself. I go to their rooms sometimes, look at the tangible evidence of the years they have spent on this planet—please God, with their mother and me: the little cars and trucks they delighted in having when they were five or six, now tucked away on shelves inside their closets, with one or two still left here and there in a particular room for them to see in a quick glance as they go on to other matters; the books, some going back to the days when they listened to us doing the reading, some the first objects of their newly achieved literacy, some the works of art that link so-called youth with so-called grown-ups, such as *Animal Farm* or Kipling's stories or those of Hemingway or Mark Twain, and finally, books such as *Invisible Man* or *Pride and Prejudice* or those convoluted Henry James novels. All this tells their English teacher mom and novel-loving dad that we're four voters now, and one soon to be, and that two are away in college, and one soon to be, and that everyone drives, and we all wonder, out loud, what's happening to America and the world, not who can come over and play Lego, or when that Red Cross swimming instructor will be able to hand out those junior life-saving cards.

I catch myself sad one morning. I think as I go from room to room of the missed chances, the missteps, the misstatements—things done I should not have done, things not done I should have done. Why didn't we help the first boy to make more friends earlier? Why did we keep him so close to us? Yet, he has lots of good friends now, and is quite comfortable traveling all over, I remind myself. *Still.* Why did I get so impatient at times with our second son? Remember that day when a friend came, and the three-year-old child was running all over the place, and fell down and cried, and I was in the middle of a conversation I had judged to be "important," and I shouted, and the child cried harder? Yet, he's a strong, even plucky young man, no crier, and he is thoughtful, and while he doesn't interrupt people, he also doesn't seem resentful or gloomy in his willingness to hear them out; and he knows when to speak up for himself. *Still.* Why, finally, did I miss some of those wonderful school celebrations the third son wanted me to join, or avoid talking with some of his teachers, because (I told myself) I was shy, or I felt my wife could talk better with people in the neighborhood, in the school. Were those self-told jokes about my hermit-like nature a transparent excuse for my pride, my egoism: stick with the writing, the teaching, where the control is yours, and the subject matter, too, directly or indirectly? Yet, this high schooler and I have a great time talking about Latin or biology or a theme that is due by the end of a given Monday. *Still.*

I say to myself, having visited all three rooms one day: "They've turned out fine." Then I arraign myself as all too full of myself, as summoning three other creatures of God for my own chronically self-serving purposes. They *have* turned out fine, I say now—but (in the tradition of a 20th-century secular world obsessed by a meliorism heavily saturated with psychology, with dreary phrases such as "child development," "parenting skills," "learning environments") they might well have turned out even better. Wasn't one boy too reticent too long in school? Didn't he take years to relax among his classmates, known these days as "peers"? Wasn't another boy a little too neat and orderly for a while, and much more relaxed with his mother than with me? Hadn't we worried a lot for a year or so about the third child's sloppiness and his preoccupation, we deemed it, with those rock albums? A half an hour or an hour, occasionally, is alright, I'd thought, then said (and to him, not only to myself and his mother), but on and on the playing of those records went. Besides, the teachers say he comes to school sloppy—or rather (I corrected them silently and with sinful pride) manages to turn sloppy within moments of arrival there.

If only I'd been with the boys when younger more of the time! If only I'd not been so taken up with my work, my damn research—all that "field-work," all those "home visits" to other people's homes, all those children interviewed, again and again, other parents' children. No wonder I think back wistfully at all the opportunities forsaken, the spells when I was traveling, or worse, plain self-preoccupied. Would I be sad that these three boys are now just about grown up, if I'd been with them more than was the case? *Really* been with them—concentrating all my mental and physical energy on their lives, the way their mother has done, with great enjoyment. (She: "They needed you to leave, to do your work. They'll always love and respect you for it." He: "Don't say that—it's a rationalization, a justification. A pity it's all over now." She: "It's never 'over'—even when we die. We remember a lot of each other, all of us do, and there were all those good times we had, *you* had." He: "There could have been more. I feel sad, bad about that.")

The other day I got upset about some stupid matter, and once again, stupidly, compounded an initial stupidity by adding to it my own stupid shouting. I slammed a cabinet door shut, a dish precariously placed fell and broke, I shouted even more—whereupon one of my sons said: "Don't worry, Dad." I found myself getting angry with him, as I do occasionally with my wife, when she, also, mobilizes a phrase meant to supply some badly needed perspective, both moral and psychological. Then I remembered an event that took place over a decade ago. The same boy had cut himself badly, and I had to rush him to the hospital. He'd cut an artery at the wrist, and I was speeding. He was sitting beside me in the car, quietly—with a certain detached interest, actually, in what was happening. I was not only upset at the traffic—the emergency allowed me to consider everyone driving to be perversely slow, or dim-witted, or obstinate, or childish, or senile—but at the boy. How many times had I told him to stay away from that drawer, with all those dangerous tools! He'd already hurt himself with the hammer. I thought we'd settled the matter then—that he ask permission to use anything at all in the left-hand side of the chest. Certainly he was old enough and sensible enough to understand me at the age of seven. Wasn't that the age of reason!

There I was, cursing the failures of the drivers of Concord, Massachusetts, while my own mind was in the above described manner proving itself to be plain crazy—and outrageously, wrongheadedly moralistic. Nor was this the only time such a way of reacting had taken place; nor was this to be the last time I would turn mean and sour in my thoughts, in my face's expression, and ultimately, in my language, when confronted with a difficulty experienced by one of my children. My own father, sadly, used to give me hell when I did something wrong that caused injury to me.

There I'd be, hurt, bleeding, in pain, and he'd shout at me: why did you do that? What's the matter with you—can't you listen and remember?

In the long stretch of psychoanalysis people like me go through (a big help in learning how to understand ourselves and others), such childhood troubles come up and get examined repeatedly, and so eventually I figured out that my father's outbursts had to do with his nervousness and fearfulness. He was scared by the trouble I'd presented to him, worried I might be in jeopardy (I broke a few bones when I was a kid, sustained my fair share of bruises, infections) or yes, worried I might be in great discomfort (I got poison ivy regularly and in bad attacks), and he put such worries in that immediate form of expression: "Why, *for Christ's sake,* did you go near that poison ivy? How many times have I showed you what poison ivy is? What's the *matter* with you?"

My mother would then get angry—at him. Her Christian ire was aroused by the swearing—but really, she was aghast that the victim was being blamed: "Will you, *for Christ's sake,* leave Christ out of it—or if you have to mention Him, remember what He stood for!" That was enough to silence him. Yet, I remember feeling the pain of his momentary, reproachful lapse longer than any caused by the actual illness or accident I'd happened to suffer—and no matter how quickly my mother had managed to intervene. In fact, I remember times when my mother's anticipated intervention worked so well that my father said nothing—but a telltale look in his eyes was there, and that was all I needed to feel dopey and wayward, well worth a stretch of gloom.

I vowed over and over never to repeat all that with my own children, and yet I was, on occasion, helpless—then devastated by my helplessness, and utterly disgusted with myself. Thank God, actually, for those perfectly normal drivers who roused me to rage that day: I got to the hospital faster on their account, because they stimulated me to dodging and zooming and using my horn—*and* they kept my mind, mostly, away from my son's predicament, meaning in this instance, away from grave temptation. I believe the psychoanalytic phrase is "repetition-compulsion." Soon enough we were at the emergency ward, my son's wound was sutured, and he seemed fine. But as he got up from the table and saw something cross my face, he was moved to say something: "Don't worry, Dad." With these words a smile, finally, broke across my face, and we were able to have a pleasant drive home. I think I crawled back in the car—glad to enjoy the sights and sounds of a particular day. I remember being startled when somebody passed me and gave me a dirty look.

On another occasion, with another son, I recall raising my voice, saying what his teachers had said, that he was not using his mind enough in school, his "God-given intelligence"—talk about parental narcissistic grandiosity flimsily masked (and rationalized) as exhortative, necessary piety. The boy was in the seventh grade, and had been goofing off. Nothing doing, I'd thought—but kept my silence. When the teachers spoke, though, I followed. But my previous, frustrated silence had exacted a cost: I shouted. I was angry for other reasons, too, and so the usual controls had given way. Complaints from me pounded forth: the messy room, the messy way of dressing, the willingness to pay complete, abjectly submissive attention to a "them," all those fellow twelve-year-old slobs—and *this* boy, who had always seemed so "independent," so eager to follow his own idiosyncratic interests: fish tanks, mechanical gadgets of all kinds, splendid forays, even then, into stories and novels and nature essays (Lewis Thomas) and the literature of travel (Steinbeck, Theroux).

When I'd had done with my tirade, I slumped into a chair, and then all of a sudden, without warning to myself, started crying. I guess I'd never heard myself speak like that to a child, any child, never mind my own. I got up quickly and left the house and got into my car and drove and drove, this time, oblivious of all other drivers. On the road I passed our family's favorite ice cream stand, Bates Farm—a splendid, homemade product dispensed against a background of grazing cows, a silo, fields of hay, a colonial New England farmhouse. I am an ice cream freak, and this was the moment for a big hunk of mocha chip—but I couldn't drive into the Farm's parking place. Somehow it seemed obscene of me even to want to gratify such an impulse—to soothe my ailing, hurting soul while that of another deserved the comfort far more. When I came back, my wife saw the look on my face, and knew exactly what to say: "Don't start in with that 'I'm sorry' routine! What you said was right, and he needed to hear it." Needless to say, as if she were a confused driver in my way, I got angry at her. I was ready to argue and argue, but realized I'd best shut up, disappear: the exile of the study, morally sanctioned by the requirement of work to do. But I could only stare out the window and feel rotten. Soon my wife was calling us all to supper, and she has never allowed grudgy or grumpy static to linger. Her cheer (I call it "forced" when I'm reluctant to let go of pride's despair) quickly swept us along, as did her delicious supper of spaghetti and baked chicken and strawberry rhubarb pie. Later the boy and I were taking some garbage to the barn, and I prepared to apologize. Only the next day did I realize how readily I'd been comprehended and anticipated. I'd scarcely opened my mouth with the words meant to affirm, in a long-winded explanatory statement, a given mistake, when I heard "Don't worry, Dad." I recall feeling like a small child who'd been forgiven, and who now could feel better. I recall my eyes filling up. He and I went to Bates Farm and got our cones.

I tell you, I say to myself sometimes, with more of those tears choking at me: to be a father is to love one's children, love them continually, love them enough to give them countless kisses and boosts, examples and assistance; but also love them enough to stumble with them, before them, on their account, love them enough to say the wrong things, do the wrong things—not because, God save us, some damn fool American "expert" told us *that,* too, but simply by reason of one's humanity put on the line, one's frailty and helplessness exposed. To be a father, moreover, is to heal those children over and over again, hold them and hug them and carry them on one's shoulders and on one's bike and beside one in the car, healing them daily as they sustain daily the world's inevitable, constant assaults, and in so doing, be healed by them: Don't worry, Dad—meaning, thank you, and I'm glad you're here to fall down and say "the wrong thing," because Mom is right, I did need to get that message, or because it's nice to see the next guy (especially when he's a passing demigod, as all parents are for a while) come down to earth—hence what we boys have been telling you ever so casually yet with conviction, time and again: Don't worry, Dad.

March 1986

INTERVIEW

JW Is there a story behind how you came to write this essay?

RC I wrote this as a result of a telephone conversation with Daniel Menaker, who is an editor and a writer for the *New Yorker*. I think he and his wife had just had their first child, and they were all excited about parenthood, and he had gotten an idea in the process of talking with some of his friends at the magazine that those of them who had either recently had children or who had them many years ago—that they all reflect upon parenthood. He asked me if I'd be willing to write an essay about what it meant to me to be a father. I said it sounded like a rather portentous subject and I didn't know exactly how to go about it. And then the matter was dropped. This conversation had taken place in the midst of another conversation we'd been having about a book review I'd written that he was editing for the magazine.

About two months later, in the course of discussing another book review over the phone, he brought this matter up again and said that a group of the writers had gotten together and talked with some editors who thought it was a very good idea. They were going to go ahead, and he asked me if I would think of writing something. So I said yes, I would. I didn't know exactly what form it would take, but I told Dan I didn't just want to sit down and write some pontifical psychological essay, which is what I thought he wanted from me. He corrected me and said, "Look, I know you well enough that I wouldn't have a chance of getting something like that from you. I know your animus toward that kind of writing, that whole tradition." About a week after that second call, he called me up to say that he was pretty sure that they had a publisher, and so I began.

I began by trying to eliminate various possibilities—an essay on how to bring up children, or how my wife and I brought up children, or whatever. I finally worked myself into a corner. I didn't think I had anything to say, because in a way, writing about parenthood is just the kind of thing I never thought I would do or should do, or that anyone should do. I told Dan this. I said, "There's already too much stuff about this." And he said, "You forget that I'm not looking for that," which I should have known right off. I mean, he himself is a short story writer and not exactly "into" what Christopher Lasch would call the culture of narcissism. So he wasn't interested in additional psychological baggage being put in print. "All I'm interested in," he told me, "is some of the memories you have to share."

Now, the word "memories" got me going. I remember that distinctly on the phone. That opened the door and freed me from the pretensions of my own trade and the gullibility of the public with respect to that trade—quotes around the word "trade," I guess. And I just sat down and started remembering some of the things that had happened to me with my wife and with the children—our family life.

And then, before I began this, I wrote down these words you see in the margin [draft 1] to give me some direction. This is what I often do when I'm going to write an essay or a story about my work. I mean, I have these certain themes. The word "reflection" obviously was what I was trying to do about this experience.

JW "Orderliness and peace"?

RC "Orderliness and peace." My own struggles with my children when they were very "disorderly," when I needed some peace from them. I always kept my study open, and they would come running through when I was working and disrupt everything and sometimes pull things from tables, and books would come down, and I think those were my initial memories.

JW "Roaming boys haunted."

RC Those words represent qualities of feeling I have as I go through the house now, roaming through the boys' rooms and feeling the house haunted by their absence. Each had a separate bedroom, and I often do that—go to their rooms and remember them as they were years ago. And then this is important, the words "healing" and "redemptive." This essay was, in a way, an opportunity to talk about some of the wounds and pain that I must have felt, and the guilt and the shame of not being as adequate, perhaps, a father as I, in my ideal life, in my ideal imagination, would want to be, and the "redemption" which is a preoccupation anyway, I guess, of all of us, or ought to be, so we're told by the ministers and priests and rabbis. How you somehow come to terms with your inadequacies and your failures is how all that may be redeemed.

These words represent themes in my mind's life, and I think I was connecting them to this particular essay because of its subject, because nothing could be more important than this subject.

JW It looks as if you may have had the title very clearly in your mind before you began writing the essay.

RC Yes. In the process of writing these words down, I was remembering things about the kids, and I specifically remembered with an enormous amount of feeling one of the episodes I describe—rushing Bobby to the emergency room of Emerson Hospital because he had nicked an artery. And he knew the difference; he knew it was an artery and not a vein because he saw the blood pumping with some periodicity, even though he was just a kid, under ten, I think he was.

JW The doctor's son.

RC The doctor's son, who's now on his way to becoming a doctor himself. But he said to me, "Dad, this is an artery that I hit," and I was just so flustered, and both, in a way, startled and pleased but also horrified. In a sense, when he said that, it added even more urgency to this scene. I had tied my sweater around his arm very tightly to diminish blood flow to the low part of his arm. Then I decided the sweater wasn't tight enough, so I got a sheet. I ripped a sheet. I was going through hell! I got him in the car and must have gone ninety miles an hour. Here that word "orderliness" becomes relevant again, because the car seats were getting covered with blood, and his clothes, and it was a messy, urgent scene.

What I remember is his calm in the midst of my agitation, and that reassurance—that he was telling me not to worry. And only in retrospect do I realize what a powerful moment that was. It still brings tears to my eyes at times, in telling about it, or thinking about it. And it also summarizes a lot of his personality, which is very much like my wife's personality.

JW The line about the detached interest that he takes in all of this sure conjures up his calmness.

RC It does conjure him up, and it conjures up my wife, who also has a calmness to her, an ability to comment on things in a relatively evenhanded way, whereas I am always the one who is more up and down and agitated and/or depressed, and sometimes both at the same time!

JW As soon as you had that title, it sounds as if you could sense that you were onto something really very deep and important to you.

RC Well yes. I've never had a title provided by one of my children, and this title is my son's. Those three words were his. I'd never before done that, nor since, and so obviously, I guess, I was really putting myself and my family on the line in a very personal and powerful way, drawing on a very powerful experience, and challenging myself to do justice to his words. I'm saying this now, of course, whereas back then I don't think I thought any of this consciously, but I think I was challenging myself to do justice to those three words, and really to my son, to the memory of my son, his importance in my life, his dignity. Quite a challenge for me. I'm not in the habit of drawing on my own family, though I've made a profession of drawing on other people's families!

JW And you touch on that in the essay.

RC Right.

JW Did it come out in one sitting?

RC Yes.

JW It's largely unchanged from the first draft.

RC I wrote this all at once. I couldn't have done this in two days. I remember thinking that I had to get into it with some kind of intellectual beginning, probably intimidated by the *New Yorker*, so I started out mentioning these books. It starts out with the memories, but then I draw upon that side of them, namely their books, their intellectual sides, which I suppose I needn't have.

JW I see that you started with "the boys are gone," and then added three: "the three boys are gone." Then, from "the boys are no boys" to "the boys are no longer boys." You begin with these two simple, direct sentences and then follow them with this very long sentence that leads the reader into their rooms, and that idea of orderliness, that contrast between the orderliness of their rooms now and what it must have been like when they were strewn with toys.

RC Well, all this was unconscious. I mean, I did not consciously think that. I do remember putting the "three" down, because I felt the reader should know that there were three sons. At first I was writing for myself—"the boys are gone"—and then I remembered that someone's going to read this and I should give them some facts. And that's probably the theme of this whole piece: I'm talking to myself, and I'm drawing on my memories and experiences, and I'm reminding myself here, right away, that they're no longer boys. So that sets the tone of speaking to yourself and reminding yourself and having a conversation with yourself and reflecting, drawing on your own experiences.

But you're right. God, that is a long sentence.

JW It's a high-wire act.

RC When does this sentence end?

JW At the end of the paragraph.

RC Wow! There's a lot of information there, everything from Lego to Henry James! I love that combination, as a matter of fact! If Lego won't bring Henry James down to earth, I don't know what will!

JW That sentence seems to set the mood.

RC I guess it does. It's the way I feel sometimes when I go into their rooms. I look at the books, or I look at the toys. I'll look at their desks. I'll look at the way they in turn remember and see things, the posters, the things on the walls. I'll even open up their closets and look at their clothes hanging. I don't want to turn this into something morbid or kooky, but, I mean, it's just me kind of immersing myself occasionally in memories and their worlds as they are left to us, because now all three rooms are very much empty, and they only come back occasionally, at holiday times or on vacations. They're all in their twenties.

JW I know that 1985 was a rough year for you. Your parents were both sick, and I wondered if that mood had informed this too.

RC My parents died at the very end of 1985. This was written in the spring, the beginning of the year, but they were sick. My mother quite clearly was dying, and my father less clearly, but on his way. They were both in their eighties, and no question, that's part of this too. I was in some way looking back, perhaps not only at my children and their lives but my own life as a child with my parents. Also, my parents were extremely close to my children. My children would often visit them without their mother and me, and that meant an enormous amount to my parents. Bobby, whose three words are the title, Bobby was especially close to my father and has some of his way of thinking—analytical, a fixer and a doer, a scientific sensibility that I always associate with the two of them. It's no accident, I think, that Bobby's going to be a surgeon, just as it was no accident that my father was constantly able to fix things and had my brother and me in awe of that ability when we were children. That lives on, because I've never been able to have that kind of evenhanded, detached ability to analyze why something isn't working, the way my father and Bobby both could. So, in my own family's life, I'm kind of in between my father and my son in a certain emotional way. But there is no doubt that in 1985, given the failing health of my parents, I was doing a lot of looking back and tapping into my own childhood—which I'm supposed to do anyways as a child psychiatrist and as a psychoanalyst. That's what we're trained to do. But here, I was doing it in a much more personal manner and not to treat anyone except perhaps myself, to just reconnect myself with my kids and with my own childhood.

Actually, I remember going back to the home where I grew up in Milton, just taking a solitary trip there to see it. I knew my parents were not going to be around too much longer, and I was doing a lot of thinking about my own childhood and my life with them as a boy, and I think in a way there is an echo of that in this piece: I am doing this with my own sons, even as I was also doing it with my parents during that calendar year.

JW I see such similarities also in your voice as a father and the voice of your father as you've described it in other writings, perhaps particularly in the introduction to *The Call of Stories*.

It seems like such a difficult double whammy—so many parents seem to "lose" their children at almost exactly the same time that they lose their parents. The parents die, the children leave home.

RC Right. But that hasn't yet turned into a big federal case in American cultural analysis—God save us from it. But you're right. It does happen around that time, if you're lucky and your parents live that long. It is something to think about, that double loss of one's parents, and in a way, one's parenthood at the same time.

And you know, our own life as fathers and mothers is its own struggle to redeem what we went through as children with our parents, because all parents make mistakes, and all childhoods are filled with both accomplishments and achievements and disappointments. I mean more or less—some more, some less. We're not talking here about those who have almost unimaginably terrible childhoods—on the brink of starvation, or constantly fighting disease, or threatened by terrible violence—children with very little that they can hold on to. But for most of us who've had a relatively comfortable life, there were still disappointments, failures, and unpleasant memories, and we try to redeem that when we become parents—probably in order to make our own mistakes rather than repeat the mistakes that we went through! All of that is a big challenge, because we're always doomed to some extent to repeat mistakes, and so it's a struggle.

I think when you're losing your own parents while at the same time you're sensing your children leaving you, you in your own way are being moved both to remember your own past and think back on the past of your children, and this can be a very memory-filled time in a life, and I think that may have fueled this essay or story or whatever you want to call it.

JW That, I guess, is what fuels that third sentence, which in turn fuels the whole essay. I hadn't noticed the length of it either, until I sat down and started trying to come up with questions to ask you. Not noticing the length of a long sentence is, I guess, proof that it works. I was just trying to look at how you set the mood of this piece in the beginning, and I started looking for the end of that sentence, and then I started turning pages—

RC There isn't too much editing there, is there?

JW No. It seems to have just poured out straight from the heart.

RC I think it did. I think I was singing, like some old, broken-down opera singer trying to belt out a song even if the voice is cracking, partially due to the vocal cords becoming so aged, and partially due to the emotion of the situation that was clouding up the eyes and cracking the voice.

But, I guess, by the second paragraph I'm back. I guess I break that, sort of catch myself. And having remembered all of this, that's when I start to try to come to terms with it, and I think, to confess, because this is a confessional essay. I'm trying to level with myself, and I ask the reader to join in. There's an irony here: I'm a child psychiatrist and a writer, and people look to me, perhaps quite wrongly, for some kind of wisdom in these matters, and in a way what I'm saying is look, here I am, a fellow human being who may know books and may know his Freud and his Anna Freud, and his Erik Erikson, and may have a certain kind of an education, but ultimately what I am is a fellow human being, and a journeyman, a voyager who's stumbled and fallen down. Let me tell you about some of the mistakes! And some of the stumbling and some of the evidence of pride and vanity and what George Eliot calls "unreflecting egoism" at work here in my life, whether you call it an Augustinian confessional or just plain old "I confess," like the person that went before a judge in a local court.

I noticed, by the way, looking at this now through the eyes of someone doing the analysis, that the first page, even in the original, is virtually uncorrected. But then I have a lot of trouble here, later on, and there's more scratching out, and I don't know what that's about. This, of course, is pitiable intellectuality at work. When you see a word like "meliorism" being added, then you know you're in trouble!

JW When such words appear in this essay, they seem to be used with some irony.

RC I hope so, I *hope* so!

JW So when you actually started writing this, you were writing it for Dan Menaker and this book.

RC I was writing it for Dan Menaker and for the collection of pieces that were going to be written by *New Yorker* editors who were parents and writers as well as editors. I finished it and sent it to him. He called me up and was quite pleased with it, and then I didn't hear anything for a long time. I think at that time we were in a recession, the recession in the middle of Reagan's first term, and I think it had hit the book business.

JW Trickle-down economics!

RC The trickle-down effect, and I think the publisher whom Dan approached backed out, said they weren't sure that there was a market for a book such as this at the time. Dan was stunned. And then we joked on the phone. He said, if the book were filled with a lot of psychological essays, then there'd be a market for it—if it was filled with essays by people telling parents what to do and what to think and how to behave with their children, then there'd be a market for it. The other contributors were short-story writers. They were poets, they were novelists. The genre of this collection was not psychology, psychological advice to parents, and that's what the publishers wanted, and when they didn't get it, I think they backed out. So Dan and I had a very philosophical conversation over the phone. I said, hey, we've learned something about America, and about publishing, and we've learned in a sad way what isn't available generally to a lot of parents: mainly, any encouragement to stop and think about the story of their lives as parents, rather than to think about how to mend this and what to do under these circumstances, through psychology or sociology or education or whatever, all these fix-it routines of American culture, and all the psychological self-consciousness, which is really a curse on American life, for so many of us—what is wanted by publishers to this day, and I suspect will be to the end of this century, and I'm afraid the end of the next one to follow, at the rate we're going.

I think turning in on oneself, remembering, trying to figure out what you've done and where you're going through this kind of personal reflection is probably what a lot of us as parents could *use* occasionally. But there's no sanction or medium for that in our society. The sanction is for getting a book that tells you—well, *this* is what happens to the child at *this* age, and *this* is what happens at *that* age, and *this* is how you should behave with the child, you should do *this* and *that*, and you shouldn't do *this* and you shouldn't do *that*. It's all so admonishing.

There is so little wisdom and so much that passes for what's called child psychology and advice these days—very little wisdom. Lots of techniques, lots of clever, and not so clever, and actually rather banal wordiness about what to say and what to do and how to look and what "attitude," quote unquote, to have, but no wisdom, very little wisdom. And yet, ordinary working people, who make no pretense to intellectuality, are filled with the wisdom of their lives. And at times I think what this culture does to all of us is rob us of the sense of our own growing wisdom that comes with age and experience, from what my father used to call the college of hard knocks, where you fall down enough times to begin to learn how to not fall down—all of that, an achievement in life.

JW Some critics have questioned the eloquence you've documented in uneducated people that you've spoken to. I've heard you address that issue before, especially with regard to *The Old Ones of New Mexico*. This criticism has always puzzled me, because the implication is that you've got to have a certain degree of education and refinement in order to speak eloquently, which is just plain wrong. But why, do you suppose, is it that so many of the so-called educated in the country seem unwilling to acknowledge the eloquence and wisdom of ordinary language?

RC They don't listen to their own wisdom. This is a tragedy that results from the impact of social science and psychological advisory warnings thrown out at us every other minute. There is eloquence in so many of us, regardless of our background—rich, poor, black, white, educated, uneducated. We forget that. Look at some of the Harvard students whom you and I have talked with: they arrive with an eloquence that's been earned out of their lives; and gradually they lose a lot of that as they're intimidated by professors and by Harvard itself and by a notion of Harvard that they acquire in their minds, and of course, they are intimidated by one another, too. Let's not just blame the professors. And they lose some important qualities or are afraid to express some important qualities that they have within themselves—common sense, shrewdness that isn't phony, thoughtfulness, and God forbid, *passion.* You're not supposed to express too much passion, you're supposed to be "cool"!

JW They get scared out of their unhyphenated wisdom.

RC Right! They get scared out of their unhyphenated wisdom. Well said. It's a tragedy.

JW Sort of ironic that many of the people our culture turns to as sources of insight and wisdom attend so carefully to the words of ordinary people. I'm thinking of Walker Percy sitting in the Waffle House with a notebook, eavesdropping on the truckers in the next booth. Or people like you, or Studs Terkel, going out and talking to people who haven't spent their lives earning degrees.

RC What you at times find in such situations is a kind of unashamed passion and emotionality, and yes, sentiment that isn't being apologized for, that may have its own flaws, moral and psychological, but nevertheless is honest life coming through and being expressed. And if you'd been brought up too much in a world of artifice, intellectual artifice and university, psychoanalytic artifice, and the overly self-conscious world that I was trained in for so many years, I tell you it can be a breath of fresh air to be in the Waffle House or in an ordinary living room where people say what's on their minds and don't feel any need to correct themselves, or interpret themselves, or apologize for what they've felt or said, or try to emulate others, always in that upwardly mobile way that the universities encourage and seduce people into believing to be important. Well, now we're bringing into this discussion my rampant anti-intellectualism, which I don't think is actually in the piece but probably informs it indirectly, doesn't it?

JW Well, I think there's a certain *ambivalence* about all of that. I mean, on the one hand there's your acknowledgment of the stories and novels that the boys have in their rooms.

RC And the pride that those books are in the rooms.

JW Right, but also in the third paragraph you write: "in the tradition of the 20th-century secular world obsessed by a meliorism heavily saturated with psychology, with dreary phrases such as 'child development,' 'parenting skills,' 'learning environments.'"

RC Right, there it's coming out: my scorn of academic pretentiousness—of my own temptation in that direction, maybe! And also, later on in the piece, I think I use the phrase "repetition-compulsion." I use that and I put quotes around it and I distance myself from it, but that phrase is part of me, and that's the way my mind works, and I'm, in a way, saying look at me, pitiable creature that I am, this is the way I think, and it helps me to understand something, it helps me to understand my relationship with my father and things that I keep on doing, based on what I experienced with him. But I'm struggling against that way of thinking, too. Not only do I want to free myself up, so that in a way I don't keep on repeating things that come out of my childhood, but I am also struggling (here's the irony!) against the word or phrase that describes that psychology of mine—words and phrases which are perhaps all too confining and maybe don't do justice to the complexity of my relationship with my father and to the complexity, by extension, of all of our humanity, you know, which simply is not going to be addressed by phrases such as this here, used in the paragraph I've created.

The hyphenation, I suppose, is implicitly at its best an acknowledgment that it's too damn complicated for one word, but two doesn't work either, and especially words like those two, which both explain but also have their own limitations.

JW A more recent trend than the hyphen is the slash. The slash seems to have become the preferred weapon of a lot of jargonists. It's as if they're saying, "I don't want to impose any kind of tyrannical editorial authority on you here, poor common unempowered reader, so I'll throw out a few words and you can exercise your right to choose the one you like!"

RC That inclination or habit I have yet to learn, or desire to learn. That's awful in a way, isn't it?

JW That's a lot of what Camille Paglia is raging against, and that's the uncrazy part of her work I respond to—her attacks on fatuousness and smugness in her profession.

RC Overwrought, pretentious, abstract thinking.

JW And little wisdom.

RC And little wisdom. Of course, this conversation risks our own arrogance because, you know, the implication here is that *we* possess wisdom. But it's a tragedy that so often wisdom isn't even seen as something one lacks and one struggles for. It's just missed, the ordinary wisdom that novelists have given us, and the Bible has given us, and, I think, parents all the time give to children—the earned knowledge out of suffering, out of the troubles we've had. That, to my mind, is what wisdom is: not philosophy, not psychoanalytic knowledge, not intellectual achievement, but a kind of sense of things that comes out of a lived life.

JW I think my favorite pieces of your work are the moments of reflection. In the longer documentary efforts they often occur juxtaposed against the comments of the people you're meeting. Some of your essays seem very personally revealing. I'm thinking of the first-person personal reflections—"The End of the Affair," and "Shadowing Binx," and this piece, "Don't Worry, Dad." But I sense somewhat of an ambivalence in you. I know I've heard you mention before that you were always hearing the echo of your mother's voice, talking about the sin of pride—

RC Just came to me as you were talking about it. I had thought of that as you were forming your sentence!

I'm embarrassed and I feel ashamed at times. Those are the emotions I feel, and guilty and wrongheaded, when I start drawing too *much* on my personal feelings and start using the word "I," simply because I have to live with that voice, those words of my mother's. It's a big part of my life. We would come home from school with our report cards. If they were very good, she would always give us the cautionary reminder about watching ourselves lest we become too full of ourselves, watching ourselves lest we become "prideful." Of course, when I was in analysis in New Orleans, my analyst used to say to me, "Hey, look, what did your mother want from you? Everyone has this 'pride,' " he reminded me. "It's a necessary part of building up your life! You have to develop a concern for yourself or you'll get nowhere. And be no one." So I said, "Well, my mother was worried about the excesses." She drew on the Old and New Testaments, which are constantly warning people about pride. To balance my mother's way of thinking and the observations of my analyst—it's a dialectic of sorts for me. I understand that at times, when I speak out of personal memory and experience, then possibly a certain kind of genuine feeling and honorable series of experiences might be offered to the reader. But I just worry about the danger of paying too much attention to myself and pointing at myself in what seems like—to use a word that she also would use—an unseemly way. "Unseemly" was one of her words.

JW Were you ever tempted to bring home a really crappy report card?

RC No, because there was another side of all of this. I wanted those damn grades to be good. And my dad wanted them—and he had no worry about "pride"!

JW I think of that photograph of you and your schoolmates when you were in grammar school, where you're sort of glaring at the camera in your little black leather jacket.

RC Yeah, I *did* have a leather jacket—and years later, when I was a so-called teenager, I caused a lot of trouble for everyone, myself included, by plenty of rebelliousness. Anyway, there is the struggle to feel relaxed about what I suppose these days in literary criticism is called the presentation of the self, although I don't even like that talk. It seems like such a bullshitty way of putting the matter. Too abstract, I guess. At times you're putting yourself on the line, so to speak, and some people, I think, do it with more comfort and ease than others. For me, doing so is fraught with those childhood memories of reprimands and caveats from my mother.

JW Well, some of your most personal writing that I'm aware of appeared in the *New Oxford Review* column.

RC At the time I wrote this essay, I was writing in a similar vein for that magazine, which is relatively obscure. I don't say this in any pejorative sense. It's a small magazine, no big circulation. Somehow, I felt at ease publishing the essay we're discussing there. Maybe this is tapping into, again, a psychological interpretation. Maybe because it's a religious magazine, and because it draws on the kind of Christian reflection that my mother was comfortable with, maybe I felt some permission to be more personal there, because it was under that kind of auspice or aegis. The religious orientation of the magazine buffered the self-critical tendencies I learned from my mother to impede this kind of writing.

I sure drew on the personal in the very first thing I wrote, which at the time I assumed might be the *only* thing I'd ever write, namely "A Young Psychiatrist Looks at His Profession" [*Atlantic Monthly* (July 1961)]. Maybe because I thought that was a one-time thing and I wasn't conscious of being a writer, even. That essay was kind of an explosion of disappointment and anger, as well as an effort to find the good in this profession that I'd struggled with for so many years. I have also written about my parents, as you mention, in "The End of the Affair" [*Katallagete* 4, nos. 2–3 (Fall–Winter 1972)], with some direct personal writing. It's interesting to note that I wrote that essay for another relatively obscure magazine, a place where I didn't think too many people would be reading it: *Katallagete*. I think there's some sense of "you mustn't speak too loudly about yourself for too many people, because if you do, that means you're in some ways sinning, you're getting too much attention." This sounds crazy. Maybe it is, but I think there is something to it—my struggles with my mother's biblical injunctions.

JW Where was "Shadowing Binx" first published?

RC That was also in an obscure publication, *Literature & Medicine* [4 (Autumn 1985)]. So there is a consistent effort to hide, relatively speaking, some of this kind of writing. These pieces were written at a time when I was also writing for more high profile publications like the *New Yorker*, the *New York Review*, and the *New Republic*.

JW Well, "A Young Psychiatrist" was something of a trumpet blast in the *Atlantic*.

RC That was a trumpet blast, but I think the history of that piece would be consistent with what I'm describing, because it was suggested to me by someone, and he really had to struggle to get me to do this. Whitney Ellsworth was working at the *Atlantic* then, and he really had to push me long and hard. He really dragged that piece out of me. He really did.

Part of it was fear, too, because it was a critique of a profession I was just entering at the age of about thirty. And I'd never written before, and as I said, repeating myself, never intended consciously, at least, to write again. Some of my friends felt that I was drawing on my friendship with William Carlos Williams, that it had some of his cranky disdain for "principalities and powers." And I guess they were right.

He read that essay. He had another year or two left of life. I must admit with great pride, which I'm not going to apologize for at this moment, that he liked it and he told me so. He saw two things that I wrote besides my thesis on him. He liked something else I wrote on children that appeared in the *New South*. He'd been pushing me toward doing that, writing directly about the southern children I met, without resorting to the jargon of the social sciences, and I sent that up to him and he said, "*Now!*" He said, "Now you're getting someplace!"

He and Margaret Long were two novelists and poets who pushed me. She was the editor of the *New South*. She'd written a number of novels, and she was dragging that kind of writing out of me the way Whitney dragged that piece for the *Atlantic* out of me, and Williams was saying, "For crying out loud, give us these kids, not your profession. Give us *their* words, not what you learned in *school*." "School" was an epithet for him. Remember, he says in *White Mule*, I think it is, "Schools, those factories of despair."

JW Which sounds so much like Orwell.

RC That's right, they all come together, these folks whose writing I now teach. Thank God! The alternative would be that I'd be crazy! But if you can bring it all together, these various voices in your life that meant something, then it shows a certain kind of structure, I guess, that will keep you on this side of the sanity divide.

JW It's kind of funny and ironic that one of the most prolific writers of our time began so reluctantly with these older writers and editors trying to *drag* stuff out of you.

RC Well—I think we're back to parenthood in this discussion here! There are dads and dads, moms and moms.

JW Well, so you sent "Don't Worry, Dad" off to *NOR*—

RC I sent it off to *NOR* and they published it and they got a lot of mail on it, and so did I. I was surprised. I got a lot of letters, and I got telephone calls from people who told me that they had been so moved and they had been moved to tears. And the fact is, I myself was literally moved to tears toward the end as I was writing this. I got all choked up, which really does not usually happen when I write. And even now, when I go over this, as I did this morning in preparation for our talk, I get choked up at certain points in the piece.

JW It's so important to distinguish between sentimentality and sentiment. The relation of the two is somewhat analogous, I think, to the relation between overwrought abstractions and real wisdom, to go back to an earlier part of this conversation. The former is a form of fakery, and the latter is earned. We aim for wisdom, and sometimes we try to fake it with puffed-up intellectuality; we aim for genuine sentiment in our communications of the heart, and sometimes wind up faking it with inflated, nebulous feelings. But "Don't Worry, Dad" builds genuine sentiment through its particularity—the dialogue and vivid detail. Certain lines in this essay just resonate. I mean, you jotted down at the beginning of your first draft "redeemed," and that one line, that one moment when you write "He and I went to Bates Farm and got our cones" just resonates with that sense of redemption.

RC It's the working out of all this anguish and conflict—whatever. But the choking and the anguished voice that I feel when I read it to myself, it's an inner choking. I think every parent knows this, and I think many of us remember it from our own childhood struggles when we become parents.

Which is what the task of this piece was, according to Dan Menaker, to write about that, and that's what I tried to do.

JW I'm looking through the second draft now for changes. There really are so few—no major changes in the second draft.

RC You'll notice, by the way, on the first draft, where I crossed out "but as psychiatrists."

JW On page 4, yes. "Telling ourselves, occasionally, we're basically alright, but as psychiatrists"—you changed that to "a big help in learning how to understand ourselves and others."

RC I was threatening to become pontifical and play the hand of the expert, which would have been a devastating failure. But the temptation is there, if you want to analyze the original manuscript!

JW Here, on page 5 of the first typed draft, you made a change. We were talking about language and abstractions. The abstractions that you use in this essay seem to be used with some irony, and here, where you originally wrote "through the process of personal amplification"—

RC Oh that's awful! That's a terrible thing to write! Thank God I got rid of that!

JW You replace the phrase with this wonderful repetition of "stupid." "The other day I got upset about some stupid matter, and once again, stupidly, compounded an initial stupidity by adding to it my own stupid shouting."

RC I noticed that this morning. It's interesting that I'm doing that. I'm crossing out "personal amplification," which is a form of stupidity!

JW So that's an implied fifth use!

RC As I say, this piece may be about a little bit of redemption—the writer paring things down and getting rid of his blind spots and pretensions, which is part of what writing ought to be about for all of us, a form of learning a little bit of discipline, a little bit of self-restraint, a little bit of self-criticism, I guess. Of course, this is me, my mother's son talking. My father's son too, with that Puritan tradition. You can't just write for aesthetics. You write for some kind of purpose, moral purpose. And I know there's a big split among writers and literary critics about this.

JW You seem to have received an education that would have made it next to impossible for you to embrace abstract language and jargon. Your parents' fondness for the novels that they loved, and primarily those nineteenth-century novels, and Perry Miller's influence. From what I know of him, someone who had been through a horrible war, he sounds as if he just didn't have a whole lot of patience for bullshit.

RC He didn't. He was a very earthy man.

JW And then Williams: "No ideas but in things."

RC Very earthy also. I think for me, the embrace of the social sciences—starting out even when I did some of that experimental psychology work with Richard Solomon, and going on to the work that grew out of my medical school education—I think for me it was an effort to be both rebellious but also conforming. Because my father was a scientist, and in a sense there was a part of him that asked for a level of science that I never adequately was able to offer him or myself. But I did struggle with the matter. And I think social science was the nearest I could come to it, because I couldn't be the kind of hard scientist that he was. I didn't have the intellectual equipment—well maybe, to be fair to myself, the *emotional* equipment. And I think part of me, when I was in medical school and during the early mid-fifties, was struggling for some kind of scientific home, a language of science and a way of thinking that was called scientific so that I could consider myself in that sense, maybe, my father's son.

And I think I failed. Of course, ironically, he had no use for the social sciences, so I failed on his terms. He had a wonderful skepticism about psychology and sociology, as did my mother. Whatever psychology and sociology they were interested in obtaining they got from George Eliot or Tolstoy. Or Dickens. Or Chekhov. So you know, I was fighting my own struggles with them and with their heritage that they'd handed on to my brother and me—and it's no accident I think that my brother became a professor of English at the University of Michigan. But I was struggling for this heritage and I think maybe rebelling—I don't want to say glibly "rebelling" against it, but I was trying to find some territory of my own, and I stumbled into a swamp! It may have taken me a little time to figure out how to get the hell out of there before I drown. And I did get out, I think by the skin of my teeth. I said good-bye, at last, to the language of experimental psychology and psychiatry and psychoanalysis, although holding on, I still hope, to whatever good knowledge I learned from certain analytic supervisors and, Lord knows, whatever good knowledge I learned from my friendship with Erik Erikson and Anna Freud, but that was a bit later. I think by the time I got to know them in the sixties, I had also gotten to know Ruby and Lawrence and some of those kids in the South, black and white, who enabled me to connect with Erik Erikson and Anna Freud in a way that I wouldn't have been able to connect with them had I gotten through my training and then met them without that intervening period of years in the South, doing that work in all those homes with those families going through school desegregation.

By the way, listening to myself talk, I've never heard myself realize this before quite this way. Because you know, I could have connected with Erik Erikson and Anna Freud as yet another child psychiatrist, a young analyst who took courses from them. But I didn't, I connected with them after living and working in the South, and doing that work and then writing to them and getting into a correspondence with them and then getting to know them. It was a different way of meeting them.

JW I see similarities, too, between the particularity of the writers, a lot of the writers you admire, certainly someone like Williams, and the particularity and precision of practical sciences like engineering and like medicine.

RC That's true, that's part of what the practical sciences offer. My father could have been a physicist, or a physical chemist. He'd majored in physical chemistry, which is really very tough. I could never even contemplate taking that in college. Some premeds went on to take it even though it wasn't required. But I had neither the intelligence or capability or emotional ability, I think, to immerse myself in that. But that's what he knew very well. But there was always in him the fixer, and the guy who wanted to connect that kind of knowledge to the actual world. You're right, that practicality, and that concreteness. He had that. He loved to fix things around the house, just as my son Bobby does. Loved to apply knowledge to everyday life. Used to make toys for my brother and me. Had a workshop and would make things. He'd come from England, from Yorkshire, and he had a very good sense of language, just plain ordinary language—strong, vigorous language such as the English have, all of them, whether they're educated or not. And I remember being conscious of language because I had to make sense of the fact that my mother and father spoke different versions of English with different accents and came from different parts of the English-speaking world.

JW Sioux City, Iowa, and Leeds, England?

RC Sioux City and Leeds are not exactly neighboring towns!

JW Looking back over the drafts again, I see that here, on page 6 of the typed draft, you got rid of "stupidity." From "There I was, cursing the stupidity of the drivers of Concord" to "the failures of the drivers of Concord."

RC I guess one of the keys in all this is that I should only use that word "stupid" directed at myself! I was censoring myself from judging others. There's the Puritan tradition working its way into my writing. Always turn on yourself before you think you have a right to turn on others. Of course that itself becomes a form of *pride*: this is never-ending, this kind of self-scrutiny!

The confrontations between Jane and me in this essay kind of echo what went on sometimes between my parents.

JW For example, on page 10, where she says, "Don't start in with that 'I'm sorry' routine"?

RC Right, exactly. She's telling me, "I've had enough of that, I'm not interested in it," and really this is as strong as she'll get, because she criticizes me in a quieter way than my mother and father would criticize one another. But she makes her point, and I think it lasts longer for me.

But I guess what I was trying to say was, there was a kind of an echo—

JW Kind of a parallel—

RC A parallel, that's the word. There's a parallel which is totally unconscious. I just happened to notice it now. And why wouldn't there be? It's a part of any family's life—parents are struggling with one another as they think about their kids, and as that happens they remember how *their* parents managed.

JW On page 8, you at first added "repeatedly," then changed that to "over and over," which sounds much nicer. "Over and over, never to repeat all that . . ."

RC I think that's just earthier and blunter and less affected. What interests me is how little editing there is in that paragraph. I usually have to do so much more editing.

JW There's so little in this piece. It just seems like it tapped into something. Did you pace a lot, thinking about this piece?

RC I paced in their rooms, and then I came down to my study, and I thought of their rooms as I wrote this. I thought of their rooms, and I remembered myself as a child with my parents. That's what was happening in my mind as I was writing. I wrote it in the morning. I couldn't have written it if any of them were at home. I couldn't have written it. Two of them, Bob and Dan, were off in college then, and Michael had left that day for school.

JW Here, on page 8, is "repetition-compulsion." And this fine moment: "I remember being startled when somebody passed me and gave me a dirty look." Very funny, following as it does your frantic race to Emerson.

RC Well, that conveys how self-absorbed we're capable of becoming in this life! Here [page 9] I've added "previous, frustrated" silence. And this other change, getting rid of "a damn" is interesting, too.

JW "The usual controls." Now, in the original draft, when you were talking about the books in the boy's room, you left the parentheses blank.

RC I had forgotten! I ran upstairs to his room! Not then, but obviously when it was typed up.

JW This is a real moment here! Empty parentheses in a Robert Coles manuscript! I never thought I'd see empty parentheses in an essay of yours!

RC I had to go back to his room and check because I couldn't look around the way I usually can in my study to fill up the parentheses that you're so familiar with! I had to go up a flight of stairs! How could I forget? He used to love those books. We used to get whole stacks of those Steinbeck paperbacks.

JW And here, when you're describing Bates [page 10], you changed "amid" to "dispensed against a background." "Amid" seems like an echo of that language of your father's that you use sometimes a little ironically, as if to acknowledge that it's just a little archaic. And "amid" also doesn't seem as visual.

RC "Dispensed against a background" is escalating the scene, I think. It's much more vivid. "Amid" just plays it down.

JW "Amid" makes it sound like you're standing shoulder to shoulder with the cattle.

RC Well, maybe I belong there, dispensing bullshit, or cowshit!

JW This is followed by a long stretch with absolutely no editing. You must have gone through this a few times, though, because this is in pencil and the rest is in pen.

RC You see, here is the confessional thing—that I thought I had to tell the truth, that I was crying, and yet I couldn't quite say that I was crying, so I put it that way, so I put it that way: "I recall my eyes filling up." A little awkward, even a little pretentious, but I think the tone works because there's an understatement there—or embarrassment. Someone like me isn't supposed to cry at my age or something. You're supposed to fight that.

JW But it echoes the previous sentence, both in the structure—I recall, I recall—and also just feeling like a small child who'd been forgiven. And then that's sort of consistent with that feeling of being a small child: the eyes filling up.

RC Which is the way it often happens with a child: tears well up, but children don't always just *cry*, exactly.

JW And then your crescendo ending, which goes back to that wonderful long sentence that pulls you into the essay.

RC There's where I do release some of my feelings about my profession and struggle with my embarrassment of what all this is about. It's a struggle for some genuine emotion, liberated from self-consciousness and psychology, which is a big struggle for all of us, and I think I'm trying to draw the reader into it all, too, so maybe the reader will also be free. It's a kind of liberation theology at work here! Readers of the world, unite! Break out of the bind that we've gotten into from all these experts—the arrogance, the all-knowing, jibberish-talking pundits of psychology and psychiatry or whatever.

JW Well, I hear echoes of previous statements that you've made about Williams and your father: that phrase "some damn fool American expert."

RC Right, that's my father talking. That is my father. That is my father's voice. Including the "American"!

JW Never British!

RC Oh boy, this is like a psychoanalysis! Oh, look at this mess.

JW Yes, the ending changed a lot. You worked with it a lot in the first draft, too.

RC Well, I introduced the boys here at the end, which is very important.

JW Instead of one boy, all three.

RC Right. Each one of them appears in these pages.

JW Why do you do this? At the end of the written draft the writing sort of drifts toward the right-hand margin.

RC I think this is my way of coming to some completion. I feel that I'm struggling, because I have to break free of the constraints of writing, and this is my way of saying this has got to *stop*.

JW So you're sort of narrowing the parameters of the *page*?

RC Right, and saying I've got to end!

JW You're saying, "I've only got this margin now to work in"!

RC I'm fighting against the constraints of the page, and against the constraints of writing itself, and trying to say: finale, *end*, break free, free of words. There's a struggle here, there's a struggle between the constraints of writing and the constraints of the piece itself. I'm now turning into a critic, I'm becoming self-conscious, but I think this is the struggle for that last sentence, for saying good-bye.

JW Because your instincts are to fill up the page?

RC Right! And you can keep on doing that forever, more and more pages, and I'm saying enough! No more pages!

JW On your first attempts at the ending, did you feel you were just lacking the right conclusive rhythm?

RC I guess. See, I think this is an important shift at the end. I'm reminding the reader that the boys are my teachers. The original way was really wrong. The original way is an intrusion of my egoism into this piece. It shows you that I still have a lot to learn on that score, as my mother told me I always would! And at the end I remind myself—hey, this whole piece is about what you learn from your children. It would have been a fatal mistake to have edited that. That's important. It's interesting, that omission.

JW The omission of—

RC Kissing them.

JW "And hug them and kiss them." I wonder if it's because you'd already said "give them countless kisses."

RC Yes, that's right, that's right. Otherwise it would have been Puritanism at work! But you're right, that's what I did. Gotta be careful about making psychological interpretations without checking the paragraphs! I was too fast on the draw there.

JW My sense from having talked to you is that you really had to struggle in the early years to find your way of writing, and you did that with the help of these editors. By now, you've written so much I get the feeling that you're very good at being able to let go of a piece of writing, and just not become totally bogged down in it. This essay seems to be exceptional for how it poured out, in almost final form.

RC Yes, I do know how to let go. I feel, at a certain point, this is all I have—and maybe I feel that too soon, some critics would say. But I very strenuously edit myself, and the second time around edit myself again when it's typed up. But then I feel mostly that that's it, that I can't do much more, and I've got to go on. I've never been one to hold on too tightly to the work, once I've given it my all. So I just hand it on to the world, or for that matter, put it aside, which I've done occasionally, just throw it out, feeling it's not worthwhile. But I'm not one to tinker repeatedly over a long period of time. Maybe I haven't invested enough of myself in my work. I'm being my psychoanalytic devil's advocate now, criticizing myself. Maybe this is hastiness in the service of fickleness toward one's own work, but I do work hard at editing, and then I feel that's all there is.

Also, I have to worry about something: I don't trust my judgment of my writing once I've finished it. I tend to be so critical that I think at times I let this go for fear that if I don't let it go, I'll tear it up. And then again, maybe some people would say: I wish you did more of that tearing up! But regardless of that, ending a piece of writing can be an emotional problem for me. I tend to get depressed and extremely critical of whatever writing I do, good or bad, and I'm sure that emotion came across with this piece too. I felt inadequate at the end, and somehow a failure. So I need to let go, hand it over to an editor or to another person, for fear that it won't be handed over to anyone but will be handed over to the wastepaper basket!

JW That reminds me of what Flaubert said, that novels are never finished, only abandoned in despair.

RC We tend to have exacting consciences. We have ideals and we try to live up to them, but we always fail, as inevitably we would. And I think we wouldn't want it any other way. If we didn't have some sense of impending failure, or the distinct possibility if not likelihood of failure, then we'd be so intoxicated with ourselves that we'd be unbearable, probably our writing with it. It's a struggle, and it damn well should be, I guess—a struggle for honesty and clarity against the various limitations or burdens or excesses of our "nature."

Don't Worry, Dad

[illegible]

¶ The boys are gone, I stay to myself. The boys are men, not boys, I remind myself. I go to their rooms sometimes, look at the tangible evidence of the years they have spent on this planet — please God, in their closets + etc: the little cars + trucks they delighted in having when they were two or six, now tucked away on shelves inside their closets, one or two still left here + there in a particular room for them to see in a quick glance as they go on to other matters; the books, some going back to the days when they listened to us during the reading, some the first effects of their newly achieved literacy, + some stories that link so-called youth to so-called grownups, such as Animal Farm or Kipling's stories or those of Hemingway or Mark Twain, + finally books such as Of Mice and Men or Pride and Prejudice or those convoluted Henry James novels which tell their English teacher mom + novel-loving dad that we're [illegible] voters now, + one soon to be, + that one away in college, + one soon to be, + that everyone drives, + we all wonder, out loud, what's happening to America + the world, not when can I come over + play Lego, or when that Red Cross swimming instructor will be able to hand out those senior life-saver cards. ¶ I catch myself and one morning I think as I go from room to room of the missed chances, the missteps, the misstatements — things done I should not have done, things not done I should have done. Why didn't I help the third boy to make more friends earlier? Why did we keep him so close to us? Yet he has lots of good friends now, + is quite comfortable travelling all over, I remind myself. Still! Why did I get so impatient at times with our eldest son? Remember that day when a friend came, + the three-year-old child was running all over the place, + [illegible]

[illegible]

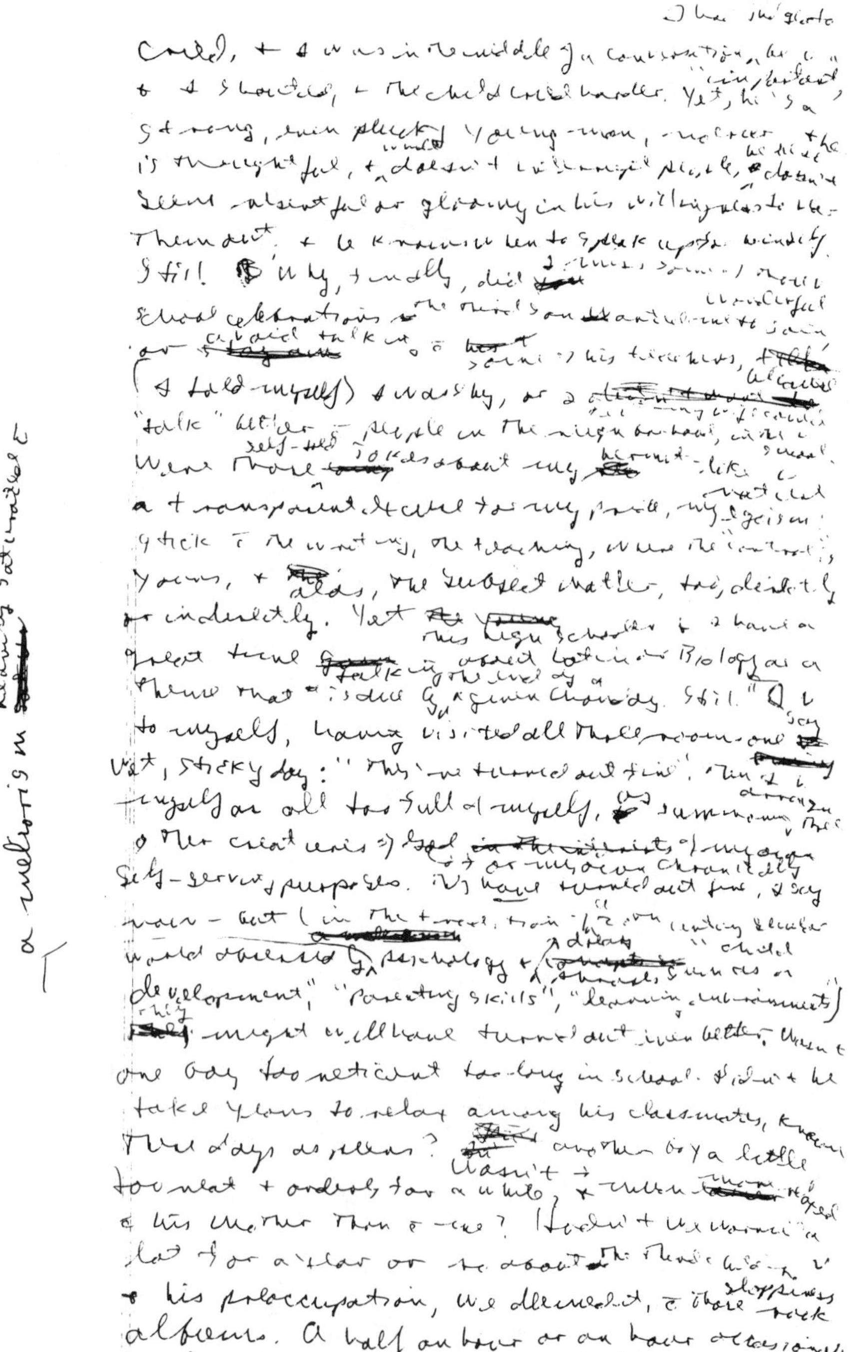

—2—

I have tried to

Could, + I was in the middle of a conversation, he ... + I shouted, + the child could hardly ... Yet, he's a strong, even sturdy young man, ... + he is thoughtful, + doesn't ... seem ... or gloomy in his willingness to ... Then ... + he ... to speak up ... Still, why, + ... did ... school celebrations ... wonderful ... or ... talk ... his teachers, ... (I told myself) ... "talk" ... people in the neighborhood, ... Were those ... jokes about my ... a transparent ... my pride, my egoism ... stick to the writing, the teaching, ... Yours, + alas, the subject matter, too, directly or indirectly. Yet this high schooler ... a great ... Biology ... Still" ... to myself, having visited all those rooms one ... wet, sticky day: "This one turned out fine". ... myself as all too full of myself, ... summoning ... other creatures ... self-serving purposes. It's turned out fine, I say now — but (in the ... century) ... would ... psychology + ... "child development", "parenting skills", "learning environments") ... might well have turned out even better. Wasn't one boy too reticent too long in school. Didn't he take years to relax among his classmates, ... those days as [illegible]? Another boy a little too neat + orderly for a while, + ... his mother than ... ? ... for a year or two about ... his preoccupation, ... those ... albums. A half an hour or an hour occasionally is alright, I'd thought, I'd said (+ ... not

a meliorism heavily saturated

[illegible]

ē rueful smile,

— 3 —

only myself + his mother) but on + on + on, all on [playing]
of those decades ago. Besides, the teachers say he comes
to school sloppy — or rather, ^dresses irresponsibly, + manages to turn in
written comments - ... [sloppy]
If I'd been ē the boys when younger — more of the
time! If I'd not been so taken up ē my work, my
doctoral research — all that "field work," all those
"visits", to other people's homes, all those [being] children
interviewed, again + again interviewed, other parents'
children. No wonder I think back wistfully at all
the opportunities forsaken, the spells in an uncertain, deadly
or worse, plain self-preoccupied. Would I be sad
that these small boys are now just about grown, [up]
if I'd been ē them more + more + more than was the [case?]
Really been ē them — concentrating all my mental
+ physical energy on their lives, the way their mother
has done, ē great enjoyment. [She: "They need you
to leave, to do your work. They'll love + respect you for
it later." He: Don't say that — it's a rationalization
+ justification ... it's all over now." She: "It's
never 'over' — even when we die. We remember
a lot of each other, all of us do, + they recall all those
good times we had, you had." He: There could have
been more. I feel sad about that."] The other day
I got upset about some stupid matter, + once I'd
seen how stupid it is to compound stupidity through again
personal amplification, I said "damn," + I
slammed a cabinet door shut, + one of my sons
said: "Don't worry, Dad." I found myself getting
annoyed ē him, as I do occasionally ē my wife, when
she, also, mobilizes a phrase meant to supply some
badly needed perspective, moral + psychological both.
Then I remembered an event that took place over a
decade ago. The same boy had cut himself badly, + I had
to rush him to the hospital. He'd cut an artery
at the wrist, + I was speeding. He was sitting

–4–

Beside me in the car, quietly — in a sedate, detached, controlled way on what was happening. I was not only upset at the traffic — the emergency — [illegible] done, drawing a blank, or dim-witted, or obstinate, or childish, or similar — feet at the boy. How many times had I told him to stay away from that door, and all those dangerous tools he'd already hurt himself with — the hammer! I thought we'd settled the matter then — that he ask permission to use any of them at all in the left-hand side of the chest. Certainly he was old enough and sensible enough to understand me at the age of [illegible]. Wasn't that the age of reason! There I was, working the streets of Concord, Massachusetts, and while my dear [illegible] was in the above described manner proving himself to be plain crazy — and outrageously, warily-headedly moralistic. Nor was this the end, since such a way of reacting had taken place, nor would it be the last time I turned mean and sour in my face, in my expression, and ultimately, in my thoughts, language, in the face of a difficulty experienced by them. My own father, sadly, used to give me hell when I did something wrong that caused injury to me. There sit he, hurt, bleeding, in pain, and he'd shout at me: Why did you do that? What's the matter with you — can't you listen & remember? In the long stretch of psychoanalysis people like me go through (a big help in learning how to understand ourselves and troubles come up and [illegible]) I eventually figured out that my father's outbursts had to do with his [illegible] and fearfulness. He was scared by the trouble I'd presented to him, worried I might be in jeopardy (I broke a few bones when I was a kid, sustained my fair share of childhood infections) — yes, worried I might be in great discomfort (I got poison ivy regularly, and in bad attacks) and such worries in that immediate

—5—

of our transgression: "Why, for Christ's sake, did you go near that poison ivy? How many times, have I showed you what poison ivy is? What is the matter with you?" My mother would get angry at him, then her Christian ire was aroused, but really, she was aghast that the victim was being blamed: "Will you, for Christ's sake, leave Christ out of it — or if you have to mention Him, remember what He stood for!" That was enough to silence him. Yet I remember feeling the pain of his unwarranted lapse longer than any caused by the actual illness or accident I'd happened to suffer — and no matter how quickly my mother had managed to intervene. In fact I remember times when my mother's intervention was anticipated so well that my father said nothing — but a tell-tale look in his eyes was there, and that was all I needed to feel deeply and wayward, worth a stricken gloom. I vowed never to repeat all that with my own children, and yet I was, on occasion, helpless — then devastated by my helplessness, and utterly disgusted with myself. Thank God, actually, for those properly normal drivers who were resourceful to rage that day. I got to the hospital faster on their account: they stimulated me to dodging and zooming and using my horn — and they kept my mind, mostly, away from my son's injury, in this instance, away from grave temptation. I believe the psychoanalytic phrase is "repetition compulsion"! Soon, though, my son's wound was sutured, and he seemed fine. But as he got up from the table and saw something crossing my face, he was moved to say something: "Don't worry, Dad". Upon those words a smile, finally, broke across my face, and we were able to have a pleasant drive home. As I crawled back in the car — glad to enjoy those sights and sounds of a particular day. I remember him startled when somebody passed me and gave me a dirty look.

— 6 —

On another occasion, I [illegible] another son, I'm raising my voice, saying what his teachers had said, that he was not using his mind enough in school, his [illegible] "[illegible]" — talk [illegible] [illegible] grandiosity thinly masked as [illegible], piety, the boy was in the senior grades, & had been goofing off. Nothing doing, & so thought — but keeping my silence. When the teachers spoke, though, & [illegible]. But my silence had [illegible] & shouting. I was angry for other reasons, too, & so a dam had given way. Complaints & [illegible]: the messy room, the messy way of dressing, the [illegible] to pay complete, [illegible] attention to a "[illegible]", all those [illegible] year old [illegible] — & this boy, who has always seemed so independent, so eager to follow his own idiosyncratic interests: fish tanks, mechanical [illegible] all kinds, & splendid [illegible], into stories & novels & natural essays (Lewis Thomas) & the literature of travel ( ). When I'd had [illegible] my tirade, I slumped into a chair, & [illegible] a sudden, [illegible] to myself, started crying. I guess I'd never heard myself speak like that to a child, any child, never mind my own. I got up quickly & left the house & got into my car & drove & drove, [illegible] of all other drivers. [illegible] the road & passed [illegible] Strand, Batch farm — a splendid, [illegible] amid grazing cows, a silo, [illegible] hay, a [illegible] New England farmhouse. [illegible] ice cream stand [illegible], & this was the moment for a big [illegible] of mocha-chip — but I couldn't drive into the farm's parking place. Somehow it seemed obscene, even, to want to gratify such an impulse — to soothe my ailing soul with that [illegible] comfort far more. When I came back, my wife —

—7—

What to say!" don't

Saw the look on my face, & knew exactly I stand in & that (insanely) routine! What you said was right, & he needed to hear it." Needless to say, as if she were a confused dancer in company, I got angry at her. I was ready to argue & argue, but realized I'd best shut up, disappear; the stillness of the study, usually conducive of no-nonsense work to do. But I could only stare out the window & feel rotten. Soon my wife was calling us all to supper, & she has never allowed grudgy or sulking static to linger. Her cheer (I call it "forced" when I'm in reluctance to let go of parent's despair) quickly swept us along, as did her delicious supper of spaghetti & baked chicken & strawberry-rhubarb pie. Later the boy & I were taking some garbage to the barn, & I was ~~ready~~ prepared to apologize. Only later did I realize how readily I'd been conquered & anticipated. I'd scarcely opened my mouth, the words meant to affirm in a long-winded [illegible] a mistake, in [illegible], when I heard "Don't worry, Dad". I recall feeling like a small child who'd been forgiven, & who now could feel better. He & I went to Bates farm & got our canes. I tell you, I say to myself sometimes, [illegible] tears choking at me, to be a father is to love one's children, love them continually, love them enough to give them countless kisses, & boosts, counsels & assistance — but also love them enough to stumble [illegible] them, before them, on their account, love them enough to say the wrong things, do the wrong things, (that because, Lord knows, some damn fool "expert" told us that, too!) [illegible] of one's humanity put on the line, one's frailty & helplessness exposed. To be a father, moreover, is to want those children over & over again, hold them & hug them & kiss them & carry them on one's shoulders & on one's back &

(over)

Beside one in Iraq, healing them daily as they sustain daily the world's inevitable, constant assault, & ~~[illegible]~~ it claims, being healed by them: Don't worry, dad — Tommy, thank you, & I'm glad you're here to tell me down & say "the wrong thing", because mom is right, I did need to get that message, or similarly because it's nice to see the next guy (especially when he is a passing demi-god, as all parents are to a child) come down to earth, ~~so to speak~~ you might say.

~~So, again, don't worry, dad~~

I know what I [illegible] say now & the next [illegible] & the next time: Don't worry, dad.

Don't Worry, Dad

Robert Coles

The three boys are gone, I say to myself. The boys are no longer boys, I remind myself. I go to their rooms sometimes, look at the tangible evidence of the years they have spent on this planet -- please God, with their mother and me: the little cars and trucks they delighted in having when they were five or six, now tucked away on shelves inside their closets, with one or two still left here and there in a particular room for them to see in a quick glance as they go on to other matters; the books, some going back to the days when they listened to us doing the reading, some the first objects of their newly achieved literacy, some stories that link so-called youth with so-called grown-ups, such as Animal Farm or Kipling's stories or those of Hemingway or Mark Twain, and finally books such as Invisible Man or Pride and Prejudice or those convoluted Henry James novels which tell their English teacher mom and novel-loving dad that we're four voters now, and one soon to be, and that two are away in

- 2 -

college, and one soon to be, and that everyone drives, and we all wonder, out loud, what's happening to America and the world, not who can come over and play Lego, or when that Red Cross swimming instructor will be able to hand out those junior life-saving cards.

I catch myself sad one morning. I think as I go from room to room of the missed chances, the mis-steps, the mis-statements -- things done I should not have done, things not done I should have done. Why didn't we help the first boy to make more friends earlier? Why did we keep him so close to us? Yet, he has lots of good friends now, and is quite comfortable travelling all over, I remind myself. Still. Why did I get so impatient at times with our second son? Remember that day when a friend came, and the three year old child was running all over the place, and fell down and cried, and I was in the middle of a conversation I had judged to be "important", and I shouted, and the child cried harder. Yet, he's a strong, even plucky young man, no crier, and he is thoughtful, and while he doesn't interrupt people, he also doesn't seem resentful or gloomy in his willingness to hear them out; and he knows when to speak up for himself.

- 3 -

Still. Why, finally, did I miss some of those wonderful school celebrations the third son wanted me to join, or avoid talking with some of his teachers, because (I told myself) I was shy, or I felt my wife could "talk" better w/ people in the neighborhood, in the school. Were those self-told jokes about my hermit-like nature a transparent excuse for my pride, my egoism: stick with the writing, the teaching, where the "control" is yours, and also the subject matter, too, directly or indirectly. Yet, this high schooler and I have a great time talking about Latin or Biology or a theme that is due by the end of a given Monday. Still.

I say to myself, having visited all three rooms one warm, sticky day: "They've turned out fine". Then I arraign myself as all too full of myself, as summoning in three other creatures of God for my own chronically self-serving purposes. They have turned out fine, I say now -- but (in the tradition of a 20th century secular world obsessed by meliorism heavily saturated with psychology, dreary phrases such as "child development", "parenting skills", "learning environments") they might well have turned out even better. Wasn't one boy too reticent too long in school? Didn't he take years to relax among his classmates, known these days as peers? Wasn't another boy a little too neat and orderly for a while, and much more relaxed with his mother than with me? Hadn't we worried a lot for a year or so about the third child's sloppiness and his preoccupation, we deemed it, with those rock albums. A half an hour or an hour occasionally is alright, I'd thought, I'd said (and to him, not only myself and his mother) but "on and on" the playing of those records go. Besides, the teachers say he comes to school sloppy -- or rather, I corrected them silently and with sinful pride manages to turn sloppy within moments of arrival there.

If I'd been with the boys when younger more of the time! If I'd not been so taken up with my work, my damn research -- all that "fieldwork", all those "home visits" to other people's homes, all those children interviewed, again and again interviewed, other parents' children. No wonder I think back wistfully at all the opportunities forsaken, the spells when I was travelling or worse, plain self-preoccupied. Would I be sad that these three boys are now just about grown up, if I'd been with them more and more and more than was the case? <u>Really</u> been with them -- concentrating all my mental and physical energy on their lives, the way their mother has done, with great enjoyment. (She: "They needed you to leave, to do your work. They'll always love and respect you for it." ~~later.~~" He: "Don't say that -- it's a rationalization, a justification. ~~and~~ A pity it's all over now." She: "It's never 'over' -- even when we die. We remember a lot of each other, all of us do, and there were all those good times we had, <u>you</u> had." He: "There could have been more. I feel sad about that.")

The other day I got upset about some stupid matter, and once again ~~saw how stupid it is to~~ compound stupidity ~~through the process of personal amplification. I said "damn" & and~~ I slammed a cabinet door shut, whereupon one of my sons said: "Don't worry, Dad." I found myself getting ~~annoyed~~ angry with him, as I do occasionally with my wife, when she, also, mobilizes a phrase meant to supply some badly needed perspective, moral and psychological both. Then I remembered an event that took place over a decade ago. The same boy had cut himself badly, and I had to rush him to the hospital. He'd cut an artery at the wrist, and I was speeding. He was sitting beside me in the car, quietly -- with a certain detached interest, actually, in what was

- 6 -

happening. I was not only upset at the traffic -- the emergency allowed me to consider everyone driving to be perversely slow, or dim-witted, or obstinate, or childish, or senile -- but at the boy. How many times had I told him to stay away from that drawer, with all those dangerous tools. He'd already hurt himself with the hammer. I thought we'd settled the matter then -- that he ask permission to use anything at all in the left hand side of the chest. Certainly he was old enough and sensible enough to understand me at the age of seven. Wasn't that the age of reason!

There I was, cursing the ~~stupidity of~~ the drivers of Concord, Massachusetts, while my own mind was in the above described manner proving itself to be plain crazy -- and outrageously, wrong-headedly moralistic. Nor was this the only time such a way of reacting had taken place, nor ~~would it~~ be the last time I turn[ed] mean and sour in my thoughts, in my face's expression, and ultimately, in my language, ~~in the face of~~ a difficulty experienced by one of ~~them.~~ My own father, sadly, used to give me hell when I did something wrong that caused injury to me. There I'd be, hurt, bleeding, in pain, and he'd shout at me: why did you do that? What's

- 7 -

the matter with you -- can't you listen and remember? In the long stretch of psychoanalysis people like me go through, a big help in learning how to understand ourselves and others, such childhood troubles come up and get eyamined repeatedly, and so eventually I figured out that my fahter's outbursts had to do with his nervousness and fearfulness. He was scared by the trouble I'd presented to him, worried I might be in jeopardy (I broke a few bones when I was a kid, sustained my fare share of bruises, infections) or yes, worried I might be in great discomfort (I got poison ivy regularly and in bad attacks) and put such worries in that immediate form of expression: "Why, for Christ's sake, did you go near that poison ivy? How many times have I showed you what poison ivy is? What's the matter with you?" My mother would then get angry -- at him. Her Christian ire was aroused -- but really, she was aghast that the victim was being blamed: "Will you, for Christ's sake, leave Christ out of it -- or if you have to mention Him, remember what He stood for!" That was enough to silence him. Yet, I remember, feeling the pain of his momentary lapse longer than any caused by the actual illness or accident I'd happened to suffer -- and no matter how quickly my mother had managed to intervene. In fact, I remember times when my mother's anticipated intervention worked so well that my father said nothing -- but a tell-tale look in his eyes was there, and that was all I needed to feel dopey and wayward, well worth a stretch of gloom.

I vowed never to repeat all that with my own children, and yet I was, on occasion, helpless -- then devastated by my helplessness, and utterly disgusted with myself. Thank God, actually, for those perfectly normal drivers who roused me to rage that day: I got to the hospital faster on their account; because they stimulated me to dodging and zooming and using my horn -- and they kept my mind, mostly, away from my son's predicament, meaning in this instance, away from grave temptation. I believe the psychoanalytic phrase is "repetition-compulsion". Soon enough we were at the emergency ward, my son's wound was sutured, and he seemed fine. But as he got up from the table and saw something cross my face, he was moved to say something: "Don't worry, Dad." With these words a smile, finally, broke across my face, and we were able to have a pleasant drive home. I think I crawled back in the car -- glad to enjoy the sights and sounds of a particular day. I remember being startled when somebody passed me and gave me a dirty look.

On another occasion, with another son, I recall raising my voice, saying what his teachers had said, that he was not using his mind enough in school, his "God-given intelligence" -- talk about parental narcissistic grandiosity flimsily masked (and rationalized) as exhortative, necessary piety. The boy was in the seventh grade, and had been goofing off. Nothing doing, I'd thought -- but kept my silence. When the teachers spoke, though, I followed. But my previous, sometimes frustrated silence had exacted a cost: I shouted. I was angry for other reasons, too, and so the usual controls ~~a dam~~ had given way. Complaints from me pounded forth: the messy room, the messy way of dressing, the willingness to pay complete, abjectly submissive attention to a "them", all those fellow twelve year old slobs -- and _this_ boy, who had always seemed so "independent", so eager to follow his own idiosyncratic interests: fish tanks, mechanical gadgets of all kinds, and splendid forays, even then, into stories and novels and nature essays (Lewis Thomas) and the literature of travel (Steinbeck, Theroux).

When I'd had done with my tirade, I slumped into a chair, and then all of a sudden, without warning to myself, started crying. I guess I'd never heard myself speak like that to a child, any child, never mind my own. I got up quickly and left the house and got into my car and drove and drove, now oblivious of all other drivers. On the road I passed our family's favorite ice-cream stand, Bates Farm -- a splendid, home-made product, amid grazing cows, a silo, fields of hay, a colonial New England farmhouse. I am an ice-cream freak, and this was the moment for a big hunk of mocha-chip -- but I couldn't drive into the farm's parking place. Somehow it seemed obscene of me even to want to gratify such an impulse -- to soothe my ailing, hurting soul while that of another deserved the comfort far more. When I came back, my wife saw the look on my face, and knew exactly what to say: "Don't start in with that 'I'm sorry' routine! What you said was right, and he needed to hear it." Needless to say, as if she were a confused driver in my way, I got angry at her. I was ready to argue and argue, but realized I'd best shut up, disappear: the exile of the study, morally sanctioned by the requirement of work to do. But I could only stare out the window and feel rotten. Soon my wife was calling us all to supper, and she has never allowed grudgy or grumpy static to linger. Her cheer (I call it "forced" when I'm reluctant to let go of pride's despair) quickly swept us along, as did her delicious supper of spaghetti and baked chicken and strawberry rhubarb pie. Later the boy and I were taking some garbage to the barn, and I prepared to apologize. Only later did I realize how readily I'd been comprehended and anticipated. I'd scarcely opened my mouth with the words meant to affirm, in a long-winded explanatory statement, a given mistake, when I heard "Don't worry, Dad". I recall feeling like a small child who'd been forgiven, and who now could feel better. He and I went to Bates Farm and got our cones.

I tell you, I say to myself sometimes, with some tears choking at me, to be a father is to love one's children, love them continually, love them enough to give them countless kisses and boosts, examples and assistance but also love them enough to stumble with them, before them, on their account, love them enough to say the wrong things, do the wrong things not because, God save us, some damn fool American

- 12 -

"expert" told us that, too, simply by reason of one's humanity put on the line, one's frailty and helplessness exposed. To be a father, moreover, is to heal those children over and over again, hold them and hug them and kiss them and carry them on one's shoulders and on one's bike and beside one in the car, healing them daily as they sustain daily the world's inevitable, constant assault, and so doing, being healed by them: Don't worry, dad -- meaning, thank you, and I'm glad you're here to fall down and say "the wrong thing", because mom is right, I did need to get that message, or ~~similarly~~ because it's nice to see the next guy (especially when he's a passing demi-god, as all parents are for a while) come down to earth, ~~you~~ might say, hence what ~~I say~~ ever so casually yet with conviction ~~now and the next time and the next time~~: Don't worry, dad.

JOYCE CAROL OATES

'Naked'

Since the publication of her first book, a collection of stories entitled *By the North Gate* (New York: Vanguard Press, 1963), Joyce Carol Oates has produced scores of others, including novels, stories, poetry, plays, and nonfiction. Many of the stories that make up her sixteen collections have been widely anthologized. Indeed, her stories have appeared so frequently in *Prize Stories: The O. Henry Awards* that twice she has received the Special Award for Continuing Achievement in that series. Among her many other awards are National Endowment for the Arts grants, a Guggenheim fellowship, and a National Book Award for her novel *them* (New York: Vanguard Press, 1969).

After receiving her undergraduate degree from Syracuse University and a master's from the University of Wisconsin, Oates taught at the University of Detroit and the University of Windsor. She is now Roger S. Berlind Distinguished Professor in the Humanities at Princeton University. With her husband, Raymond Smith, Oates also runs the Ontario Review Press, publisher of the distinguished *Ontario Review.*

I first wrote to Oates in February 1992 to ask if she'd be willing to participate in this project. "If you can locate material pertaining to a recent, representative story of mine, at Syracuse, I'd be happy to answer your questions by mail," she wrote back within a week. "Virtually all of my writing *is* rewriting."

I decided to choose a story from what was at the time her most recent collection, *Heat* (New York: Dutton, 1991). I chose "Naked" for the simple reasons that I liked it more than any other story in the collection and that Kathleen Manwaring, of the special collections department at Syracuse, had informed me she'd located a good deal of draft material for this story.

Manwaring sent me the draft material as it had arrived at Syracuse: sixty-four pages of handwritten and typed notes and typed manuscript. A few notes were scribbled on pages from other manuscripts I didn't recognize. (Oates later informed me that occasionally, while working on the *Ontario Review*, she jots down notes on whatever scrap paper is handy, including unsolicited manuscripts that arrive without self-addressed stamped envelopes.) Other pages had been typed on from both ends, so that two sets of typeface approach one another toward the middle of the page, like tiny pica battalions marching toward the breach.

For the purposes of this project, as well as for the sake of clarity, I have tried to organize Oates's draft material into three discrete sections. The first contains seven pages of handwritten and typed preliminary notes. (I have not included the three pages of notes written on some other, unidentifiable writer's manuscript.) The second section includes four distinct versions of the story's opening passage. The third section contains thirty additional pages of draft material that roughly illustrate the story's narrative progression. As anyone can see from the numerous gaps and repetitions in this section, these pages do not represent a single, uninterrupted draft. No such draft appears to exist; "I never write a complete draft straight through," Oates said in the interview. These pages provide, however, a useful glimpse into Oates's process of composition and development as well as a basis of comparison to both the first published version of "Naked" (*Witness* 2, no. 4 [Winter 1988]) and the subsequent version collected in *Heat*.

NAKED

She was hiking alone in a suburban wildlife preserve two miles from her home when she heard, behind her, erupting seemingly out of nowhere, children's shouts, squeals, and laughter. She turned to see a small pack of black children running along the wood-chip trail. The eldest, a skinny boy of about eleven, in soiled white T-shirt, oversized pants, and sneakers worn without socks, seemed to be shouting at her and gesticulating urgently with both hands—"Hey! Lady! Hey, *you*!"—though his high-pitched jeering words were not wholly intelligible. It was late in the afternoon, in spring, the first really warm, sunny, pleasurable day in weeks; the air was damply tremulous; the earth exuded a sense of quiveringness, scarcely restrained life. She had been hiking for an hour, pushing herself, walking quickly, enjoying the strain of leg, thigh, arm muscles, and a light film of perspiration had gathered over her, and her thoughts, scattered and inchoate initially, had gradually slowed, steadied, crystallized until they were not thoughts at all so much as simply impressions and gliding wordless images as in a dream. And the children, led by the strangely intense, even angry black boy, surged up like unexpected images in that dream.

"Yes? Are you talking to me?" she asked.

The boy laughed as if in delight and derision. Had he not been so young she might have thought him drunk or high on a drug. He came barely to her shoulder, easing toward her like a wiry little animal out for blood. He addressed her in a stream of soprano sounds underlaid by contempt, but she could make out none of the words except perhaps "Lady" or "Where you goin', lady?" and his aggressive intensions bewildered her rather than frightened her since the children were so young, the youngest no more than eight or nine, and very small, and there were two or three girls among them. "Yes? What is it? What do you want?" she asked with a mother's slightly strained calm. They're only children, she told herself even as, instinctively, she took a step backward.

And in the next instant they were upon her.

Even as it was happening, as the children swarmed over her, pummeling her with their fists, pounding, kicking, tearing, the eldest leaping up on her to bring her heavily down, savage and deft as a predatory animal, even as she struggled with them, flailing her arms, trying too to strike, punch, kick—for she was a woman of some strength, very fit, unshrinking, resolute—she was thinking, *This can't be happening!* and *They're only children!* She'd known from her first sighting of them that they were not children from the University Heights area in which she lived but from the ragged edge of the old industrial city below the bluff, that steep drop to a neighborhood of row houses, tenements, railroad yards, factories, and condemned mills on the river she and her family rarely glimpsed except from the interstate expressway elevated over its ruins, but she was a woman in no way racially prejudiced who had grown up with blacks, gone to school with blacks, Chinese, Hispanics, and other minorities, as they were familiarly called, and she was determined to instill in her children the identical unjudging uncensorious liberalism her parents had quite consciously instilled in her. So it did not strike her, as perhaps it should have, upon occasion at least, that these minorities might look upon her as conspicuously different from themselves and that, against the grain of all that was reasonable, charitable, and just, they might wish to do so and take satisfaction in it. And this demonic little pack of children who had so totally surprised and overcome her—who beat her, tore her clothes from her, emptied her pockets, all the while squealing and laughing as if what they did were only in play—she simply could not believe they were capable of such a thing: and with such nightmare quickness.

She was forty-six years old, in very good health, a woman of intelligence and independent character, the mother of two young children and the stepmother of a young teenager, wholly unskilled in physical exertion or prowess, as clumsy in this bizarre struggle as a fish hauled from the water and thrown down upon the ground without ceremony to gasp and thrash about and drown in an alien element. Her screams were breathless and incredulous. Her wild blows found no marks or glanced harmlessly off forearms, shoulders, lunging heads. *They're only children!* she was thinking, and as a mother she did not want to hurt children even had she been capable of doing so. The thought came to her too that if she surrendered, if she submitted, put up no further struggle, they would take what they wanted and leave her alone.

And so it was. When she stopped fighting they stopped hitting her, but in the fierce hilarity of their excitement they stripped her clothes from her, turning her, rolling her, tugging at her jeans, whooping with laughter as they tore away her brassiere and underpants, yanked off by sheer force her running shoes, pulled off her socks. She was too overcome by shock to beg them to stop, and the mad fear struck her that they meant to devour her alive: set upon her like ravenous animals, tear the flesh from her bones with their teeth, and eat. For what was there to stop them?

Then they ran away, and were gone, and she was left alone dazed and sobbing in a place she could not have named. The attack had probably not taken more than two or three minutes but it had seemed interminable, and afterward she lay for what seemed like a very long time not daring to move for fear of discovering that they'd crippled her—for her back and buttocks had been soundly kicked. *This is what you deserve,* a voice meanly consoled her, but she was too weakened, too much in pain, to respond.

She guessed she must be alone in the preserve since no one had come in answer to her calls for help.

So she lay still and tried to gather her strength, tried to think what had happened, what she must do next. Her sobs were erratic and resigned rather than the high breathless sobs of hysteria for she was not a hysterically inclined woman; she was a woman who might quell hysteria in others. *It's all right. You're going to be all right. The worst is over.*

So she spoke frequently to her own children, half chidingly, half in affection.

But her clothes had been taken from her. And her car keys.

And her wallet too, of course, and her wristwatch, and her gold chain—yanked so violently from her neck that the catch snapped and her skin was lacerated as by a wire noose. Only the rings on her left hand remained: one of the children had tugged fiercely at them, so hard she'd felt her finger turn in its socket, but her finger must have been swollen; the rings hadn't budged.

Savages, she thought.

Filthy little animals, she thought.

But why had they hated her so, to beat her as well as rob her, and to humiliate her by stripping her clothes from her?

She sat up. Brushed her hair out of her sweaty face. The thought came to her that there was an emergency telephone she could use near the parking area—but almost in the same instant she knew that the emergency phone she was thinking of, and could see so precisely, so desperately, illuminated by a cool blue light, was on a post behind her office building at the university.

She spent a wretched half hour, or more, looking for her clothes. Every part of her body ached as if she had been thrown from a great height, her bones shaken to the marrow but somehow unbroken, able to bear her weight. Her scalp stung where a clump or two of hair had been torn out. Her nose had been bloodied. Both her eyes were swelling and would surely turn black, and her vision was blurred as if she were under water for one of them had tried to rub dried leaves in her eyes: a playground tactic, she supposed, a nasty playground tactic; probably everything that had been done to her was play of a kind, the moves known in advance, deftly and gracefully orchestrated. But she had not known.

She didn't want to think why the children, strangers to her, had hated her so. Hadn't she been quite cordial to the boy, unalarmed, even trying to smile as he approached her? She was by nature and by training an unfailingly friendly woman; she practiced friendliness as a musician practices an instrument, and with as unquestioned a devotion. And there was the unwanted but undeniable privilege of her white skin, which brought with it a certain responsibility not only to be good and decent and charitable but to be nice in being so.

Walking on the wood-chip trail was not painful but walking into the underbrush hurt her feet; the soles were shockingly tender, softer than the palms of her hands. It was disorienting that in this open, public place, where any stranger might suddenly appear, she should be walking with her breasts loose and exposed and that between her legs air touched her in a space that widened and narrowed as she walked. Her vision blurred in the hazy sunshine as with increasing desperation she searched for her things. Surely the children wouldn't have troubled to carry them far? Surely she would find them tossed into the underbrush? Her jeans, her khaki jacket, her shoes, socks, underwear, however ripped and defiled? But her eyes leapt only upon useless things, teasing shapes: newspapers blown into the brush, banks of white wood anemone, smashed bottles and beer cans winking up out of the shadows. She wept in abject frustration.

She was a woman of generous instincts, but her instinct failed her now. What to do? Where to go? She didn't have her car keys and her car was locked—she'd acquired fro n her husband, a fastidious man, the habit of always locking her car—so if she had wanted to make her way shyly to the parking lot and sit in the car awaiting discovery and rescue she could not do so.

She felt an attack of faintness. The image of a fleshy cartoon woman came to her, a balloon woman, big breasts and belly and pubic hair, hoisted up into the sky. People, mainly men, gathered to gape, smirk, point their fingers. Aloud she cried, "What am I going to do!"

As if in answer, a car pulled into the graveled parking lot not far away. She heard car doors slamming and men's voices. In a panic she plunged into the shrubs to hide, ran without caring about her bare feet and the branches and prickles that tore against her naked body. Like a hunted creature she squatted and hid even as she knew that she should call for help; she had only to raise her voice calling "Help!" or "Help, please!"—a timid, hopeful, desperate appeal—and the nightmare would be over.

She could even call out to her rescuers—she had no doubt they would be rescuers; nearly everyone who came to the preserve was connected in some way with the university—that she had been stripped of her clothing and could they please bring her a blanket or something with which to cover herself; and she could, assuming the circumstances were right, insist that she was not hurt and did not want the incident reported to police, nor did she want, or require, medical attention.

But she said nothing. She crouched low behind a thick bank of bushes and flowering dogwood, her sweating forehead pressed against her knees, her arms gripping her legs in a frantic embrace. The terror of being discovered naked as she was, battered, bruised, disheveled as a wild animal, was simply too much for her: she wanted only to hide and not be seen. Nothing mattered to her but that she not be seen.

So she hid, and the men's voices quickly faded, for they must have taken one of the other trails and would not find her. If they had seen her car in the lot they would probably not have really noticed or remarked upon it. It's all right, she consoled herself repeatedly, not knowing what she meant.

She was a woman who had married late, by choice, and had had her children late, also by choice; thus she'd formed habits or practices of solitude that were closely bound up with, perhaps inextricable from, her character: her private, secret, abiding self. Her blond sunlit good looks had never mattered greatly to her except as they buoyed up her naturally exuberant spirit; she thought it simply a matter of tact to hide from others, including her husband, the small doubts and shifts of mood that frequently overcame her. It was a matter of pride that everyone who knew her should think her unfailingly good-natured, resilient, happy and confident always; or nearly always.

And now, what to do? How to spare herself further humiliation? She had fled from the men who might have helped her; thus, what to do?

She would have forgiven the children their savage assault, she thought, if only they had left her her clothes.

There seemed to her no alternative that was not hideous, shameful. She would end up crouching in the bushes at the side of the road and flagging down a car with the hope that whoever was driving the car might be a person she could trust. A man who was a stranger would be the worst prospect, yet a man who knew her was scarcely better—might in fact be worse, since then word would be spread of her plight and the sordid incident exaggerated. If it were a woman perhaps she could bear it, but if it were a woman who knew her, or knew of her, from her work in the community or her photograph in the local paper, then too the tale would be spread everywhere at once and the rumor would be that she had been sexually assaulted. Even people who wished her well would repeat the tale and thrill to it; some would wonder why she'd been alone in the wildlife preserve; some might even hint that she'd had it coming to her—independent as she was, married to a well-known department chairman at the university, with an excellent job of her own in the university's development office. So the ugly tale would be told and retold numberless times, out of her control. She would be, simply, the woman who was found naked in the Meadowbrook Wildlife Preserve.

And her children would hear of it at school, her six-year-old daughter and her nine-year-old son; they'd be teased, taunted, made to believe things that weren't true. And her stepson—the boy would be crushed with embarrassment for her. And there was her husband, of whom in this context she could barely think: so ambitious, so caught up in his work, so concerned with his reputation in the community. After his relief passed that she hadn't been seriously hurt, she knew he would feel a kindred humiliation.

And if she sought help there would be police to contend with, probably. It was clear from the sight of her that she'd been beaten. The police would insist on questioning her, and how to tell them that her assailants had been mere children, not teenagers but children? And girls among them? And black? *I am not a racist*, she would tell the police carefully. Excising all emotion from her voice: *I am not a racist.*

"I can't risk it."

As in a waking delirium she saw herself, a naked, spectral figure, floating in directions parallel to but hidden from the roads that led to her home, following a variant of the route she would have taken by car. Those familiar suburban-country roads she drove every day. She was only two miles from home, possibly less: couldn't she make it on foot, alone and unassisted? With no one knowing? She calculated it must be about six-thirty. And since she was often home late, after dark, delayed at the office or socially or with errands, her family would not begin to miss her for hours; her husband had lately become involved in fund raising for the university and he too kept an erratic schedule: sometimes, arriving home, she'd learn from the girl who watched the children that her husband had telephoned to say he would not be home for dinner. And her stepson was in and out of the house. The girl would feed the smaller children at six-thirty; thus she had no immediate cause to feel anxiety or guilt about them apart from the anxiety and guilt she felt at the possibility of their learning of her humiliation or, worse yet, seeing her in the state she was in.

For then they would never see *her* again, as the person she was.

She said aloud, licking her cracked lips, "I can't risk it."

She waited until the sun slanted through the trees and the western sky turned bluish orange, mottled like a bruise. Around her birds were calling to one another with renewed urgency, quickened by the diminution of light: lovely high-pitched cries like ribbons, wires, threads of sound; she listened, hearing each note with unnatural clarity. She had never heard such sour ds before.

"I want my home again. My own place."

She had established in her mind's eye a map to guide her through the woods and back fields:

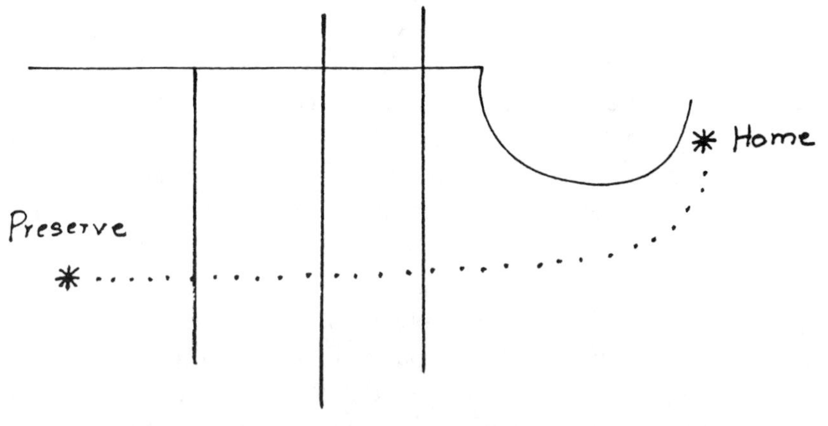

The distance between her present position in the preserve and her home was approximately two miles. There was no reason she could not cover it on foot, without being seen! Unavoidably, she would have to cross three roads, but only the first, bordering the preserve, was large; the others were only residential lanes. It would all be a matter of timing.

Her destination was, not her own front door or even, at least initially, her back door, but the ravine at the rear where she could hide in the shadows and observe the lighted windows of her house: noting the comings and goings of her family, should they be visible. For she did not want them to see her naked, no, not even her husband, not in this debased state of nakedness, with the look of a victim in her face and her body scratched and bruised. Her breasts ached as if the outermost layer of skin had been peeled off; the nipples were hard and puckered in fear. That boy with the mean eyes and jeering mouth had kicked her in the pit of the belly until she'd turned away retching and gasping for breath, but such an outrage would never happen to her again.

Once home, undetected, she could steal away upstairs and revert to herself again. She would bathe, doctor herself up, dress, reappear. If she acted quickly enough, the smaller children would not yet be in bed or asleep. She would prepare a meal, something simple, for her husband and stepson. Or she would join them at the table if they were already eating. She would tell her husband she'd lost her car keys in the woods and had decided to walk home without telephoning him or anyone: no need to fuss; he could drop her off in the morning and she could pick the car up then. It was locked, it was safe. (For the children were surely too young to steal a car!) "You walked home?" her husband would ask, mildly surprised, and she would say, "It wasn't far. I enjoyed the exercise."

Afterward, she would begin the effort of forgetting as resolutely as, years ago, before she was married and living in a fine home, she might have washed a wall of one of her rented apartments preparatory to painting it. *And no one would know.*

None of the children would sense that anything had happened to their mother, for their attention was focused almost exclusively upon themselves: which was only natural and good. Nor would her husband sense anything, for his imagination was absorbed primarily in his own work, his own being; he wasn't a young man any longer but a man at the peak of his powers, or a little beyond: now it was younger men who drew his attention, who fascinated and repelled.

And what in fact would there be for this busy successful well-liked man to notice if she, his wife, his happy confident wife, gave no sign of unease? They rarely had time for love now, in the old, intimate sense. But they were companions and sometimes plotters together, conspirators.

Could you identify the children if you saw them again, Mrs.—?

Yes. I don't know.

What was the color of their skin?

I am not a racist.

How painstakingly she was walking, barefoot! How treacherous the seemingly soft, moist earth, laced with invisible stones and bits of branches! When she left the path, making her way toward the edge of the preserve bordering the road, her feet sank in muck and she had to stifle a scream of panic, for what if this were a bog or even quicksand that might swallow her up without a trace?

But she kept going. There was no other way for her except forward.

She had never noticed how, in the woods, there were so many dead trees: dried lifeless stalks from which dried lifeless leaves, last year's leaves, hung in tatters. And the continuous scurrying of invisible birds, animals. And the continuous wind. On all sides mysterious sounds of rustling, stirring, shifting, as if a gigantic organism were defining itself, never quite rising to consciousness. She felt a thrill of deep calm fear, thinking this thought. It was not one she'd ever had before.

At the road she waited. She was prepared to wait for a long time. In the silence of the countryside the approach of a car and its passing and its subsequent retreat were clearly disparate. If she didn't lose her courage at the last moment and if she didn't step down on something sharp she really should have no difficulty getting across the road and hiding in the wooded area beyond.

A car passed, and another. After an interval another. And then there were several in a row, then what sounded like a diesel truck, heaving and sighing, and then there was silence. She peered excitedly out of the underbrush, seeing nothing but pavement and the farther side of the road. It was nearly dusk but not quite! A figure running across the road, a figure of pale astonishing female nakedness, might be visible for miles.

She was trembling. With oneiric clarity she saw the distance between herself and her home across which she must fly, saw herself crouching in the ravine at the foot of the hill, waiting. She did not trust her family not to stop loving her should they see her; thus they must not be allowed to see her, or to know!

Stooped almost double, she prepared to run. Drew a deep breath as years ago as a girl she would prepare to dive from the high board, eager not merely to reach the water below but to execute a perfectly calibrated dive, entering the water with the deft grace of a hand slicing a porous surface at a slant, unhesitating. For pride would allow no lesser performance!

She threw herself blindly out of hiding and began to run, her forearms steadying her breasts from beneath, and no dive or flight or plunge or physical ecstasy in her life had prepared her for this effort, running naked and wincing, gasping for breath through her opened mouth, eyes wide and stark and fixed on the farther side of the road, not daring to look elsewhere. And then almost at once she was there, and safe, seemingly, scrambling through a shallow ditch and into the field beyond. But somehow she had cut her foot. Stepped on glass and cut her right foot at the heel.

It's all right she told herself. *You're all right.*

She told herself impatiently, *The bleeding will wash the dirt away.*

She walked on, limping. She wasn't going to examine her foot. To her left there were no houses within sight, and to her right there was a farmhouse a short distance away but partly screened by trees, and should someone happen to be looking out a window as she passed it would not be evident that she was naked. Despite her wildly pounding heart she felt a surge of hope, almost of elation.

She was, and had always been, a woman of principle: a woman who believed in intelligent, considered, but not overconsidered action. Everyone who knew her respected her; yes, and some who did not know her quite as she knew herself envied her, and that too was good, or at least provided satisfaction. She could not be exposed now and would not be, but she would have to guard against waves of panic and faint-headedness and the possibility of losing her way, going in circles, as, once, not so long ago, she'd become lost in the wildlife preserve, doubling back on her trail and crossing it until she realized her error and returned safely to her car. Now that she had crossed the first and most dangerous of the roads she would have to keep it firmly in her mind's eye perpendicular at her back, envisioning the next road (how far away was it? She did not think it could be far) perpendicular before her.

She would have thought this interior land merely empty, but there was much evidence of human intrusion: piles of trash scattered along a farmer's lane as if people came here regularly by night and by stealth to dump their unwanted things—rotted tires, automobile parts, an upended refrigerator, a scorched mattress. Like a scavenger, and as eagerly, as unreasonably hopeful, she searched amid the trash for something she could wrap around herself, lifting and dropping a strip of canvas stiff with filth, and what appeared to be a child's playsuit, and other items of clothing that were mere shreds, tatters. She was excited yet dreamy too: standing for a long purposeless moment staring at the debris of strangers, wondering at lives so parallel to her own yet unknown to her. Gnats swarmed about her as if attracted by her very nakedness and the sweaty smell about her. Her right foot throbbed with something like pain but she refused to be drawn into examining it. Vaguely she thought that might be a trick, a trap of a kind.

She walked on, limping, until the farmer's lane ended abruptly in a final pile of trash, out of which something scuttled and ran into the underbrush to hide—a rat, judging by its size.

Her head rang with accusations. *How dare you. How dare touch. My skin doesn't define me. My color, my skin.* She was thinking suddenly of her husband and the happiness of his first marriage, of which he would never speak except crudely to deny it. As if mere words *now* might erase what had been *then* and, having *been*, flowed inexorably into what *is*. "You must think I'm a fool." Her voice sounded loudly but did not startle her.

Now: should she continue in a straight line across an open field in which swaths of wild rose with their deathly thorns were growing or should she take, thus risking the loss of her sense of direction (the road perpendicular at her back, the next road perpendicular, or approximately, before her), the edge of the field where it might be safer? She had forgotten the children, or nearly. They had nothing to do with her since they hadn't known her, and they certainly had nothing to do with her now.

She must have made a decision to make her way along the edge of the field but how slowly she was walking, how timidly—both her feet were bleeding now—thinking how, if she bled, the bleeding would wash away the filth and purify the wounds. Wasn't it puncture wounds in such instances that were dangerous?

She was thinking too what a curiosity it was of female life that, bleeding so frequently, bleeding amid cramps and occasional nausea and faintness, a woman had faith nonetheless that the bleeding would not go on and on until she bled to death. And there was the secrecy of the bleeding—well hidden inside the clothes, always well hidden, discreet and not to be spoken of. Yet how real, such doubleness! She had always liked it, really. She would never give it up, no matter that in a few years the cycle of her body would shift, and she would not bleed again in that way.

Beyond the field the lane began again, broader now, less rutted and less painful underfoot. She believed she knew the property—an old, inoperative farm—but she did not know the owners. Unless she was emerging at a place she hadn't calculated?

A chill began to lift from the darkening earth, though the sky was still fairly light, streaked with clouds. And the birds continued to call to one another, more urgently it seemed.

An error now would be fatal.

Not single pains but a wash of pains rose and throbbed in her body. She did not think of them, but increasingly they penetrated her consciousness and left her panting, whimpering. Her eyes—her head—her scalp—her belly, buttocks, spine—her feet. Forever would she walk in this no-man's-land so strangely close to familiar suburban roads yet hidden from them. The undeveloped still-wild countryside, no longer lucrative for farming, not yet sold for residential building, custom-made homes like the one she and her husband lived in—how strange *she* should be *here*. It was a place for death, for nude female bodies: victims of assaults, murders. She was not one of those women.

Yet she might lose her strength and collapse, might faint, and in a day or two or three she would be found comatose, perhaps dead.

A woman's body, it would be reported. *A woman's nude body* would be the initial report. Balloon breasts and fleshy hips and thighs, a patch of pubic hair at the fork of the legs, eyes rolled whitely up into the skull. It happened all the time. Not a person but a body. And all the prior history of her life—her achievement, her winningness, her sunny smile and resolute optimism, and her love for her family and theirs for her—would be summarily erased. She would become a story, a fiction.

Thus buoyed by anger she walked faster. In the growing dusk she could not make out whether, at the road, she would encounter a facing house, but the sound of an occasional car meant that the road was ahead and proof she was not lost.

Then it happened that a dog began barking excitedly close by, and to her horror the animal trotted up the lane as if to attack her, a dun-colored dog the size of a Labrador retriever but of no distinct breed: it barked, it snarled, the hackles on its shoulders were raised, its long clumsy tail thrashed from side to side. She was in terror of dogs since as a young child she'd once been bitten, or so she believed, though her mother had assured her she hadn't actually been bitten, only badly frightened by a German shepherd, and now she was seized with panic, backing off and murmuring to the aroused animal words plaintive and submissive: "No. Please. Go home. Go *home*." The dog approached to within a few yards, then stopped, crouching, barking in such a frenzy she supposed its owner would hear and come out to see what was going on. There was a farmhouse not far away, a hundred yards perhaps from the lane.

As if for her very life she was begging and pleading in an undertone: "Good dog. Nice dog. Go *home*." She wondered if her nakedness excited the dog, if it could smell her fear, the sharp rank animal odor of her helplessness.

She backed off. She picked up a large tree branch, held it threateningly overhead, and backed off. The dog continued to bark but did not follow. Its tail was thrashing energetically. Did that mean it might be friendly? But she could not take a chance, for as much as the prospect of being attacked by the dog, the prospect of having to call for help terrified her.

Some minutes passed. She thought how people would laugh at

her—the dog's owner, if he came out into the lane to investigate. A disheveled naked woman confronted by a barking dog, trying to protect herself with a branch. How had her life come to this?

Gradually the dog's barking subsided, and it appeared that a crisis of a kind had passed. It allowed her to pass by, then trotted as if indifferently in her wake, nosing about, sniffing at her heels. She felt its damp cool muzzle against her bare legs and the backs of her knees.

Its owner did not appear.

She was nearing home. Crossed the second road in a delirium of a plunge. Running, sliding somewhere, and staggering downhill. A swampy place. She snatched at bushes to steady her, like a drunken woman; leaves tore off in her fingers.

She should never have married, she was thinking. She'd been happiest alone.

The effort of hypocrisy wearied her.

The need to urinate came suddenly and so violently it was like a knife blade thrust up inside her. She squatted in a place already soft with mud and released a pungent burning liquid from her bladder, not in a stream but in tentative little spasms. When she was at last finished she wiped herself awkwardly with a wad of leaves. She was thinking, *At least no one has seen.*

Her face burned, her hands shook. A memory came to her as if emerging from a previous lifetime of having as a small child squatted in the grass to urinate and watching the liquid streaming from her—the strange helplessness of something happening to her she could not control. And someone had called to her, to reprimand her. Or had someone laughed at her?

At least, this time, no one had seen.

The house floated in the darkness.

How many hours had passed she did not know. Or if it were a single hour, distended as in a dream.

Why did you do such a thing? he was demanding and she said *I do what I want to do*, though until that instant she had not known that this was so.

She had had her children after all as she'd determined to have them. She would not have had two children had she not wanted them, for one would have done. Two was incontestable proof.

And the stepson who eyed her with suspicion, liking her sometimes and at other times not at all. For he was in no way hers and could not be cajoled into thinking so.

Inside the floating house indistinct figures moved. Some of the windows were lit, others darkened. *Why on earth did you do such a thing?* he would ask, for it was his right.

There, at the top of the incline, was the house, the rectangular box, in which she lived. She crouched in the underbrush blinking and rubbing her eyes so that she could see clearly, for it was crucial now that she see. Was the house hers? Or had she taken a wrong turn, become confused in the dark? She had never seen her house from such a position of course and would not perhaps have identified it. She saw movement by one of the windows—a figure that must have been that of her husband, though not quite so tall as she would have imagined her husband—and shortly there came another figure to join him, male or female she could not determine; it must have been the stepson, the fourteen-year-old, and how strange that, seeing him, seeing both of them, having wanted so desperately to get home, she felt no emotion at seeing them, or the indistinct shapes she believed must be them—no more than if they were strangers.

I do what I want to do. So in the dark below the house, squatting where no one could see, she waited naked—until such time as it would become known to her why she was waiting.

INTERVIEW

JW Would you describe how this particular story first occurred to you?

JCO The idea for the story may have sprung from a certain landscape near my house, and my imagined journey, naked, home. The journey is then experienced by a fictional person, or persona; the landscape is altered; over a period of perhaps two weeks the initial concept becomes altered, deepened, until it strikes a certain mythic resonance. (But not too "nakedly" mythic, because I don't want to write allegory.)

JW You appear to begin with handwritten notes. What can you tell me about this note-taking stage? How does it fit in to your general pattern of working? Do you set the notes aside for a time before beginning an actual draft?

JCO When I finish a piece of writing I try my best to forget the preliminary stages, which involve a good deal of indecision, groping, tension.

Most of your questions are not answerable by me, and I don't want to do what many, or most, writers find very tempting in such circumstances—invent.

JW The story's title seems to have occurred to you fairly early, during the note-taking stage. Do you usually hit on the title before you begin drafting?

JCO Titles sometimes come at once, or after some brooding. This did come immediately.

JW The draft material includes a number of pages with distinct opening paragraphs. What can you recall about how that opening unfolded for you?

JCO I don't understand this question.

JW I've tried to reconstruct a complete initial draft, but it appears from the material I've seen that you may work on discrete sections at various times in the drafting stage. Am I right to assume you do a lot of cutting and pasting?

JCO Yes.

JW Do you use a typewriter for stories and a word processor for novels? Why is the old cut-and-paste method more effective for you in your shorter narratives than the electronic cut-and-paste of a computer?

JCO I always write in longhand and type on a typewriter. For a while, I used a word processor, then got rid of it.

JW Once you finished the initial notes, did you write one complete draft straight through?

JCO No, I never write a complete draft straight through. The voice of the narrative is always changing.

JW The notes also reveal that you decided early on not to give the woman a name. Was this something that occurred to you from the first moments that you sensed this story's outlines? Why didn't you want to name her?

JCO The story is, in part, a feminist/woman's story.

JW The map also appears in the notes. Why was it important for you to illustrate her route rather than simply allow her to describe it in her mind?

JCO Why not? Our minds do operate visually.

JW You once remarked on the "graceful synthesis of the 'naturalistic' and the 'symbolic' " that Joyce achieved in *Ulysses*. "Naked" also achieves this, balancing allegorical significance with naturalistic vividness. What particular challenges did this fusion present as you wrote the story?

JCO Again, the question—or an answer—eludes me.

JW When writing a story that has strong allegorical implications, do you have to make a special effort to guard against a tug toward philosophical abstractions that might dilute verisimilitude?

JCO Yes. By grounding the story securely in the here and now.

JW Rereading the story, I noticed a repetition of a particular sentence pattern: "She was a woman who . . . ," or "She was a woman of . . ." Could you comment on the effect of this repetition?

JCO The "effect" can only be gauged by the reader, a neutral observer, not the writer.

JW You have in the past drawn a distinction between your various writing voices, particularly the meditative voice you've said fills your journals and the voice you use in writing fiction. In this story, I wonder whether revision wasn't in part a process of transforming the meditative, philosophical impulses into character, setting, and incident. You seem, for example, to have eliminated or reduced certain moments, the woman's explicit philosophical ruminations on beauty and childbirth, for instance. Could you comment on this?

JCO *You* have done so, quite adequately!

JW Another example of this sort of paring, I think, occurs when you decided to remove a line that occurs late in the early drafts: "She was capable of anything now." While originally explicit, you chose to allow this to remain implicit in later versions. Why?

JCO Less *is* more.

JW Reading "Naked," I couldn't help thinking of Cheever's story "The Swimmer." Did you contemplate any parallels as you wrote this story?

JCO No.

JW The two stories are dissimilar in more ways than they're alike, of course, but both have an allegorical resonance and a linear, sequential narrative strategy—characters, wearing little or nothing, wending their way home on a kind of suburban odyssey. Cheever commented how difficult it was to contend with the deceptive simplicity of this kind of linear strategy, and I wonder if you found this to be a challenge as well. (There is, for example, an interesting point in your notes, where you wrote: "A STEADY PROGRESSION AS SHE MAKES HER WAY HOME OF 'TRUTH'—THAT THINGS ARE NOT SO PERFECT REALLY.")

JCO ?

JW Toward the end of your character's journey, she experiences a sense of time "distended as in a dream." How difficult was it to depict her sense of unreality and disorientation while simultaneously relying on the story's donnée that dictate a linear progression—the attack, the sunset and dusk, the long walk home?

JCO No more difficult than anything else; perhaps it was easier, as, as a story nears its completion, momentum carries it along.

JW Her sense of unreality, of course, is conveyed from the very beginning, even before the actual attack. And then afterward, as she's walking through the woods, she notices for the first time how many dead trees there are: "She felt a thrill of deep calm fear, thinking this thought. It was not one she'd ever had before." This points toward her perception of a new reality, yet also seems to hint at a possibly rather unnerving sense of excitement she feels facing this challenge. Do you see this as an especially crucial moment in the story?

JCO Yes: the uncovering of deeper layers of personality.

JW One aspect of "The Swimmer" that's always troubled me is what I perceive to be a certain trickiness in its ending: Neddy's house turns out to be empty, revealing at the last moment that the author has withheld crucial information from the reader. No such puncture of narrative reliability occurs, however, in "Naked." The change has to do with her *perceptions* as much as with her new reality, a new reality we've witnessed unfolding from the start. At the end, she *perceives* things differently: her family appear as strangers as she glimpses them through the windows of her house, which in the evening light seems almost to be floating, suspended. How difficult was it to arrive at this ending?

JCO The ending was imagined from the beginning. The ending (my own glass-walled house seen from a woody slope to the rear) *was* in fact the beginning.

JW Something else that heightens her disorientation and clearly distinguishes her odyssey from Neddy Merrill's is her near-complete isolation on the journey. There's a real sense of wilderness in this exurbian setting. Is this in part why you used the repetition of the wild animal metaphor?

JCO Perhaps.

JW I see from the notes, however, that you had originally considered forcing her to pass along the edges of a small business district, as well as a more settled residential area, where she was to have near-brushes with bicyclists and a boy shooting baskets. Why did you choose to abandon this route?

JCO For the economy of drama.

JW I was struck by the number of subtle revisions that occurred between the time this story appeared in *Witness* and then finally in *Heat*. You made many changes in punctuation, as well as a number of alterations in paragraphing and the order of certain phrases. Do you typically make this many changes between the time a story first appears and the time it's collected?

JCO Since I love to revise, revising between magazine publication and book publication is a pleasure. I nearly always do so.

JW Do you typically find yourself continuing, in late revision, to experiment with alternative forms of punctuation?

JCO Yes.

JW I know many writers have passionate theories about punctuation, eschewing certain parts of the keyboard. Your style offers a lot of variety. You don't seem hesitant about using italics or any particular punctuation marks. Are you guided by any especially strong biases when it comes to punctuation?

JCO Style is an expression of a character's voice, and must therefore vary from work to work.

JW In the *Paris Review* interview, you said: "I am inclined to think that as I grow older I will come to be infatuated with the art of revision. . . . I am in favor of intelligent, even fastidious revision, which is, or certainly should be, an art in itself." Has your approach to revision changed over the years?

JCO Yes, this mode of composition is typical of my stories. And novels. It's a slow, painstaking, perhaps needlessly fastidious process, involving, as you've gathered, not only revising and rewriting but retyping. In this way I cultivate the "voice" of the narrative, I suppose. Events in a plot tend to be pared back, because the work's inner essence or integrity can usually be expressed by fewer outward episodes than I'd originally anticipated.

The process is extremely slow, and requires many hours. So I'm continually surprised by critics' assumptions that I write quickly and that it is somehow "easy."

JW Looking over the story again, do you see anything you might be inclined to change now?

JCO No. If I did, I would change it.

not fearful of lonely places and not in fact fearful of this peculiar child tho' his expression — mean, jeering, moron resolute — shld. have alerted her to s'thg very wrong.

"Yeh! You! Lady! Where you goin'?" What's wrong? His voice rose in (hilarity). He glanced o'r shldr. at his companions, who quivered w/ excitement. Like young dogs in a pack. The ♀ hes't, transfixed. She was in no way racially prejudiced: she'd grown up w/ blacks, gone to school w/ blacks, Chinese, —, other minorities. So it did not strike her, as p'haps it shld have, that these minorities l'k'd upon her as dif. from th'selves; or that this ragged little gang of children, the eldest no more than 11, the youngest very young, and small — eight or nine — mgt. be dangerous.

"Is s'thg wrong?" she asked. She was not a schoolteacher but as a mother of two y'g children she fell from time to time into a teacherly sort of diction. "What do you want?"

The boy glared at her w/ hatred. Yet there was (hilarity) in his the gleam of his wet teeth, and the mocking bulge of his eyes. He signalled to the others — boys, girls — all as raggedly dressed as he, and as wiry and supple and resolute. — and screamed & they sprang toward her, punching and mauling. She cld not believe it — cld not believe it! They were only children! "Stop! Wait! What are you —" she cried, baffled. She shld. have turned & run but it was too late. In an instant they were upon her,

— One afternoon in early May a woman was hiking alone in a suburban wildlife preserve when a gang of children swarmed over her and attacked her. Their object was theft — of her wallet, wristwatch — but in the wildness of their attack they —

— She was about to turn back on the hiking trail when she heard a boy call out s'thg loud, jeering, & unintelligible. "Yes? What?" she said, shading her eyes, staring.

— One aft. in early May a woman was hiking alone in a suburban wildlife preserve when she heard a raised voice behind her, and turned. It was a black boy of p'haps ten eleven, in T-shirt, shorts, sneakers w/out socks. He was grinning at her strangely, and he was gesturing w/ both hands. "Hey! Lady! You!" he said. She stared at him, and at the small gang of children straggling on the woodchip trail behind him, they were black, though in fact they were shades of black. "Yes? Are you talking to me?" she asked. The boy was skinny and came p'haps to her shoulder. But he was quick, & his grin easing springing toward her like a wiry little animal out for blood. Behind him the other children followed, staring wide-eyed, grinning excited. "What do you want?" the ♀ asked. She stood turned at the waist; in jeans, khaki jacket & shirt, jogging shoes. She was a tall, generously built ♀, 46 yrs old,

3 She ~~got~~ lifted 'self to hands & knees, panting (& sobbing.) Hair in face— breasts loose/... So exposed... What if s'one came along? S'one who knew her?

4 (She l'k'd for clothes ~~but found n'thg~~ except) underpants torn in pieces... thrown into (underbrush). S'thg tossed -> branches of a tree high o'rhead—s'thg white & filmy. But p'haps it was (n'thg) of hers.

5 For some time, crouched o'r, in dread of being seen, she l'k'd for her clothes on the trail & in the underbrush. (The childrens' gleeful screams / cries echoed in her ears.) There was a ringing in her ears. Her vision blotched & the ground veered up -> her; she found 'self on her knees, ~~so~~ lgt-headed.

The attack passed...

"What can I do? Where can I go?"

— She was naked, smeared in dirt, mud, rotted leaves. Body bruised, eyes burning. (Boy yelled 'Get 'er eyes! 'er eyes!')

— She walked limping, wincing— barefoot. Now, & why, had they taken her shoes from her? Her socks....

It was a nightmare, ~~but too keen, too vivid, stark, to be a mere nightmare,~~

— ~~The Preserve~~ She th't of her children, at home; her daughter who was 13, & her son 8; & her (babysitter) stepson w/ whom she was just now on amicable, (lightly) terms... They would be astonished & frightened to know what had happened to their mother— that so competent, self-sufficient ♀. In the household, she minimized (Fuss). She was soothing, placating.

1 — She was alone. ~~The~~ Her assailants were gone. She lay still as if paralyzed, fallen from a great height. Her eyes were open but ~~filled w/~~ opaque ~~w/ a film of~~ hurt, incredulity, rage, shame. They'd torn her clothes from her, taken away her wallet, her car keys, the wristwatch from her wrist.... One of them had tugged at her ~~ra~~ rings, so hard she'd felt the finger ~~jerk~~ turn in (~~pull from~~) its socket, but he, or was it she, had given up. Her finger must have been swollen; the wedding band & engagement ring, both antiques, had not budged.

They're only children.

~~Animals.~~ Filthy animals. Savages

2 — They were gone but she was ~~terrified of their return. Or~~ unable to move, ~~of~~ ~~Her clothes torn from her! Wad of hair torn from her head!~~ She lay on her side, naked, protecting 'self w/ her arms, sobbing into the soft, ~~spongey~~ ~~so~~ spongy soil. A fragrance of leaves, rot, wet, decay, woodchips.... Calls of birds, thin as wire, lifting like confetti. So beautiful. Eyes burned.

X She sat up, l'k'g for her clothes. (LEAVES) It was horrible to her— the children had torn her things from her, (gleeful, savage, mean, =)— but where had they thrown them? Her wallet & car keys were gone— but wldn't they throw the wallet down? Old children so young steal a car? —& there were too many of them to fit inside, weren't there?

So her th'ts ~~rattled~~ (careened) rapid fire, in no logical sequence.

END — ~~Slowly & cautiously~~ Limping, exhausted, she climbed the hill to the house. ~~Was it here?~~ The grass was wet but her feet were so numb she scarcely felt it. Her hair was stuck → her sweaty face, she bled from a dozen cuts & scratches, ~~but~~ s'thg had turned to grit in her ♡. But she was home. She'd done it. She h't.

— Slowly, limping, she climbed the hill toward the house. ~~She felt a curious sort of~~ Her eyes were fixed on the windows...

— She th't, Now I am capable of anything. — There followed then (after 'a') — a dreamlike sequence of seemingly unrelated events... She was ~~—~~, & ~~then~~ she was

— That ngt, she had no dinner; ran a bath & soaked in it for a long time.

NAKED NAKED NAKED

— In the shadows below the house, well out of range of its ~~aura~~/nimbus of light, she waited, shivering & resolute, ~~unhurried~~ ~~naked. In time, the way wld. be clear for her to re-enter her life, she supposed. It~~ It wld. not be long, she supposed, before the way wld. be clear for her to re-enter her ~~—~~ life, if she wished. She wld. do e/thg as she'd planned & no one wld. know & in time she mgt. forget

— Afterwd., those hours wld. fade as a dream fades, vivid as pain at the time, ~~insubstantial~~ in retrospect, blurred and uncertain.

— ~~She had lost her fear~~

— ~~A naked ♀ crouched & waiting.~~

— She lost patience suddenly & ran → house, shouting for them to come out. Why shld

— Eventually, she would return home.

— ~~Surely th-~~

— ~~"And why did you walk home?"~~

— She thought, Now I am capable of anything.

— ~~She came finally to her own house. — In a matter of minutes the way wld. be clear for her to silently enter her house, and begin the effort of forgetting.~~

~~And yet, what (Bliss!) Though she was exhausted, smeared w/ dirt, bleeding from a numberless cuts & scratches... She th't, Now I am capable of anything~~

— And if they didn't know her?

— She began to resent her family, so unthinking in their (feeling) for her.

— A bus passed. Silhouettes in the windows.

— ~~A trash-scattered clearing — a dirt lane, farmer's, led to a trash-littered clearing; s'one had dumped a mattress there... Crates, household bags of (garbage).~~

— This is the account of those hours, of which no one else knew

— She climbed the hill → the house, badly limping, ~~exhausted~~. Her hair was in her face, stuck — sweaty; ~~she~~ she ~~—~~ bled from a dozen cuts & scratches, but she was too exhausted to feel, or to care about, pain

NAKED.

This story is about the strangeness of the familiar, when one element is altered. The consequent alteration of all elements. If X, then Y; then Z. But 'Z' is a wholly unexpected development.

A woman is walking/hiking in a park. One must imagine a university//// suburban area, near which is a slum of a kind.

"The university / University Heights area, and a steep drop, a steep incline, to the ragged edge of an old industrial town/ old mill town on the river/// where factories, warehouses, decrepit old buildings were being converted into condominiums; to the surprise of all except the future-minded, who had bought the condemned properties cheaply.... But the city w/ its welfare rolls, unemployment rate of 20%, 'ethnic mixture' as it is euphemistically called, remains, infrangible, "the problems will not go away" / aren't likely to fade."

The woman, unnamed, married late; had her children late; two of her own, and one by her husband's previous marriage. She was 46 years old; the children 6, 8, 14. The step-son, 14, a 'difficult' boy whom she means to win over, in time; married now 9 years.... though she'd been pregnant before they were married. (this exposition won't figure in the story, I hope; but I might as well set it down. for the margin.)

"Then they were upon her."

1. walking in park alone; children swarm over her, tear off her clothes, jeer & mock her, toss pebbles/dirt/leaves/branches/ debris at her; she fights them off, panting, demonic creatures, her own children gone mad, her boy , 2 years old, in a temper tantrum/rage... She screams for them to leave her alone, their attack seems, is, senseless. They knock her down, pull off her slacks, her panties, laughing wildly, (high on crack?) her brassiere, tossing leaves & mud in her hair, "Get 'er eyes! 'er eyes she hears one of them say.
The attack is over w/in two or three minutes and she is lying/ alone/ left on the ground, sobbing, dazed, incredulous, naked.
The children run away with her clothes and her wallet, car keys, etc. her car, parked at the / only a few hundred feet away, is useless. she will have to get help.
but, naked, she is in terror of someone seeing her.
she thought: in a few hours, this story would be all over town; meaning, not the larger town, which, for the University Heights people scarcely existed, but the residential area/ the neighborhood/the community on the hill.
the thought of everyone talking about her--her extraordinary experience--shame/humiliation//she can't bear. "It would be exaggerated into a sexual assault," she thought. That in particular she could not bear.
And those who had never liked her, much, or were jealous of her & her husband, would gloat over it. "Did you hear--?" "Did you hear--?" and they'd recount the story, many times magnified/sensationalized/altered, until the woman, who had always been independent/strong-minded, one of the most self-sufficient women of the community, would be a victim pitiful; . They would say, "What was she doing there alone?"
Thinking of all these things/// Also: the police. The ambulance squad. She wasn't hurt, really, only a few bruises, cuts, scratches, the worst of it a skinned / palm of her hand which she'd done herself, and her knee, when she'd fallen; dirt in her hair, on her face; leaves rubbed in her hair; recalled a boy / girl saying, rub that shit in her eyes! her eyes! the bitch's eyes! white bitch's eyes!
No; she could not bear to be questioned by the police; an object of pity. her story in the local weekly newspaper. (But could she keep her

name out of it? they would respect her identity: her husband was an important man in the community/ powerful/ University/community reputation. She calculated rapidly: her husband would telephone X who was a close friend of Y who owned the newspaper and thus.... "ButI can't risk it."

She lay there in the dirt sobbing. Thinking, I can't risk it.

2 So: she decides to wait until dark; to hide/ in the woods; and make her way home. since the car is useless. so she hides in the woods, behind a / in a dense thicket, her skin scratched, insects, newly awakened after the long winter, buzzingabout her. the woods, which she'd delighted in, the white dogwood, pink dogwood, blooming like xxxxx spectacles/festive/ the (wildflowers) underfoot. the quiveringness of life / fecundity to come / soon, within weeks, a near tropical humidity & torpor. And she'd been so happy, at the start of her walk! And she'd felt so much in control of her life, so superior!.... The day, involving personal / a number of appointments, a very good/ telephone call that morning, her career, herm sense of self-worth, triumph, 111///so xxxxxx ironic now.

She walks tentatively, wincing, pebbles & bits of broken glass underfoot. It is about 2 miles to her house, on a lane of the U. Heights, hill; fortunately xxxxxxxx overlooking an undeveloped slope, xxxx through which she could make her way undetected.

1 Her mind calculated rapidly: she would hide until dark; she would make her way by back routes, crossing fields in a crouch, through woods, avoiding roads, avoiding open areas. once she got home, it would be easy, even , if her husband & children were not downstairs, to slip inside...go upstairs... get to herm bedroom. Like a (mathematician)...she plotted the way from the rear of the house, she's standing in the grass in the xxxxx dark just out of the range of thexx window's aura of light...nimbus of light...and she waits xxxx until no one is visible. (the kitchen windows are larger enough/ downstairs, much glass/ the living room lights rarely switched on until dark/// her husband comes home late, and if she isn't there he will assume she's late too, their schedules overlap in the evening; children in their rooms, or watching tv., the 'recreation' the TV room at the end of the house. She knows that, ifm she gets home, she will be able to make her way unseen up to her rom...barring terrible misfortune/chance....
"And no one will know." Her control, resumed. (MAP of route)

3' She hides in a dense thicket, hugging her knees. she could begin her/// then gets restless; it's quiet; at a distance, traffic, aircraft, train... she makes her way flinching through the woods, toward the edge, is confused, goes the wrong way, her difficulty, the great risk being to / when she has to cross a road.
the way home: she knows the roads, the route by car, but has to re-think, re-imagine, how to make the brief journey on foot w/out being seen. obsessed w/ not being seen.

her breasts, her thighs, hips, her nakedness seems large, balloonlike, a balloon woman floating in the sky. All that is her publicly--the place at which everyone looks: her face, her eyes: her spirit/ personality shining out of her eyes., would nowbe lost. Seeing her as a spectacle, an object of astonishment & xx pity, people would immediately look at her nakedness. her pubic hair, her exposed breasts, vulnerable, revealed, soft, sagging, the contours of flesh. she was not a slender woman; had never been; ample flesh on thighs, hips, slightly raddled; her legs thick above the knee, fairly attractive beneath; small hands, feet, ankles. not fat but solid; fleshy woman. "But txxx this isn't me! This doesn't define me!"
She could not bear it/ felt sick/ that, seeing her, her discoverer would look past her/ignore her and focus upon her nakedness. And then he'd say, "I saw this naked woman!--I was / couldn't believe my eyes!"
But why did she imagine it would be a man who discovered her; it could as easily be a woman. And she would say: "It was the most astonishing sight--"

— Parking lot – car doors slam, voices; she hides, in sudden terror. They wld see her car there but prbbly take no real notice....

— She hides at the edge of the woods; crouches; finally sits, her head against her knees, hugging herself. waits. how slow, how incalculably slow, the coming of dusk! Birds overhead; squirrels; rustling in the bushes; undergrowth. her heart beats slow & hard & she wonders if she can learn to live w/ mortification; could live with it. If we were all naked? always? what alteration in our lives? in civilization? the idea fascinates.... Perhaps nudists colonies/ cultists believe in a personality in the body; or, conversely, they don't believe in the body at all but see through it; ignore it. & what would a menstruating woman do? a pregnant woman? are some allowed to clothes themselves, at ~~specific~~ times?

(3) urinates, in fright and spasms. Squatting, like prim./'savage,' wipes self w/ leaves, then hand

— when it was dusk she stood, and made her way, wincing, across the gravel, to her car. as she approached ~~she remembered--she had not~~ brought (x?) along; it was in the trunk.

A ....she thought she might find her clothes scattered in the woods, along the trail, but she did not. or her car keys flung down. looking, desperate ...gasping. what would they want w/ her things? would they steal her car?

rehearsed –

— her ~~story~~: she'd lost her car keys, walked home, would get the car tomorrow. her husband would ask why she'd walked home, why not stop at a house/ find a telephone & call? and she'd say she preferred to walk home: "It was a lovely evening." And so it was.

4 C~~rosses the road~~, walks, her feet now bleeding, parallel to the road, in a wooded area. so many hills/bumps; a ragged terrain. debris, newspapers blown into woods; a car's headlights & she crouches, her heart beating wildly. Now I know what a fugitive feels like...a desperate person.... homeless/ derelict. Waits; the car passes; she continues. Down a hill, a brook, little creek, has to wade across, the water very cold; shivering; it's getting colder now; the sun gone; she gives in to a convulsive shiverin fit; teeth chattering; hugs herself Stop. Stop. Just Stop. You're going to be all right.___ (urinates)

— a ~~hill~~, and now she's approaching another road, or should be; a figure in her ~~head~~--

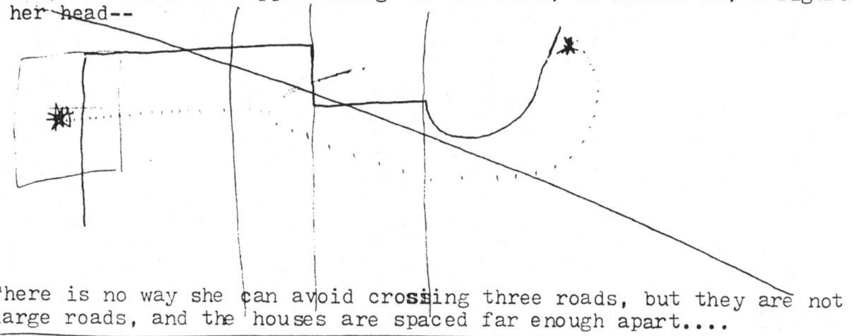

There is no way she can avoid crossing three roads, but they are not large roads, and the houses are spaced far enough apart....

— ~~She had a picture in her mind but~~/ The ~~picture~~/map in her head must have been wrong because she could see traffic to the left, a thinning patch of trees, but the road / that road really should have been farther away; so she was veering off to the left, and should straighten her course.

5 ....came to an open area, parking lot behind a converted pickle factory where antique shops, a second-hand bookstore, a trendy furniture store' paint-it-yourself furniture stop, Fortunately, these shops were all

She nr shopped there — but knew the layout.

closed... a light burning in the bookstore, but no one there. she
walks swiftly, not minding that herfeet are being lacerated by the
gravel, hides panting behind the building; makes her way to the side;
there is the largest road shemust xxx cross...and facing it is a
house,, so she can't cross directly here, has to go up a bit, a distance,
then crosses, crouched, covering herself, her heart beatingviolently
now. how exposed! how wraithlike she'd look in the dark, if someone
happened to look out the window! she ran stooped along a grown-over
lane or alley; could see houses, windows, on either side; no one here
she knows; then, an old barn/ building. dog begins to bark, terrifying
(2) her. a dog trots up to her sniffing. barks. but seems friendly,
tail thumping; undecided whether to be friendly, or not. hackles on
shoulders going down.... subsiding. "Go home. Please. Go home."
she has lost her authority; has to regain it; tries... picks up a
branch , waves it. the dog watches, now silent; after a while, but
indifferently, turns away, his atttention elsewher...distracted from
her///follows her for a while, trotting ahead, off to the side, sniffing.
finally, he's gone. (unexpected) — (feel/urinates)
6 she crosses another road. bicyclists. /// now, a ~~nicer~~ neighborhood/
the residential area, homes on larger lots; in which she & family live.
only a half-mile from home. she knows . slightly, the peple in this
house; a large colonial; dog too; cars in the driveway; teenaged boys
~~children~~ playing basketball... she has to double back, and cross the
road, makeher way a ~~few hundred~~/ short distance down. (Greek inscription!)
7 ....her own street/ lane, xxx running parallel, xxxxxxxxxxx on a hill
above. she is about / would be hardly more than two or three minutes
from home now if circumstances were otherwise. Neighbors. For some reason,
it w'ld be worse/. Obsessed w/ not being seen. What if she'd come so far, & was →
8 she looks at her ?/ smashed watch/ xxxxx crystal cracked; time stopped
at 6. 6:20 P.M. wedding band, ~~another ring--the children didn't notice,~~
or want.
climbs hill at (wrong place) neighbor's; retreats, guilty—JUNK (back there even)
9 beneath her house, makes her way slowly & carefully uphill. the
garage is visible; the liiacs; forsythia; azaalea bushes...the flower
beds she worked in, x to relieve strain of (marriage/ career).

[A STEADY PROGRESSION AS SHE MAKES HER WAY HOME OF "TRUTH"--THAT THINGS
ARE NOT SO PERFECT REALLY.]

10 her impatience w/ husband & his ego-involvement, his greedy/ seemingly
insatiable need to be placated, praised.... Isn't my love enough for
you? she'd wondered. Hex slipped easily into depressive mood xxx from
which only 'good news' jolted him; his career; men friends. their praise,
comradeship, meant a good deal to him. she'd felt some slight envy, mild
jealousy; for her worth too came froma network of male colleagues/ associ-
ates; the praise of women was pleasant but not somehow crucial. AND I
KNOW BETTER. I KNOW DAMNED BETTER. ....

11 She crossed to the side of the garage, panting .... Her house! her
house! It was strange to see it from this angle, in the dark; hiding
like a thief; she saw her house mainly from the front, and, at night,
only from the front; the outside light hadn't been turned on--which
was good. her husband sometimes turned it on for her if she came home
late; she never failed to turn it on for him. ~~But, good.~~ A movement
in the kitchen one/ her step-son walking going past a window; the living
room lights notyy yet switched on. ~~her husband was~~ home, his car in the
garage, but in his study. (She would not wanth to frighten the children
by appearing to them, naked, stricken, dirty, burrs/ weeds in her hair,
no doubt a look of (misery)/ exhaustion in her eyes; it might traumatize
them for life, her little girl, particularly; but also her son.... " I
owe it to them notxx to frighten/ terrify them." She waits w/ x increasing nervousness. now her step-son & husband are in thek kitchen talking.
now the phone must have rung--the hus. answers it ~~step-son leaves. hus-~~
band leans against walls, talking. / etc. (AND IF THEY DID NOT KNOW HER?)
SHE RECALLS A GREEK INSCRIPTION: xxxxx When my ship sank, the others
sailed on. →

men who might be h— us.—boy, stepson. she w'ld have to come closer to see.

NAKED

by Joyce Carol Oates

Were they shouting at her?--or about her? Or had their noise nothing to do with her? There appeared to be a gang of them, children, not teenagers, the eldest no more than eleven, the youngest very young, and small--surely no more than eight or nine--and she'd been aware of them for several strained minutes, annoyed rather than uneasy, but reluctant to look in their direction: she wasn't the sort of adult who oversees other people's children, or other people generally. This damply sunny May afternoon she had gone after work to hike for an hour in a suburban wooded area known locally as the Preserve--its official name was Meadowbrook Wildlife Preserve--and she was about to return to her car when the children seemingly erupted out of nowhere, a hundred feet or so behind her on the woodchip path, calling loudly to one another, laughing, shrieking, like wild animals she might have thought if she were the sort of person who had such censorious thoughts which she wasn't. And the children were black, and she was white, and that too was a thought, or an observation, she didn't allow herself to think.

She was a woman of ~~forty-six who'~~d married late, by choice, and had her children late, also by choice, thus she'd formed habits or practices of solitude which were closely bound up with, perhaps inextricable from, what she would have called her character; her private, secret, abiding self. Sun-lit, resilient, happy and confident always, she practiced friendliness as a musician practices his instrument, and with as unquestioned a devotion. She was fit, healthy, energetic, attractive; with two young children of her own and a fourteen-year-old

NAKED

by Joyce Carol Oates

There appeared to be a gang of them, children, not teenagers, the eldest no more than eleven, the youngest very young, and small--surely no more than eight or nine--and she'd been aware of them for several minutes, annoyed rather than uneasy, and reluctant to look in their direction: she wasn't the sort of adult who oversaw other people's children, or other people generally. She had gone after work to hike for an hour in a suburban wooded area known locally as the preserve--its official title was Meadowbrook Green Acres--and she was about to turn back when the children seemingly erupted out of nowhere, a short distance behind her, calling loudly to one another, laughing, shrieking, like wild animals she might have thought if she was the sort of person who had such thoughts which she wasn't. And they were black, and she was white, but that too was a thought, or an observation, she didn't quite allow herself to think.

She was a woman of forty-six who'd married late, and had her children late, thus she'd formed habits or practices of solitude which were closely bound up with, perhaps inextricable from, what she would have called her character; her private, secret, abiding self. Sun-lit, resilient, happy always, a look of genuine joy in her smile and the lighting-up of her eyes, she practiced friendliness as a musician practices his instrument, and with as sincere a devotion. She was very attractive, only just lapsing from beauty; fit, healthy, energetic, resilient; with two children of her own and a step-son--her husband had been previously married; and an excellent part-time position as assistant director of the development office of a presti-

NAKED

by Joyce Carol Oates

She was hiking alone in a suburban wildlife preserve two miles from her home when she heard, behind her, erupting seemingly out of nowhere, children's shouts, squeals, and laughter. She turned, more startled than annoyed, and saw a small gang of black children running along the woodchip trail. The eldest, a skinny boy of about eleven, in soiled T-shirt, oversized pants, and sneakers without socks, appeared to be shouting at her, and gesticulating with both hands. "Hey! Lady! Hey you!"--though his high-pitched jeering words were not really intelligible. He was grinning at her but his expression showed anger, even contempt. She stared bewildered at him and at the others, younger children, straggling behind him--the youngest, who was very could have been no more than eight or nine. "Yes? Are you talking to me?" she asked. The boy continued to address her but she could make out only the word "lady"

NAKED

by Joyce Carol Oates

She was hiking alone in a suburban wildlife preserve two miles from her home when she heard, behind her, erupting seemingly out of nowhere, children's shouts, squeals, and laughter. She turned to see a small gang of black children running along the woodchip trail. It was late in the afternoon, in spring, the first really warm, sunny day in weeks; the air was damply tremulous; even the earth exuded a sense of quiveringness, scarcely restrained life. The children were not from the University Heights area in which she lived but from the ragged edge of the old industrial city below the bluff, that steep drop to a neighborhood of rowhouses, tenements, railroad yards, factories and boarded-up mills on the river she and her family rarely glimpsed except from the interstate expressway elevated over its ruins. It was unusual for children so young to appear unsupervised by adults in the preserve, which stretched for acres along the bluff, whether black or white

NAKED and then

by Joyce Carol Oates

Were they shouting at her?--or about her? There appeared to be a gang of them, children, not teenagers, the eldest no more than eleven, the youngest very young, and small--surely no more than eight or nine--and she'd been aware of them for several minutes, annoyed rather than uneasy, but reluctant to look in their direction: she wasn't the sort of adult who oversees other people's children, or other people generally. This damply sunny May afternoon she had gone after work to hike for an hour in a suburban wooded area known locally as the preserve--its official title was Meadowbrook Wildlife Preserve--and she was about to turn back when the children seemingly erupted out of nowhere, a short distance behind her on the woodchip trail, calling loudly to one another, laughing, shrieking, like wild animals she might have thought if she was the sort of person who had such censorious thoughts which she wasn't. And the children were black, and she was white, and that too was a thought, or an observation, she didn't allow herself to think.

She was a woman of forty-six who'd married late, and had her children late, thus she'd formed habits or practices of solitude which were closely bound up with, perhaps inextricable from, what she would have called her character; her private, secret, abiding self. Sun-lit, resilient, happy and confident always, a look of genuine joy in her smile, she practiced friendliness as a musician practices his instrument, and with as unquestioned a devotion. She was fit, healthy, energetic, attractive; only just lapsing from beauty; with two young children of her own and a step-son of fourteen--her husband's from a stepson--her husband's from a previous marriage; and an excellent part-time position as an assistant director of the development office of a prestigious private university. To herself she was a creature of small ambiguities, hesitations, and doubts; subject to interior moods as wayward as weather in springtime, yet always within her control. Frequently she murmured aloud, How lucky I am! not in pride or boastfulness but in simple wonder, How lucky I am! worrying that perhaps she did not deserve her happiness. And now on this damply sunny May afternoon of no portents or apprehensions her luck had run out.

The children who swarmed over her and attacked her were not children from the University Heights area in which she lived but from the ragged edge of the city below the bluff, that steep drop to a neighborhood of rowhouses, tenements, railroad yards, factories and boarded-up mills on the river she rarely glimpsed except from the interstate expressway elevated above its ruins, and she would have fled them had her fear been keener or her sense of proportion less adamant for she kept thinking, even as the leader of the pack, a skinny boy with a ~~high-pitched jeering cry, ran~~ boldly up to her, and led the others on, They're only children, and even as they surrounded her with hyena squeals of excitement and hilarity she told herself, They're only children, as if they were kin to children she might know, or her own children. She screamed for them to stop--to go away! Screamed and shrieked and struck out at them! And when she was down and they were upon her tearing at her, hair, clothes, the contents of her jacket and jeans pockets, even at her running shoes--even at her flesh--she had no defense except screaming and begging and sobbing, her flailing but seemingly futile blows and kicks, a desperate struggle against demonic beings--boys, girls, indistinguishable--so much smaller than stepson--her husband's from a previous marriage; and an excellent part-time position as an assistant director of the development office of a prestigious private university. Frequently she murmured to herself "How lucky I am!" not in pride or boastfulness but in simple childlike wonder, "How lucky I am!" knowing that perhaps she did not deserve her happiness. But now her luck had run out.

The children crashing through the Preserve in her wake were not children from the University Heights neighborhood in which she lived but must have been from the ragged edge of the city below, that steep drop, linked of course by streets and foot paths,_even a weatherworn wooden

than she, a

than she, and so much stronger.

And hungrier: for in the midst of her terror was a deeper terror, that they meant, really, to devour her alive.

than she, and so much stronger.

Almost, she was in terror that they would devour her alive. Tear the bleeding flesh from her bones, tear with their teeth, set upon her like starving animals, and eat. For there was nothing to stop them--they had overpowered her virtually at once.

She was alone. The children were gone. She lay still, on her side, panting, sobbing, seemingly naked. She lay as if paralyzed; as if thrown from a great height. <u>They're only children. Filthy savages. Animals.</u>

ment, and with as unquestioned a devotion.

2

from themselves, and that, against the grain of all that was reasonable, rational, and just, they might wish to do so, and take satisfaction in it. And this demonic little pack of children who had so totally surprised and overpowered her--who beat her, tore her clothes from her, emptied her pockets of their belongings, all the while squealing as if what they did were only in play--she simply could not believe that what was happening was happening: and so quickly.

She was forty-six years old, the mother of two young children and the stepmother of a young teenager, unskilled in physical prowess, hesitant about defending herself even in the midst of this bizarre struggle, clumsy, on her back and on the ground, as an enormous fish hauled from the water and thrown down without ceremony to gasp and drown and die thrashing about in an alien element, all effort futile. Her screams were not loud but breathless and incredulous. Her blows found no marks, or glanced harmlessly off forearms, shoulders, lunging heads. Could she have articulated her predicament she would have said that she wanted to defend herself without injuring her attackers because they were only children and did not know what they were doing except perhaps for their leader and he she could not have injured, and jeans pockets, even at the laces of her running shoes, *even at her flesh*, she had no defense except breathless incredulous screams and flailing blows and kicks, a frenzied struggle as of a large fish hauled from the water and thrown down without ceremony on the ground to gasp and drown and die in an alien element, all effort futile. *No*! *Please*! *Stop*! *Let me go*! There were eight or ten of them, or were there a dozen, or only six, demonic beings--boys, girls, indistinguishable--so much smaller than she, and so much stronger.

Her terror was that they would devour her alive. Tear the bleeding flesh from her bones, tear with their teeth, set upon her like starving animals, and eat. For what was to stop them?--she was down, and they were upon her.

#

She was alone. Her assailants were gone. As abruptly and without warning as the attack had begun, now it was over. No more than two or three minutes had passed and now she lay panting and sobbing in a tangle of underbrush, smelling the moist soft earth, her eyes opened but unseeing. She dared not move for fear of discovering that she could not move.

They're only children.

Filthy animals. *Savages*.

They'd beaten her, torn her clothes from her, run off with her wallet, her car keys, her wristwatch--and she'd been powerless to stop them, even to impede them. Every part of her body hurt as if she'd been thrown from a great height yet miraculously lived, had not died. They'd torn out a clump or two of hair, they'd bloodied her nose, kicked her face, her head, one of them had tried to rub dried leaves into her eyes, a playground tactic she supposed, maybe all of it was a playground game of a kind, a familiar action, the and jeans pockets, even at the laces of her running shoes, even at her flesh, she had no defense except breathless incredulous screams and flailing blows and kicks, a frenzied struggle as of a large fish hauled from the water and thrown down without ceremony on the ground to gasp and drown and die in an alien element, all effort futile. How quickly it had happened, how without warning, this desperate fight against demonic beings--boys, girls, indistinguishable--so much smaller than she, and so much stronger and hungrier.

Of the screams, cries, squeals, none was distinguishable either except now and then, heard through a hazeoof pain,

She was alone. Her assailants had run away. As abruptly and without warning as the attack had bggun, now it was ovef

She was alone. Her assailants had run away. As abruptly and without warning as the attack had begun, now it was over. Only seconds had passed--no more than a minute or two. Was it possible?

however torn beyond use, for how could these things have vanished? How could the children, though they hated her, hate her that much?

But she found nothing. Her desperate eye leapt eagerly upon debris,

however torn beyond use, for how could these things havd

than she, and so much stronger.

Afterward she would recall her terror that they meant to devour her alive. Tear the exposed flesh from her bones, tear with their teeth, set upon her like starving animals, and eat. For what was to stop them?--they'd overpowered her within seconds. They could do anything they liked screaming words unintelligible except for obscenities and now and then the word "lady" almost indistinguishable from the rest.

than she, and so much stronger.

Almost, she was in terror that they would devour her alive. Tear the bleeding flesh from her bones, tear with their teeth, set upon her like starving animals, and eat. And eat, and eat!--for what was to stop them? They had overpowered her within seconds and thrown her down.

And then it was over, and the children had run away, and she was alone. Lying in the moist spongey soil

---

her finger must have been slightly swollen, her rings hadn't budged. A wedding band, and a small antique opal surrounded by tiny diamonds. . . That was all they'd left her.

She was lying on her side still protecting herself with her arms. Her knees drawn up, her back curved like a bow. She was sobbing into the spongy earth, helpless, humiliated, not knowing what to do if she couldn't find her clothes, or if they'd torn them to pieces. Her breasts ached, so strangely exposed to the outside air; the nipples hardened, puckered in fear. There was a rich fragrance of rotted leaves and earth, wet woodchips, and overhead on all sides the calls of birds, thin as wires, lifting like confetti. So beautiful, their calls. So seemingly bodiless.

After a while she sat up; brushed her hair from her face; blinked to get her eyes clear. Was no one around? Was the Preserve deserted? How far would she have to go for help? The thought came to her, too quickly, thus erroneously, that there was an emergency telephone near moves known in advance, deftly and cunningly orchestrated. But she had not known.

She lay as if paralyzed, coiled on her left side, still protecting herself, or trying to, with her arms. Her knees were drawn up to her chest and her back was curved like a bow. Helpless, humiliated, numb with pain and shock she sobbed into the spongy earth not knowing what she would do. Why had no one come when she'd called for help? Why except out of sheer hateful meanness had the children stripped off her clothes?--even her shoes, even her socks! There'd been a clumsy hilarious struggle with her jacket, her shirt, her brassiere. Turning her, pummeling her, kicking her into submission. The shrieks! The wild laughter! And the nightmare quickness of it.

<u>Savages</u>.

<u>Animals</u>.

As she lay unmoving she began to be aware of a rich fragrance pulsing about her, of rotted leaves and earth and damp pine needles. And overhead the calls of birds, crossing and criss-crossing like sky writing.

She sat up slowly and painfully, brushing her hair out of her face. She'd called for help but no one had come and she could not remember another car in the parking lot beside her own. How far would she have to go for help? If she couldn't find her clothes or if the children had torn them to pieces what would she do? What should she do?

The thought came to her that there was an emergency telephone in the preserve but almost in the same moment she knew that the emergency phone she was thinking of, and could envision so precisely, illuminated by a ceaselessly burning blue light, was on a post behind her office building at the university.

She was standing, swaying on her feet. Her breasts throbbed with pain as if the outermost skin had been peeled away; the nipples were hardened and puckered. One of the children had kicked her between the legs and when she'd turned to shield herself he'd kicked her in the buttocks and spine. It's all right! she told herself in the fierce magisterial voice she used sometimes with the children. You'll be all right! The worst is over! She didn't want to think why the children, who did not know her, had hated her so.

She spent a half-hour or more looking dazedly for her clothes reasoning the children wouldn't have troubled to carry them very far, or her wallet either, surely they would have taken what they wanted and tossed the rest away, and her car keys too--could children so young actually steal a car?--be ignorant enough to do so? She winced, walking, for the soles of her feet were shockingly tender, softer than the palms of her hands/ and there was something ~~bizarre and frightening~~ about her breasts exposed loose in this open, public place where anyone, any stranger, might suddenly appear. Strange too, seemingly unnatural, was the airy space between her legs, the space that widened and narrowed as she walked.

What had they done with her clothes? She could not believe, looking about on the paths, in the undergrowth, along the grassy space above the bluff, that she wouldn't see in the next second something, anything, that was hers, her jeans, her khaki jacket, her brassiere however torn and defiled, but there was nothing--only the repeated desperate leap of her eye onto things of no use, the teasing glimmer of old newspapers blown into the bushes, banks of lovely white wood anemone, the winking of smashed bottles, beer cans.

By degrees a new, numbing horror came upon her: the understanding that the worst was not over yet. For what could she do, naked? How could she get home, how spare herself further humiliation? Her car was useless to her without the keys even could she have managed (and how could she have managed?) to drive home naked; she was certain she'd locked the doors, for her husband was fussy about such things and she'd acquired the habit too, to placate him, so she couldn't sit in the car huddled and waiting for someone to come along. What could she do except crouch half hiding in the bushes at the side of the road and flag down a car hoping that whoever was driving the car was a person she might trust, not a man, not a man who was a stranger, yet not a man whom she knew either--God, she could not bear it!--and if it was a woman what if it were a woman she knew or who knew her from the community or from her photograph in the local paper?--<u>she could not bear it</u>. Within a few hours the story would be all over town. But the assault would be amplified into sexual assault and even those men and women who liked her would speak of it with a certain thrilled outrage, <u>Did you hear</u>! <u>what a shock</u>! <u>what a horrible experience</u>! and surely some would wonder aloud what she was doing there in the Meadowbrook Wildlife Preserve alone and some might even say she was a woman who'd had it coming to her, independent as she was, seemingly self-sufficient, leaving her children with a girl all afternoon so that she could work or not even work but go off by herself indulging herself and the ugly story would be told and retold numberless times, with zest; her children would hear of it at school, very likely they would be teased about it, taunted, without knowing why, without knowing what exactly had happened to their mother, and her stepson who was fourteen and at a difficult age, difficult particularly in relationship to her, his father's second wife, would be deeply embarrassed, and come to dislike her, and none of them would ever forget. And there was her husband.

than the palms of her hands. It was disorienting that in this open, public place, where any stranger might suddenly appear, she should be walking with her breasts loose and exposed; and that air touched her between the legs in a space that widened and narrowed as she walked. Her vision kept blurring and blotching in the hazy sunshine as with increasing desperation she looked for her things. Surely the children wouldn't have troubled to carry them very far? Surely she would find them tossed into the undergrowth? Her jeans, her khaki jacket, her shoes, socks, underwear however ripped and defiled--where were they? Repeatedly her eye leapt upon teasing shapes--old newspapers blown into the brush, banks of white wood anemone, smashed bottles and beer cans that winked up out of the shadows. She began to sob with frustration.

For a while she stood paralyzed assailed by thoughts that did not crystallize or coalesce. She was a woman of generous instincts but her instinct failed her now. What to do? Where to go? The children had taken her cars keys, her car was locked, so should she have wanted to make her way shyly to the parking lot and sit in it awaiting discovery she could not do so; and there were no buildings she could recall in the preserve. The image of a fleshy cartoon woman came to her, a balloon woman, big breasts and belly and pubic hair, hoisted up into the sky for all to stare at, smirk at, pity--"What am I going to do?"

As if in answer she heard a car pull into the gravelled parking lot some distance away. Car doors slamming, men's voices. In a panic she plunged into the bushes to hide, ran without taking heed that her feet were stabbing with pain and her face and upper body were being whipped with branches, slapped and scratched. She squatted out of sight of the path like a hunted creature, her heart hammering, sweat breaking out at every pore even as she told herself that what she must do was call for help: she had only to raise her voice calling "Help!"

She began sobbing again, helpless, defeated. Crouching in the underbrush out of sight of the path half consciously in terror that someone would come along and see her although in theory at least it was her fervent wish that someone would come along and see her, and end this nightmare. Never in her life had she felt such abject despair. It was not the pain of her throbbing head or her bruised tender breasts or the numberless scratches and cuts on her body but the helplessness of her predicament. When she'd had her babies--even, the first time, with her son, when she'd endured a labor of nine sweating hours--she had never felt defeated; had never felt despair. The experience had been wholly physical but her dignity had not been threatened. She'd known what to expect and she and her husband had rehearsed their roles and though she had not been in complete control she had never seriously surrendered control; her integrity had not been violated. Almost, she had rejoiced in the pain, knowing that she would triumph over it, she would give birth to a healthy baby, and others, witnessing her triumph, would remember it always.

She would have forgiven the children their ~~assault~~, she thought, if only they had left her her clothes.

So she hid in the underbrush, dazed, weeping, seeing in her mind's eye the cartoon-like image of herself--fleshy, exposed, vulnerable, ludicrous--a naked woman--forced to flag down a car for help. She saw the image, the grotesque vision, repeatedly, and could not accept it.

And if she were rescued, there would be police to contend with of course. They would insist upon questioning her and as an adult, an intelligent, mature, civic-minded adult, she would have to cooperate. Yet how to tell them that her assailants were mere children?--the eldest no more than eleven, the youngest as young as eight or nine? How to tell them that the children were black without the word "black" sounding strident in her mouth? I am not a racist, she would tell the police. She could hear herself explaining, speaking carefully for the record, excising all emotion from her voice. I am not a racist.

And perhaps not all the children had been black. In the confusion and scramble she hadn't seen. Though the majority had been black--the biggest boy had been black--there may have been one or two who were light-skinned; maybe Hispanic; maybe white. She simply couldn't remember, thus could not swear.

Could you identify the children if you saw them again Mrs.--?

Yes. I don't know.

How many attacked you? What were their approximate ages?

I am not a racist.

A hazy sunshine was slanting through the newly budded trees. Spring had come late this year, there had been weeks of rain, chill, overcast weather. How I long for spring, she'd thought, sliding an arm around one of her children as if spring were a gift she might give to others, a womanly sort of abundance. Now the woods, the thousands of trees, the leaves, the blossoms, the languid buzzing of insects, the cries of birds, dazzled her senses. How overpowering it was, the mere fact of the world!--when one was crouching naked, timorous, not knowing what would happen within the next hour. A swarm of tiny gnats brushed across her face and she waved them away despairingly.

What to do?

How to do it?

She seemed to have decided that she could not risk being seen in the state she was in which meant that she must make her way home without assistance. Without anyone knowing. As in a dream she saw herself, a naked, spectral figure, floating in a zigzag direction cunningly parallel to but always hidden from the roads that led to her home; following a variant of the route she would have taken by automobile. For why was it not possible?--not feasible? Her watch had been taken from her but she calculated it must be a little after six o'clock. And since she was often home late, delayed at the office, or socially, or with errands, her family would not begin to miss her until well after dark; indeed, her husband, who chaired one of the largest science departments at the university and was himself involved in ambitious fund raising projects, would probably not be home until after dark, and could not worry about her. The babysitter would feed the smaller children at about six-thirty thus she had no need to feel anxiety or guilt about them save the anxiety and guilt she knew she must feel should they know of her humiliation or, worse yet, witness it--see her--in this preposterous unclothed state, as shocking to the unprepared eye as a turtle wrenched from its shell, exposed and piteous. She would do anything to save her children that vision! She would do anything to save herself that exposure!

The image of a fleshy cartoon woman, a balloon woman, breasts and belly and pubic hair, hoisted up into the sky for all to stare at, gape at, smirk at, comment upon--it filled her with revulsion. For who, seeing her body, would see her? Who, having once seen her body, would ever again see her? In her carefully selected clothes--and even her casual clothes were carefully selected--she had authority; she was certainly attractive; bright intelligent eyes, lovely smile, beautifully modulated slightly hoarse alto voice--all that was her personality, cultivated and perfected. But naked she was mainly

10

a body and how to hide that fact! How to deny it! She had never been a slender woman and at the age of forty-six though in excellent physical condition she was soft and fleshy and even flaccid at the waist and belly, there were raddled creases in her hips, her breasts were no longer the breasts of a young woman but loose, vein-etched, the nipples enlarged by nursing--who, staring at these flaws, would look up to her face and see <u>her</u>?

Aloud she said, in a voice steadier and more resolved than she would have anticipated, "I can't risk it."

#

Her plan was to wait until nearly dusk; then make her way home by back routes, avoiding roads, open areas, private property whenever possible. The more she calculated her strategy, the more determined she became. She had only about a mile and a half to walk, perhaps less, taking a route she'd never taken by car, and much of the land between the preserve and the residential neighborhood in which she lived was still woodland, seemingly wild and untended, undeveloped. Her brain worked feverishly to establish a mind's-eye map that might guide her and prevent panic and further despair--

9

without assistance. She seemed to see herself--naked, spectral, stealthy--moving dreamlike in a zigzag direction parallel but hidden

11

Unavoidably she must cross three roads but only the first, bordering the wildlife preserve, was large; the others could be safely navigated if she were cautious, and patient, (crossing at just the right place. She supposed there were smaller residential roads and lanes she'd forgotten temporarily but the map's outline was what mattered, the surge of hope it provided her, this simple algorithm of a route as the crow flies shrewdly bypassing the usual human routes.) Each time she set out, on her mental journey from the wooded edge of the preserve to the first road and beyond her vision dissolved as in a film in which too much light has flooded, but it crystalized again at the rear of her home--the foot of the deep sloping hill behind the house (where in a tangle of trees and bushes and underbrush belonging to the county she might hide and keenly observe the lighted windows of her house, the comings and goings of her family (should they be downstairs, or visible to her) and from that perspective, once she was safely and miraculously there, she had no doubt that she could make her way undetected into the house and up the stairs and into her bedroom (thus to safety) with no one knowing.

Excitedly her mind seized upon another, even more pragmatic alternative: (if it seemed too risky to take the stairs to the second floor of the house) she could duck downstairs, to the basement, and find some clothes in the soiled clothes basket, thus quickly dressing herself with no one knowing.

So she began to walk toward the edge of the woods, wincing at the roughness of the ground, narrowly avoiding a brutal crescent of broken glass that would have sliced her foot in two, but determined, even in a way calm, for her brain held in suspension two visions--that of the map, which reduced the nightmare complexity of a mile-and-a-half's she had no cause to feel anxiety or guilt about them apart from the anxiety and guilt she felt should they learn of her humiliation or, worse yet, see her in the state she was in. Like something pried from its shell, exposed and piteous.

She sd. again, aloud, "I can't risk it."

She waited until the sun began to set, then, ~~feeling~~ impatient, sure that no one was in ~~the~~ her vicinity, ~~she~~ began walking → edge of the woods. She'd established in her mind's eye a map to guide her —

It wld be less than 2 mi, this crow's-flight route. Much of the land b. the preserve & her home was undeveloped, farm- or woodland; the countryside bounding the residential neighborhoods that were yr by yr encroaching upon it. Unavoidably (rds.)

~~3 rds to cross — but only the first was sizable; the others were narrow res.~~ ~~rest~~ ~~rds~~

barefoot journey to something finite and navigable, and that of herself, or a spectral figure that was herself, crouched in the shadowy undergrowth below her home, waiting for the proper moment to allow her to emerge. It would be a matter of timing, all of it! Once in her bedroom with the door shut behind her she believed that she would revert to herself again as if nothing had happened. She would begin the effort of forgetting as resolutely and even as cheerfully as she might begin the housewifely effort of washing a wall to be repainted. (Though in this phase of her life, buoyed by affluence, it was no longer likely that she herself would wash down a wall, let alone repaint it.) None of her children would guess that anything had happened to disturb their mother for their attention was focussed almost exclusively upon themselves nor was her husband likely to guess, or to sense, for his imagination was absorbed almost always in his own work, his immediate plans for the following day, and what in fact would there be for him to notice, if she, his wife, his smiling wife, the unfailingly confident mother and stepmother with whom he'd lived for over a decade, gave no sign? Fully formed, brilliant in its plausibility, the story she would tell her husband was already lodged in her mind: she had lost her car keys somehow hiking in the preserve, had decided simply to walk home, not to trouble him, or anyone, by telephoning, and she'd pick up the car in the morning. (Which was what she would do.) You walked home? he might ask, mildly surprised and she would say, It isn't far--I enjoyed the exercise.

But how painstakingly she had to make her way, barefoot! How treacherous the undergrowth was, pricking and stabbing at her unprotected flesh! The moist earth sank beneath her weight and filled her with a primitive panic for what if this were a bog or even quicksand that might swallow her up. . . ? Every few yards she paused, looking alertly about. Overhead jays shrieked to one another as if in warning and on all sides in the directionless woods there were mysterious sounds of rustling, stirring, shifting, as if a gigantic organism were defining itself invisibly, never quite rising to consciousness. The thought both frightened and excited her for it was not one she had ever had before in her life.

Despite the map firmly suspended in her mind's eye she was veering off at a slant since a few minutes later she heard car doors slamming, raised voices, someone newly arrived in the parking area. At once, without thinking, she squatted to hide, a hunted creature, her heart hammering, sweat breaking out at every pore, even as she told herself it would be wisest to call for help--she had only to raise her voice in a timid, hopeful, desperate appeal--"Help!" or "Help please!"--and the nightmare would be ended. She could even call out to her rescuers that she'd been stripped of her clothing and could they please bring her a blanket or something with which to cover herself and she could, if the circumstances were right, insist that she wasn't hurt and did not want the incident reported to police nor did she want to be taken to an emergency room. These possibilities raced through her mind but caught hold nowhere and were lost. For she was in the grip of an unreasonable terror, a dread of being discovered naked, being <u>seen</u>, being <u>shamed</u>, and she simply could not bear it.

So she remained hiding, her forehead pressed against her bare knees and her arms gripping her legs in an embrace. The voices quickly faded. Whoever it was must have entered the woods at some distance and would not be headed in her direction; she was safe.

Probably they had not noticed her car; or, ~~if~~ noticing, had not remarked upon it. For what business was it of theirs?

After a brief wait she began inching her way forward again, toward the road, walking in a crouch with her face and breasts shielded. She could hear an occasional car now. In the silence of the countryside the approach of a car, its passing, and its retreat were clearly definable; if she didn't lose her courage at the last moment, and if she didn't step down on something sharp, she should have no difficulty getting across the road and hiding in the wooded area beyond. The preserve stretched off for acres along the granite bluff above the river and she felt certain that the new visitors would never find her. Perhaps they were lovers who had come to make love? teenagers who had come to smoke dope? and make love? She had not walked in this or any other park with her husband for years since their busy lives drew them in different directions but a memory came to her now of having walked here in the preserve with her younger children, her own children, a year or two ago, along a lovely trail lined with clumps of white birch, and she'd become temporarily confused, cutting back on her path and re-crossing it in looping asymmetrical circles for perhaps a half-hour before she realized her error and how to break out of it. She had not allowed either of the children, of course, to know that their mother was "lost" even temporarily and indeed she hadn't been very worried since the area had always seemed to her a tamed, delimited sort of nature, bordered on three sides by roads she drove nearly every day.

And here was the road. A car passed, and after an interval another, and then there were several in a row, then what sounded like a diesel truck, and then there was silence, and she peered out of the undergrowth and saw nothing but pavement and a wooded field beyond, exactly as she remembered and had envisioned with oneiric clarity in her mental map. Still, she hesitated. It was not yet dusk but several degrees above dusk; the sun of early evening sank hazily toward the horizon but a figure running across the road, particularly a figure of astonishing nakedness, might be visible for miles.

So she waited. Panic had earlier released a film of scummy sweat to cover her body, rank as an animal's, and now, as panic subsided, she began to feel chill. The air too was losing its heat almost perceptibly.

Waiting, she found herself thinking of, not her ~~body~~, but of responses to it: a man telling her she was beautiful, and another man telling her she was beautiful, and yet another, the man she married, telling her she was beautiful: but she had not believed them. Or, if believing, had not taken it very seriously. One claims beauty where one feels irresistible desire. One claims beauty in order not to feel absurd. To herself, her body in a mirror was blurred, like a deliberate smudge in a painting, for she had not wanted to see or to know too much, fearing less the encroachments of age--though these were certainly imminent, and fearful--than simple disillusion. Her husband who loved her and whom she loved very much had not told her she was "beautiful" in a long time but she did not know whether this was because she had lost whatever bodily beauty she'd had as a younger woman or because he no longer looked at her, or, looking, no longer saw. In any case she did not blame him. She was certain that, in his place, she would behave similarly.

She was beginning to feel impatient. Hungry and light-headed too. So she inched her way forward, stooped almost double, looking up and down the road--seeing nothing; hearing nothing. Should she risk it? Running naked across the Cutters Mill Road? She drew a deep breath and prepared herself as years ago, many years ago now, she'd prepared to dive from the high board, wanting not merely to dive but to execute a perfectly calibrated dive, entering the water with the grace of a hand slicing the water at a slant. For pride would allow nothing less.

So she threw herself blindly out of hiding and began to run, her forearms steadying her breasts from beneath, and no dive or flight or plunge or physical ecstasy in her life had prepared her for this effort, running naked and wincing on badly cracked asphalt, gasping for breath through her opened mouth, eyes wide and stark and fixed on the spot at the farther side of the road she would enter, to hide herself! And then within seconds she was there, and safe, undetected, seemingly, scrambling breathless through a shallow ditch, & onto the running into field beyond. But s'how she'd sto cut her foot. Stepped on glass & cut her; at the heel a field of scrubby trees and bushes--though in so doing she'd stepped down on a piece of glass and cut her foot. It's all right, she told herself eagerly. You're all right. The bleeding won't last long.

She limped forward. She wasn't going to examine her foot. To her left there were no houses within sight; to her right there was, at a distance of perhaps a quarter-mile, a single house, an old farmhouse, but it was partly screened by trees and even should someone happen to glance out a window and see her, or the blurred moving figure that was her, she doubted that her nakedness would be discernible. Despite her wildly pounding heart and the stinging in her foot--her right foot, near the heel--she felt a surge of hope, almost of elation.

For now she had crossed the largest of the roads she would have to cross and ahead lay acres of uncultivated land, an uncultivated stretch of woodland through which she should be able to make her way without being seen. (Unless there were hunters? But wasn't hunting forbidden here, as indeed trespassing was forbidden?) The primary urgency was She had mainly to only guard against losing her sense of direction, the road at her back, and perpendicular, the next road, vividly seen in her mind's eye, perpendicular as well, an unpaved residential lane on which custom-built homes like her own had

She walked as quickly as
she cld., limping.

been built on two- or three-acre lots.) She would have imagined this

interior, ~~undeveloped~~ land as merely empty but there was much evi-

dence, ~~troubling to her eye~~, of human intrusion; piles of trash scat-

tered along a farmer's lane including rotted tires, automobile parts,

an upended refrigerator, a scorched mattress. ~~Shrewdly~~ she poked/about *she found h'self*

the debris for something--~~anything!~~--that ~~might~~ clothe her, ~~however~~ *— desperate as*
~~grotesquely,~~ but she found nothing except a strip of material stiff *a beggar, & as unreasonably optimistic—*

with filth, part of an old canvas, and this she ~~let fall from her fin-~~ *threw down*

~~gers~~ in disgust. ~~She began to resent her family for their forgetful-~~

~~ness of her.~~ *"Damn! God damn!"*
limping. Time was distended as in a diynged photograph,
She walked on, ~~Time~~ no longer seemed to flow in a chronological *shapes are distended, yet—;*

sequence. (The children had swarmed over her and torn her clothes from

her only just recently, or many hours, days, even weeks, before.) Her

head rang with accusations. How dare you. How dare touch. I am not

a racist. I don't know any of you. B~~itterly~~ she imagined her hus-

band and the happiness of his first marriage of which he had never

spoken to her except evasively to deny it as if mere words could erase

all that was and, having been, flowed into what is to make it possible.

Liar. I know you. Her right foot throbbed with pain but out of spite

she refused to examine it. Let the bleeding wash away the dirt she

thought reasonably.
That she'd n' told any one, it
— It had always seemed to her a curiosity of the female life,

that, bleeding each month, bleeding amid cramps and occasional nausea

and faintness, one had faith nonetheless that the bleeding was finite;

would not continue until death. Did ~~not~~ such bleeding in secret whet

a liking for, even a skill at, secrecy? *2 She shld. not have mar'd. She'd been*
happiest alone. She
4 A chill lifted upward from the darkening earth. The ~~sun had~~ ~~clfrt~~

~~been hidden~~ for some time behind a ~~dense bank of trees;~~ the western *(happiness*
Sun below horizon

hypocrisy make he
wearns
3 & her lily-white skin!

sky was ~~mottled like a~~ bruise. The farmer's lane had ended abruptly in a final pile of trash. ~~Looking nervously about~~ she tried to determine her position but with no road in sight, neither at her back nor before her, she was ~~easily~~ confused. Should she continue in a straight line across an open uncultivated field in which swaths of wild rose were growing or should she take~~, more prudently~~, the edge of the field, to her left, though it was ~~possibly~~ out of her ~~way~~. Her eyes welled with tears for she was thinking, An error now would be fatal.

Invisible birds called to one another on all sides, quickened now by dusk. Ribbons and wires and threads of sound lovely but unintelligible to her. She did not believe she had ever heard birds calling to one another before.

She decided to walk along the edge of the field, not to risk the open area. But how slowly she walked, how fearfully--~~for~~ both her feet were bleeding, and throbbing with pain. Not a singular pain but numerous competing pains rang through her body. Her head ~~behind~~ her eyes and her scalp where tufts of hair had been torn away and the pit of her belly and her spine--she felt waves of faintness come over her and was in dread of losing consciousness in this no-man's land bordered and bracketed by suburban country roads, so ~~teasingly~~ close to her own road and her own house; hardly more than a ten-minute drive from the downtown of the city. ~~It terrified her that~~ she might collapse ~~and be unable to continue~~ and ~~even~~ her cries for help would go unheard and in a day or two or three she ~~might~~ be found comatose, ~~even~~ dead, a woman's nude body it would be reported in the news, balloon breasts and fleshy hips and thighs, a patch of dark pubic hair between the legs, eyes rolled up into the skull. Not a person but a body. And all the prior history of her life--her achievement, her winningness, her love for her family and theirs for her--summarily erased. She would have become a story, a fiction.

~~Thus~~ anger kept her going. Anger, and resolve.

Beyond the field the lane resumed, broader now, ea~~sy to walk on~~ [it less rutted], leading to the remains of an old farm; She knew the property from the road ~~but~~ [tho'] not its owners. In the growing dusk she could not see whether another house faced the farmhouse at the road or if the house she was trying to envision was a short distance away but in the shadows she might slip past unseen. This was proof in any case that she was heading in the right direction.

Then it happened that a dog began barking excitedly, and to her horror trotted up the lane as if to greet her, a dun-colored animal of no distinct breed though in size about that of a Labrador retriever; it was alternately barking and snarling, its long tail thrashing from side to side. An old childhood terror of dogs washed over her: she'd been bitten once, or so she believed though her mother had sworn she had never been actually bitten only badly frightened by a German shepherd as a small child, and now she was seized with panic, speaking plaintively to the dog as if it might understand--"No. Please. Go home. Go home." The dog stood its ground but did not advance, barking so noisily she supposed its owners would come out to see what was happening. She begged and pleaded in an undertone as if for her very life--"Good dog. Nice dog. Go home." She wondered if her nakedness aroused the dog's suspicion? She wondered if her fear could be detected, the sharp rank odor of her helplessness?

She ~~picked~~ [snatched] up a branch and held it like a club, her hand badly shaking. The dog continued to bark. Yet its tail was thrashing and thumping too which might mean it was inclined to be friendly--how could one judge? After a minute or two when the dog's barking subsided a degree she made a move to edge past it, the branch still upraised, and

At least, this time, no one had seen.

<u>Why have you done such a thing</u> he was demanding, his revulsion showing in his face, and she said <u>I do what I want to do</u> though until she did not know if this were true. He was pleading with her but as always there was a threat in his words. <u>But why this</u>!--<u>why this</u>!

this desperate strategem the dog for all its frantic bravado seemed to accept. Still, she did not dare turn her back on it and walk away; she feared it leaping at her. More than the prospect of being attacked the prospect of having to call for help terrified her. For her predicament, hideous to her, would surely have its comical overtones for others. She could expect no sympathy, still less any understanding.

The dog allowed her by, then trotted as if indifferently in her wake, nosing about, sniffing at her heels. It went silent in sudden contemplation of her: her smells. She felt its damp cold nose against her bare legs and the backs of her knees.

At the road she waited. No cars? No one? ~~She would have inched~~ cautiously out ~~but~~ saw at the ~~last~~ moment a flash of color and movement, a bicyclist, on a racing bicycle, helmeted head lowered, spine painfully bent, a young man who ~~flashed~~ past her at a formidable speed without glancing toward her. When it was safe to do so she crossed the road in as blind and as prayerful a plunge as she'd crossed the first road but this time the pavement was smoother; the road itself narrower; there was no ditch for her to scramble through; only a cluster of water willow she forced her way unhesitatingly into, taking no notice that her face and breasts were being scratched. Behind her the dog barked ~~but did not follow her.~~

She was running, sliding, falling downhill. Losing her balance in a swampy place, like a drunken woman careening from side to side, snatching at bushes to steady her. And then she had to wade through a wide, shallow stream, pebbles sharp underfoot, water freezing, and on the farther bank, panting, sobbing, the need to urinate came so violently it was like a blade thrust up into her. She squatted releasing a hot pungent liquid from her bladder, not in a stream but in frightened little spasms. When she was finished--and it seemed to take an excruciatingly long time--she wiped herself awkwardly with a wad of leaves. Her face burned, her hands shook. But at least, she was thinking, no one had seen.

A memory came to her, years old, as if emerging from a previous lifetime, of having, as a child, squatted in the grass to urinate, and watching with fascination and an emotion akin to but not quite identical with shame as the hot liquid streamed from her--the eerie helplessness of what she did, or what was being done to her, a physical episode, something both her and not her, out of her control.

At least, this time, no one had seen.

#

2 Inside the floating house figures moved indistinctly. Some of the windows were lit and blazing light, others were darkened. The effort to hold her head erect, to see, was a strain. Repeatedly she blinked to clear her vision but failed--it frightened her that she could not see what was crucial for her to see. Why have you done such a thing, he was demanding, his revulsion for her showing in his face, and she said, I do what I want to do though until this instant she had not known it. Pleading yet, as always, threatening too, he said, But this!--why this! And she repeated, I do what I want to do. Standing before him battered, disheveled, eyes swollen, bleeding from countless scratches and lacerations, naked. I do what I want to do.

3 The house floated in the night. It was hers; or the house she believed was hers. Stumbling as in a dream without end she'd made her painstaking way along the ravine, how many hours she could not have estimated, ~~unless it was a single distended hour.~~ She was no longer talking to herself nor was she raving wordless as, once, as they'd searched for a vein in both her forearms and then in her ankles to start the precious fluid going to feed the "life" so tenuously

held within the body she had raved without so much as uttering a sound. In her confusion she had erred thus was required to retrace these ~~painstaking~~ wincing steps groping through a stretch of ravaged bull-dozed land she did not recognize where new houses were being built sobbing as fire leapt up from her torn feet. I do what I want to do but who is it who does such things?

In the shadows below the house she crouched blinking repeatedly to clear her vision. When was it the savage children had torn her clothes from her and beaten her and rubbed leaves into her eyes she could not recall and was not certain, if questioned, she would wish to recall. For all of her life she had carried inside her a secret simultaneous life not only not known to others but not known fully to herself as the brain's perpetual dreaming continues even during consciousness and of this life, this intimacy, no one could force her to speak. And here was the house in which seemingly she lived, or a part of her had lived and would continue to live, a long rectangular box with a second floor, several large plate glass windows facing the rear, a two-car garage. She would not perhaps have recognized it immediately for returning to this house at night she invariably approached it from the street, from the front, and it was this vision firmly imprinted in her mind's eye but she could make out the kitchen, or part of it, and some movement there, a figure that must have been her husband though not quite so tall as she would have imagined her husband to be, and shortly there came another figure to join him, the stepson evidently, and now the telephone must have rung because her husband moved to answer it leaning in the kitchen doorway as he often did while speaking on the kitchen phone. But where were the others--the girl who was six, the boy who was eight? She wld not have had two children had she not wanted them, for one wld have done. 2 was proof & the stepson who was in no way hers was proof. They were the ones she most wanted to spare the terrifying sight of herself even should she step out of her body and run up the hill to boldly and defiantly declare herself as she was urged to do.

So in the dark below the house she waited naked and shivering until such time as it would become clear to her, what she was waiting for.

Naked

Joyce Carol Oates

She was hiking alone in a suburban wildlife preserve two miles from her home when she heard, behind her, erupting seemingly out of nowhere, children's shouts, squeals, and laughter. She turned to see a small pack of black children running along the woodchip trail. The eldest, a skinny boy of about eleven, in soiled white T-shirt, oversized pants, and sneakers worn without socks, seemed to be shouting at her, and gesticulating urgently with both hands. "Hey! Lady! Hey *you!*"—though his high-pitched jeering words were not wholly intelligible. It was late in the afternoon, in spring, the first really warm, sunny, pleasurable day in weeks; the air was damply tremulous; the earth exuded a sense of quiveringness, scarcely restrained life. She had been hiking for an hour, pushing herself, walking quickly, enjoying the strain of leg, thigh, arm muscles, and a light film of perspiration had gathered over her, and her thoughts, scattered and inchoate initially, had gradually slowed, steadied, crystallized until they were not thoughts at all so much as simply impressions and gliding wordless images as in a dream. And the children, led by the strangely intense, even angry black boy, surged up like unexpected images in that dream.

"Yes? Are you talking to me?" she asked.

The boy laughed as if in delight and derision. Had he not been so young she might have thought him drunk, or high on a drug. He came barely to her shoulder, easing toward her like a wiry little animal out for blood. He addressed her in a stream of soprano sounds underlaid by contempt but she could make out none of the words except perhaps "lady" or "where you goin lady" and his aggressive intensions bewildered her rather than frightened her since the children were so young, the youngest no more than eight or nine, and very small, and there were two or three girls among them. "Yes? What is it? What do you want?" she asked with a mother's slightly strained calm. *They're only children* she told herself even as, instinctively, she took a step backward.

And in the next instant they were upon her.

Even as it was happening, as the children swarmed over her, pummelling her with their fists, pounding, kicking, tearing, the eldest leaping up upon her to bring her heavily down, savage and deft as a predatory animal, even as she struggled with them, flailing her arms, trying too to strike, punch, kick—for she was a woman of some strength, very fit, unshrinking, resolute—she was thinking *This can't be happening!* and *They're only children!* She'd known from her first sighting of them that they were not children from the University Heights area in which she lived but from the ragged edge of the old industrial city below the bluff, that steep drop to a neighborhood of rowhouses, tenements, railroad yards, factories and condemned mills on the river she and her family rarely glimpsed except from the interstate expressway elevated over its ruins, but she was a woman in no way racially prejudiced who had grown up with blacks, gone to school with blacks, Chinese, Hispanics, and other minorities, as they were familiarly called, and she was determined to instill in her children the identical unjudging uncensorious liberalism her parents had quite consciously instilled in her. So it did not strike her, as perhaps it should have, upon occasion at least, that these minorities might look upon her as conspicuously different from themselves, and that, against the grain of all that was reasonable, charitable, and just, they might wish to do so, and take satisfaction in it. And this demonic little pack of children who had so totally surprised and overcome her—who beat her, tore her clothes from her, emptied her pockets, all the while squealing and laughing as if what they did were only in play—she simply could not believe they were capable of such a thing: and with such nightmare quickness.

She was forty-six years old, in very good health, a woman of intelligence and independent character; the mother of two young children and the stepmother of a young teenager; wholly unskilled in physical exertion or prowess; as clumsy in this bizarre struggle as a fish hauled from the water and thrown down upon the ground without ceremony to gasp and thrash about and drown in an alien element. Her screams were breathless and incredulous. Her wild blows found no marks, or glanced harmlessly off forearms, shoulders, lunging heads. *They're only children!* she was thinking and as a mother she did not want to hurt children even had she been capable of doing so. The thought came to her too that if she surrendered, if she submitted, put up no further struggle, they would take what they wanted and leave her alone.

And so it was. When she stopped fighting they stopped hitting her but in the fierce hilarity of their excitement they stripped her clothes from her, turning her, rolling her, tugging at her jeans, whooping with laughter as they tore away her brassiere and underpants, yanked off by sheer force her running shoes, pulled off her socks. She was too overcome by shock to beg them to stop and the mad fear struck her that they meant to devour her alive—tear the flesh from her bones, tear with their teeth, set upon her like ravenous animals, and eat. For what was there to stop them?

Then they ran away, and were gone, and she was left alone dazed and sobbing in a place she could not have named. The attack had probably not taken more than two or three minutes but it had seemed interminable and afterward she lay for what seemed like a very long time not daring to move for fear of discovering that they'd crippled her—for her back and buttocks had been soundly kicked—and she could not move. *This is what you deserve* a voice meanly consoled her but she was too weakened, too much in pain, to respond.

She guessed she must be alone in the preserve since no one had come in answer to her calls for help.

So she lay still, and tried to gather her strength; tried to think what had happened; what she must do next. Her sobs were erratic and resigned rather than the high breathless sobs of hysteria for she was not a hysterically inclined woman: she was a woman who might quell hysteria in others. *It's all right. You're going to be all right. The worst is over.*

So she spoke frequently to her own children, half chidingly, half in affection.

But her clothes had been taken from her. And her car keys.

And her wallet too, of course, and her wristwatch; and her gold chain—yanked so violently from her neck that the catch snapped and her skin was lacerated as by a wire noose. Only the rings on her left hand remained: one of the children had tugged fiercely at them, so hard she'd felt her finger turn in its socket, but her finger must have been swollen, the rings hadn't budged.

Savages, she thought.

Filthy little animals, she thought.

But why had they hated her so, to beat her as well as rob her, and to humiliate her by stripping her clothes from her?

She sat up. Brushed her hair out of her sweaty face. The thought came to her that there was an emergency telephone she could use near the parking area—but almost in the same instant she knew that the emergency phone she was thinking of, and could see so precisely, so desperately, illuminated by a cool blue light, was on a post behind her office building at the university.

She spent a wretched half-hour, or more, looking for her clothes. Every part of her body ached as if she had been thrown from a great height, her bones shaken to the marrow but somehow unbroken, able to bear her weight. Her scalp stung where a clump or two of hair had been torn out. Her nose had been bloodied. Both her eyes were swelling and would surely turn black and her vision was blurred as if she were under water for one of them had tried to rub dried leaves in her eyes, a playground tactic she supposed, a nasty playground tactic, probably everything that had been done to her was play of a kind, the moves known in advance, deftly and gracefully orchestrated. But she had not known.

She didn't want to think why the children, strangers to her, had hated her so. Hadn't she been quite cordial to the boy, unalarmed, even trying to smile as he approached her? She was by nature and by training an unfailingly friendly woman: she practiced friendliness as a musician practices his instrument, and with as unquestioned a devotion. And there was the unwanted but undeniable privilege of her white skin, which brought with it a certain responsibility not only to be good and decent and charitable but to be nice in being so.

Walking on the woodchip trail was not painful but walking into the underbrush hurt her feet; the soles were shockingly tender, softer than the palms of her hands. It was disorienting that in this open, public place, where any stranger might suddenly appear, she should be walking with her breasts loose and exposed; and that air touched her between the legs in a space that widened and narrowed as she walked. Her vision blurred in the hazy sunshine as with increasing desperation she searched for her things. Surely the children wouldn't have troubled to carry them far? Surely she would find them tossed into the underbrush? Her jeans, her khaki jacket, her shoes, socks, underwear however ripped and defiled . . . ? But her eye leapt only upon useless things, teasing shapes: newspapers blown into the brush, banks of white wood anemone, smashed bottles and beer cans winking up out of the shadows.

She wept in abject frustration.

She was a woman of generous instincts but her instinct failed her now. What to do? Where to go? She didn't have her car keys and her car was locked—she'd acquired from her husband, a fastidious man, the habit of always locking her car—so if she wanted to make her way shyly to the parking lot and sit in the car awaiting discovery and rescue she could not do so.

She felt an attack of faintness. The image of a fleshy cartoon woman came to her, a balloon woman, big breasts and belly and pubic hair, hoisted up into the sky. People, mainly men, gathered to gape, smirk, point their fingers. Aloud she cried, "What am I going to do!"

As if in answer, a car pulled into the gravelled parking lot not far away. She heard car doors slamming and men's voices. In a panic she plunged into the shrubs to hide, ran without caring about her bare feet and the branches and prickles that tore against her naked body. Like a hunted creature she squatted and hid even as she knew that she should call for help; she had only to raise her voice calling "Help!" or "Help please!"—a timid, hopeful, desperate appeal—and the nightmare would be over.

She could even call out to her rescuers—she had no doubt they would be rescuers: nearly everyone who came to the preserve was connected in some way with the university—that she had been stripped of her clothing and could they please bring her a blanket or something with which to cover herself?—and she could, assuming the circumstances were right, insist that she was not hurt and did not want the incident reported to police nor did she want, or require, medical attention.

But she said nothing. She was crouched low behind a thick bank of bushes and flowering dogwood, her sweating forehead pressed against her knees, her arms gripping her legs in a frantic embrace. The terror of being discovered naked as she was, battered, bruised, dishevelled as a wild animal, was simply too much for her: she wanted only to hide and not be seen. Nothing mattered to her but that she not be seen.

So she hid, and the men's voices quickly faded, for they must have taken one of the other trails, and would not find her. If they had seen her car in the lot they would probably not have really noticed, or remarked upon it. *It's all right* she consoled herself repeatedly, not knowing what she meant.

She was a woman who had married late, by choice, and had had her children late, also by choice, thus she'd formed habits or practices of solitude which were closely bound up with, perhaps inextricable from, her character: her private, secret, abiding self. Her blond sun-lit good looks had never mattered greatly to her except as they buoyed up her naturally exuberant spirit; she thought it simply a matter of tact to hide from others, including her husband, the small doubts and shifts of mood that frequently overcame her. It was a matter of pride that everyone who knew her should think her unfailingly good-natured, resilient, happy and confident always, or nearly always.

And now, what to do!

How to spare herself further humiliation!

She had fled from the men who might have helped her—thus what to do!

She would have forgiven the children their savage assault, she thought, if only they had left her her clothes.

There seemed to her no alternative that was not hideous, shameful. She would end up crouching in the bushes at the side of the road and flagging down a car with the hope that whoever was driving the car might be a person she might trust. A man who was a stranger would be the worst prospect, yet a man who knew her was scarcely better—might in fact be worse since, then, word would be spread of her plight, and the sordid incident exaggerated. If it were a woman perhaps she could bear it but if it were a woman who knew her, or knew of her, from her work in the community or her photograph in the local paper, then too the tale would be spread everywhere at once, and the rumor would be that she'd been sexually assaulted. Even people who wished her well would repeat the tale and thrill to it; some would wonder why she'd been alone in the wildlife preserve; some might even hint that she'd had it coming to her—independent as she was, married to a well-known department chairman at the university, with an excellent job of her own in the university's development office. So the ugly tale would be told and retold numberless times, out of her control. She would be, simply, the woman who was found naked in the Meadowbrook Wildlife Preserve.

And her children would hear of it at school, her six-year-old daughter and her nine-year-old son; they'd be teased, taunted, made to believe things that weren't true. And her stepson—the boy would be crushed with embarrassment for her. And there was her husband of whom in this context she could barely think: so ambitious, so caught up in his work, so concerned with his reputation in the community.

After his relief passed that she hadn't been seriously hurt she knew he would feel a kindred humiliation.

And if she sought help there would be police to contend with, probably. It was clear from the sight of her that she'd been beaten. The police would insist upon questioning her and how to tell them that her assailants had been mere children?—not teenagers but children?—and girls among them?—and black? *I am not a racist* she would tell the police carefully. Excising all emotion from her voice: *I am not a racist.*

"I can't risk it."

As in a waking delirium she saw herself, a naked, spectral figure, floating in directions parallel to but hidden from the roads that led to her home, following a variant of the route she would have taken by car. Those familiar suburban-country roads she drove every day. She was only two miles from home, possibly less: couldn't she make it on foot, alone and unassisted? With no one knowing? She calculated it must be about six-thirty. And since she was often home late, after dark, delayed at the office, or socially, or with errands, her family would not begin to miss her for hours; her husband had lately become involved in fund raising for the university, and he too kept an erratic schedule—sometimes, arriving home, she'd learn from the girl who watched the children that her husband had telephoned to say he would not be home for dinner. And her stepson was in and out of the house. The girl would feed the smaller children at six-thirty, thus she had no immediate cause to feel anxiety or guilt about them apart from the anxiety and guilt she felt at the possibility of their learning of her humiliation; or, worse yet, seeing her in the state she was in.

For then they would never *see* her again, as the person she was.

She said aloud, licking her cracked lips, "I can't risk it."

She waited until the sun slanted through the trees and the western sky turned bluish orange, mottled like a bruise. Around her birds were calling to one another with renewed urgency, quickened by the diminution of light. Lovely high-pitched cries like ribbons, wires, threads of sound; she listened, hearing each note with unnatural clarity. She had never heard such sounds before.

"I want my home again. My own place."

She had established in her mind's eye a map to guide her through the woods and back fields—

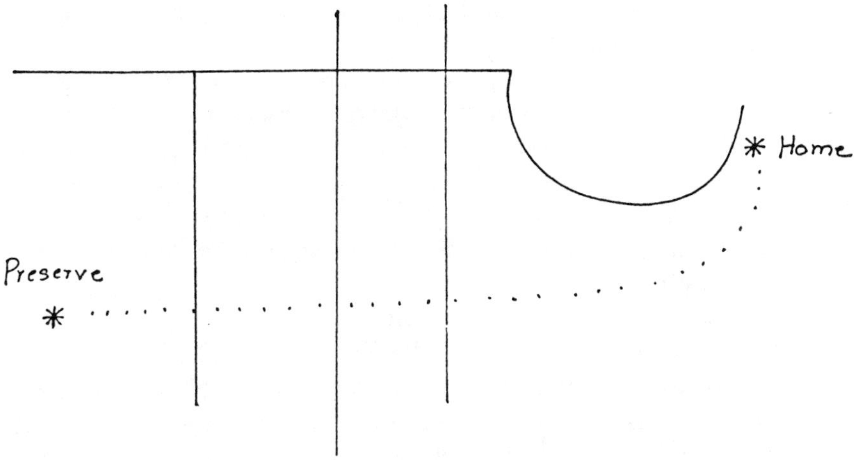

The distance between her present position in the preserve and her home was approximately two miles. There was no reason she could not cross it on foot! without being seen! Unavoidably, she would have to cross three roads but only the first, bordering the preserve, was large; the others were only residential lanes. It would all be a matter of timing.

Her destination was, not her own front door, nor even, at least initially, her back door, but the ravine at the rear of her house where she could hide in the shadows and observe the lighted windows of her house: noting the comings and goings of her family, should they be visible. For she did not want them to see her naked, no not even her husband, not in this debased state of nakedness, with the look of a victim in her face, and her body scratched and bruised. Her breasts ached as if the outermost layer of skin had been peeled off; the nipples were hard and puckered in fear. That boy with the mean eyes and jeering mouth had kicked her in the pit of the belly until she'd turned away retching and gasping for breath but such an outrage would never happen to her again.

Once home, undetected, she could steal away upstairs and revert to herself again. She would bathe, doctor herself up, dress, reappear. If she acted quickly enough, the smaller children would not yet be in bed, or asleep. She would prepare a meal, something simple, for her husband and stepson. Or she would join them at the table if they were already eating. She would tell her husband she'd lost her car keys in the woods and had decided to walk home without telephoning him, or anyone, no need to fuss, he could drop her off in the morning and she could pick the car up then. It was locked, it was safe. (For the children were surely too young to steal a car!) "You walked home?" her husband would ask, mildly surprised, and she would say, "It wasn't far—I enjoyed the exercise."

Afterward, she would begin the effort of forgetting as resolutely as, years ago, before she was married and living in a fine home, she might have washed a wall of one of her rented apartments preparatory to painting it. *And no one would know.*

None of the children would sense that anything had happened to their mother for their attention was focused almost exclusively upon themselves: which was only natural, and good. Nor would her husband sense anything for his imagination was absorbed primarily in his own work, his own being, he wasn't a young man any longer but a man at the peak of his powers, or a little beyond—now it was younger men who drew his attention, who fascinated and repelled. And what in fact would there be for this busy successful well-liked man to notice if she, his wife, his happy confident wife, gave no sign of unease? They rarely had time for love now, in the old, intimate sense. But they were companions and sometimes plotters together, conspirators.

Could you identify the children if you saw them again Mrs.—?

Yes. I don't know.

What was the color of their skin?

I am not a racist.

How painstakingly she was walking, barefoot! How treacherous the seemingly soft, moist earth, laced with invisible stones and bits of branches! When she left the path, making her way toward the edge of the preserve bordering the road, her feet sank in muck and she had to stifle a scream of panic for what if this were a bog or even quicksand that might swallow her up without a trace!

But she kept going. There was no other way for her except forward.

She had never noticed how, in the woods, there were so many dead trees: dried lifeless stalks from which dried lifeless leaves, last year's leaves, hung in tatters. And the continuous scurrying of invisible birds, animals. And the continuous wind. On all sides mysterious sounds of rustling, stirring, shifting, as if a gigantic organism were defining itself, never quite rising to consciousness. She felt a thrill of deep calm fear, thinking this thought. It was not one she'd ever had before.

At the road she waited. She was prepared to wait for a long time. In the silence of the countryside the approach of a car and its passing and its subsequent retreat were clearly disparate. If she didn't lose her courage at the last moment and if she didn't step down on something sharp she really should have no difficulty getting across the road and hiding in the wooded area beyond.

A car passed, and another. After an interval another. And then there were several in a row, then what sounded like a diesel truck, heaving and sighing, and then there was silence. She peered excitedly out of the underbrush seeing nothing but pavement and the farther side of the road. It was nearly dusk but not quite! A figure running across the road, a figure of pale astonishing female nakedness, might be visible for miles.

She was trembling. With oneiric clarity she saw the distance between herself and her home across which she must fly: saw herself crouching in the ravine at the foot of the hill, waiting. She did not trust her family not to stop loving her should they see her—thus they must not be allowed to see her, or to know!

Stooped almost double she prepared to run. Drew a deep breath as years ago as a girl she would prepare to dive from the high board, eager not merely to dive into the water below but to execute a perfectly calibrated dive, entering the water with the deft grace of a hand slicing a porous surface at a slant, unhesitating. For pride would allow no lesser performance!

She threw herself blindly out of hiding and began to run, her forearms steadying her breasts from beneath, and no dive or flight or plunge or physical ecstasy in her life had prepared her for this effort, running naked and wincing, gasping for breath through her opened mouth, eyes wide and stark and fixed on the farther side of the road, not daring to look elsewhere. And then almost at once she was there, and safe, seemingly, scrambling through a shallow ditch and into the field beyond. But somehow she had cut her foot. Stepped on glass and cut her right foot at the heel.

It's all right she told herself. *You're all right.*

She told herself impatiently, *The bleeding will wash the dirt away.*

She walked on, limping. She wasn't going to examine her foot. To one side there were no houses within sight and to her right there was a farmhouse a short distance away but partly screened by trees and should someone happen to be looking out a window as she passed it would not be self-evident that she was naked. Despite her wildly pounding heart she felt a surge of hope, almost of elation.

She was, and had always been, a woman of principle: a woman who believed in intelligent, considered, but not over-considered action. Everyone who knew her respected her, yes and some who did not know her quite as she knew herself envied her and that too was good, or at least provided satisfaction. She could not be exposed now and would not be, but she would have to guard against waves of panic and faint-headedness and the possibility of losing her way, going in circles, as, once, not so long ago, she'd become lost in the wildlife preserve—doubling back on her trail and crossing it until she realized her error and returned safely to her car. Now that she had crossed the first and most dangerous of the roads she would have to keep it firmly in her mind's eye perpendicular at her back, envisioning the next road (how far away was it?—she did not think it could be far) perpendicular before her.

She would have thought this interior land merely empty but there was much evidence of human intrusion: piles of trash scattered along a farmer's lane as if people came here regularly by night and by stealth to dump their unwanted things—rotted tires, automobile parts, an up-ended refrigerator, a scorched mattress. Like a scavenger, and as eagerly, as unreasonably hopeful, she searched amid the trash for something she could wrap around herself, lifting and dropping a strip of canvas stiff with filth, and what appeared to be a child's playsuit, and other items of clothing that were mere shreds, tatters. She was excited yet dreamy too: standing for a long purposeless moment staring at the debris of strangers, wondering at lives so parallel to her own yet unknown to her. Gnats swarmed about her as if attracted by her very nakedness and the sweaty smell about her. Her right foot throbbed with something like pain but she refused to be drawn into examining it. Vaguely she thought that might be a trick, a trap of a kind.

She walked on, limping, until the farmer's lane ended abruptly in a final pile of trash out of which something scuttled and ran into the underbrush to hide—a rat, judging by its size.

Her head rang with accusations. *How dare you. How dare touch. My skin doesn't define me. My color, my skin.* She was thinking suddenly of her husband and the happiness of his first marriage of which he would never speak except crudely to deny it. As if mere words *now* might erase what had been *then* and, having *been*, flowed inexorably into what *is*. "You must think I'm a fool." Her voice sounded loudly but did not startle her.

Now: should she continue in a straight line across an open field in which swaths of wild rose with their deathly thorns were growing or should she take, thus risking the loss of her sense of direction (the road perpendicular at her back, the next road perpendicular, or approximately, before her), the edge of the field where it might be safer? She had forgotten the children, or nearly. They had nothing to do with her since they hadn't known her and they certainly had nothing to do with her now.

She must have made a decision to make her way along the edge of the field but how slowly she was walking, how timidly—both her feet were bleeding now—thinking how, if she bled, the bleeding would wash away the filth and purify the wounds. Wasn't it puncture wounds in such instances that were dangerous?

She was thinking too what a curiosity it was of female life that, bleeding so frequently, bleeding amid cramps and occasional nausea and faintness, a woman had faith nonetheless that the bleeding would not go on and on until she bled to death. And there was the secrecy of the bleeding—well hidden inside the clothes, always well hidden, discreet and not to be spoken of. Yet how real, such doubleness! She had always liked it really. She would never give it up, no matter that, in a few years, the cycle of her body would shift, and she would not bleed again in that way.

Beyond the field the lane began again, broader now, less rutted and less painful underfoot. She believed she knew the property—an old, inoperative farm—but she did not know the owners. Unless she was emerging at a place she hadn't calculated?

A chill began to lift from the darkening earth. Though the sky was still fairly light, streaked with clouds. And the birds continued to call to one another, more urgently it seemed.

An error now would be fatal.

Not single pains but a wash of pains rose and throbbed in her body. She did not think of them but increasingly they penetrated her consciousness and left her panting, whimpering. Her eyes—her head—her scalp—her belly, buttocks, spine—her feet. Forever would she walk in this no-man's land so strangely close to familiar suburban roads yet hidden from them. The undeveloped still wild countryside, no longer lucrative for farming, not yet sold for residential building, custom-made homes like the one she and her husband lived in—how strange *she* should be *here*. It was a place for death: for nude female bodies: victims of assaults, murders. She was not one of those women.

Yet she might lose her strength and collapse; might faint; and in a day or two or three she would be found comatose, perhaps dead. *A woman's body* it would be reported. *A woman's nude body* would be the initial report. Balloon breasts and fleshy hips and thighs, a patch of dark pubic hair at the fork of the legs, eyes rolled whitely up into the skull.

It happened all the time. Not a person but a body. And all the prior history of her life—her achievement, her winningness, her sunny smile and resolute optimism and her love for her family and theirs for her—would be summarily erased. She would become a story, a fiction.

Thus buoyed by anger she walked faster. In the growing dusk she could not make out whether, at the road, she would encounter a facing house, but the sound of an occasional car meant that the road was ahead and proof that she was not lost.

Then it happened that a dog began barking excitedly close by, and to her horror the animal trotted up the lane as if to attack her, a dun-colored dog the size of a Labrador retriever but of no distinct breed; it barked, it snarled, the hackles on its shoulders were raised; its long clumsy tail thrashed from side to side. She was in terror of dogs since as a young child she'd once been bitten, or so she believed though her mother had assured her she hadn't actually been bitten, only badly frightened by a German shepherd, and now she was seized with panic, backing off and murmuring to the aroused animal words plaintive and submissive—"No. Please. Go home. Go *home*." The dog approached her to within a few yards then stopped, crouching, barking in such a frenzy she supposed its owner would hear, and come out to see what was going on. There was a farmhouse not far away, a hundred yards perhaps from the lane.

As if for her very life she was begging and pleading in an undertone—"Good dog. Nice dog. Go *home*." She wondered if her nakedness excited the dog? If it could smell her fear? The sharp rank animal odor of her helplessness?

She backed off. She picked up a large tree branch, held it threateningly overhead, and backed off. The dog continued to bark but did not follow. Its tail was thrashing energetically—did that mean it might be friendly? But she could not take a chance for as much as the prospect of being attacked by the dog the prospect of having to call for help terrified her.

Some minutes passed. She thought how people would laugh at her—the dog's owner, if he came out into the lane to investigate. A disheveled naked woman confronted by a barking dog, trying to protect herself with a branch. How had her life come to this!

Gradually the dog's barking subsided and it appeared that a crisis of a kind had passed. It allowed her to pass by, then trotted as if indifferently in her wake, nosing about, sniffing at her heels. She felt its damp cool muzzle against her bare legs and the backs of her knees.

Its owner did not appear.

She was nearing home. Crossed the second road in a delirium of a plunge. Running somewhere sliding and staggering downhill. A swampy place. She snatched at bushes to steady her, like a drunken woman; leaves tore off in her fingers.

She should never have married, she was thinking. She'd been happiest alone.

The effort of hypocrisy wearied her.

The need to urinate came suddenly and so violently it was like a knife blade thrust up inside her. She squatted in a place already soft with mud and released a pungent burning liquid from her bladder not in a stream but in tentative little spasms. When she was at last finished she wiped herself awkwardly with a wad of leaves. She was thinking, At least no one has seen.

Her face burned, her hands shook. A memory came to her as if emerging from a previous lifetime of having as a small child squatted in the grass to urinate and watching the liquid streaming from her—the strange helplessness of what was happening to her she could not control. And someone had called to her, to reprimand her. Or had someone laughed at her?

At least, this time, no one had seen.

The house floated in the darkness.

How many hours had passed she did not know. Or if it were a single hour, distended as in a dream.

Why did you do such a thing he was demanding and she said *I do what I want to do* though until that instant she had not known that this was so.

She had had her children after all as she'd determined to have them. She would not have had two children had she not wanted them for one would have done. Two was incontestable proof.

And the stepson who eyed her with suspicion, liking her sometimes and at other times not at all. For he was in no way hers and could not be cajoled into thinking so.

Inside the floating house indistinct figures moved. Some of the windows were lit, others darkened. *Why on earth did you do such a thing* he would ask for it was his right.

There, at the top of the incline, was the house, the rectangular box, in which she lived. She crouched in the underbrush blinking and rubbing her eyes so that she could see clearly for it was crucial now that she see. Was the house hers? Or had she taken a wrong turn, become confused in the dark? She had never seen her house from such a position of course and would not perhaps have identified it. She saw movement by one of the windows—a figure that must have been that of her husband though not quite so tall as she would have imagined her husband—and shortly there came another figure to join him, male or female she could not determine, it must have been the stepson, the fourteen-year-old, and how strange that, seeing him, seeing both of them, having wanted so desperately to get home, she felt no emotion at seeing them, or the indistinct shapes she believed must be them—no more than if they were strangers.

I do what I want to do. So in the dark below the house squatting where no one could see her she waited naked until such time as it would become known to her, why she was waiting.

DONALD HALL

'Ox Cart Man'

Donald Hall's first book of poetry, *Exiles and Marriages* (New York: Viking, 1955), earned him the Edna St. Vincent Millay Award of the Poetry Society of America. Since then, he has written or edited dozens of other books, including a biography of the sculptor Henry Moore, a collection of short stories, two plays, and numerous anthologies. His poetry and prose appear frequently in the *New Yorker*, the *Atlantic*, *Esquire*, *American Scholar*, *Yankee*, and many other periodicals. One of the founding editors of the *Paris Review*, Hall served as poetry editor during the early years of that quarterly, conducting some of the early *Paris Review* interviews with such notable poets as T. S. Eliot, Marianne Moore, and Ezra Pound. His many awards include a Lamont poetry prize and a Guggenheim fellowship.

Educated at Harvard, Oxford, and Stanford, Hall became professor of English at the University of Michigan. In 1975, he moved with his wife, the poet Jane Kenyon, to his old family farm in rural New Hampshire, where the couple has remained ever since.

We conducted this interview through the mail between February and June of 1992. Hall began "Ox Cart Man" in the fall of 1975, producing nearly twenty drafts before submitting the poem to the *New Yorker* in May 1976. "Ox Cart Man" appeared in the October 3, 1977, issue of that magazine; then again, slightly revised, in Hall's volume *Kicking the Leaves* (New York: Harper and Row, 1978) and again later in Hall's tenth volume of poetry, *Old and New Poems* (New York:

Ticknor and Fields, 1990). The poem was also expanded to provide the text for the children's book *Ox-Cart Man* (New York: Viking, 1979), which received the American Library Association's Caldecott Medal in 1980.

The material collected here includes five handwritten drafts, twelve typewritten drafts with Hall's handwritten revisions, a proof of the poem prior to its publication in the *New Yorker*, the *New Yorker* version of the poem, and the version that appeared in *Kicking the Leaves*. The reprint that precedes the interview is the most recent published version from *Old and New Poems*, featuring a slight revision that distinguishes it from its *Kicking the Leaves* predecessor. In addition to the various versions, Hall very generously offered to include the five letters concerning the poem from Howard Moss, Hall's poetry editor at the *New Yorker*. These letters offer a rare opportunity to examine the exchange between a poet and an editor at a major American magazine that has long been famous not only for its influence but also for its editorial inscrutability.

OX CART MAN

In October of the year,
he counts potatoes dug from the brown field,
counting the seed, counting
the cellar's portion out,
and bags the rest on the cart's floor.

He packs wool sheared in April, honey
in combs, linen, leather
tanned from deerhide,
and vinegar in a barrel
hooped by hand at the forge's fire.

He walks by his ox's head, ten days
to Portsmouth Market, and sells potatoes,
and the bag that carried potatoes,
flaxseed, birch brooms, maple sugar, goose
feathers, yarn.

When the cart is empty he sells the cart.
When the cart is sold he sells the ox,
harness and yoke, and walks
home, his pockets heavy
with the year's coin for salt and taxes,

and at home by fire's light in November cold
stitches new harness
for next year's ox in the barn,
and carves the yoke, and saws planks
building the cart again.

INTERVIEW

JW In your interview with the *Paris Review*, you describe hearing the story of the ox-cart man from your cousin Paul Fenton. Were you attracted immediately to this as a subject for a poem?

DH When my cousin Paul Fenton told the ox-cart man's story, it thrilled me—I felt an electric tingle along my spine—and I did not know why. I did not immediately know that I would write out of it, but maybe the next morning I began to draft the poem. The turn in the story is the selling of the ox, which emphasizes Total Dispersal—a phrase I found later at the auction of Paul's son Dennis's cattle farm: the thrilling notion of emptying out, getting rid of absolutely everything. It is thrilling because: *Only if you empty the well will the water return to the well.*

JW What else about this story appealed to you?

DH Surely the subject appealed to me also because I love work and ideas of work. Also, there was something immortal about the story—as if a person could come back again and again, having died, like a perennial plant. Perennial, not immortal.

JW Also in the *PR* interview, you say that "sense of continuity makes for an elegiac poetry." You also once asked Ezra Pound if the artist needs to keep moving. Your life has taken you from Connecticut and New Hampshire to Boston, Europe, the Midwest, and finally back to New Hampshire. I wondered if this return home made you especially receptive to the pattern of the ox-cart man's life, whether your having returned to your family's farm in New Hampshire somehow provided a sense of connection with this story.

DH Oh I have wandered, like many people. I heard this story from Paul shortly after returning to New Hampshire, knowing for the first time that I had come someplace to stay. Perhaps, yes, it struck me so much because of the notion of return.

JW You've described what has become your usual process of composing a poem—beginning with a flat, prosaic language to search, over the course of many drafts, for discoveries and connections to exploit. With "Ox Cart Man," you began already knowing the story the poem was to tell. How did this influence your approach to the poem and its development?

DH Many poems begin for me without any sense of where they will go; then the voyage of revision is pure discovery. But, even when you know where you are going to go, there are things to discover along the way. There are the matters of cadence, and coherence. With this poem, I had a narrative, an external coherence, but I had no idea how I would get to the end of the travel. As you see in the draft, originally I tried a grander or more general conclusion—rather than allowing it to remain implicit. Eventually it became implicit—and then *more* implicit. But all along, maybe the ox-cart's story was connected with my own work as a poet—Total Dispersal, so that the well can fill again. If so, I never knew it as I was writing. This kind of discovery—when you find out years later something about a poem, the fuel that may have fired the poem's engine all along, without your knowledge—it's an excitement.

With this poem I had a lot handed to me. Old stories are wonderful: You gather them from the air. With this poem, I had nothing to invent but strategy and language.

JW And you didn't feel constrained by what you already knew?

DH I would have felt free to alter the story if I had wanted to. The received plot was not a constraint.

JW Do you generally prefer to know less than you did in this case about a poem you're beginning?

DH I cannot say. I wish more people told me such stories! So I guess I wouldn't prefer to know less. Often I've felt great excitement in starting something because I knew nothing—except a phrase, a cadence, and the desire to explore. But even when you know a lot you don't know everything; if you knew *everything* ahead of time you would not write the poem. If we sense, sometimes, that an author knew the poem before the poem began, this sense may define or describe a failed poem.

JW You've discussed and written about your interest in Henry Moore, and quoted Moore as saying, "Never think of a surface except as the extension of a volume." The great number of drafts you do sort of resembles a sculptor chipping away to discover the form that exists within the material. In the case of this poem, I wondered whether knowing the story made you even more aware from the beginning of that form within.

DH Ever since I heard Henry Moore making that sentence, I have looked at words for the pressure at their surface. If the ox-cart man's Total Dispersal, in order to fill up again—his dying into the ground in order to rise up again in the spring—relates to poetry; the relation happens underneath the surface of the words, a volume pressing up from underneath.

The story is the surface. Against this surface a volume extends its pressure, my own psyche forcing itself up to the surface or through it—and into the story, by the language I use and the cadences.

JW You once asked T. S. Eliot, "Would you have chosen the form before you knew quite what you were going to write in it?" How did knowing this story influence your thinking at the very beginning about the prospective poem's form?

DH Form is meaning. When you decide on a form before you know what the poem is about, it's no problem. What a poem's *about* is the least of the matter. With this poem, I have no recollection of thinking ahead of time about its form—length of line, composition into stanzas, length of stanza. I suppose I improvised. In this case my improvisations reached fairly early something like the final look of the poem.

JW Moving now to the actual drafts, I see that the first draft's initial words come quite close to those of the final version. Did you sense initially that these first two lines of the early drafts were closer than others to what you were after? How important is it to you to get those first words nearly right before you can go on?

DH When I answer your questions about composition, you will understand that I am guessing. I cannot really remember what was exactly on my mind, sixteen years ago. I look at a draft and guess—and sometimes it almost seems as if I remember.

Surely my notions governing language (and in one matter the form—the narrowness of it, the relative paucity of detail) came from the impress of laconic New England speech.

The first two lines of the second draft at any rate come close to what I eventually arrived at. I was lucky. Sometimes I fumble for a long time before I find the beginning. The beginning of a poem is of the utmost importance, the *real* beginning—though it may happen halfway through the drafts of a poem. By the real beginning I mean the moment at which you catch the tone; tone proscribes the limits of the vocabulary, the possibilities of diction; in the real beginning, you catch the cadence you are stuck with—length or variety of line, general degree of line break, not to mention degrees of attention to consonance and assonance. At first these limits are not conscious, but they exist in practice; revision makes them conscious. Once you set these limits in your mind, it is like knowing the story ahead of time. You have the guidance of chosen limitations. Of course these choices limit your opportunities; but these choices give you a path to follow.

JW The initial two drafts also seem to reveal that you're not terribly concerned at that point with stanzas or lining strategies. What occupies your attention most at this stage?

DH At the beginning I search for characteristic diction and characteristic cadence, for the defining words and tone. I *listen* for it. When I get something like it, I refine it, and during the rest of the drafts I keep on refining it. My first drafts show me fumbling toward it.

JW The title of these first two drafts is also "*The* Ox Cart Man." Why did you decide to eliminate the article?

DH I don't know. I eliminate articles when I can—maybe sometimes when I can't? I want to get rid of all the little words, and "load every rift with ore."

JW You also seem at times to write on legal-size paper, at other times on regular-size.

DH The size of the page has no significance. I was writing then on yellow legal pads—I still do, from time to time. I used ordinary typing paper when I typed it up.

JW The third draft includes the final title and also shows you've nailed down the first line. Except for the use of the first person, the second line is also in its final form here. In fact, except for alterations in lining, the first stanza is basically complete. What about this early idea you're pursuing here in the final stanza—the idea of the vessel?

DH By the third version I had the cadence. Note that I cut out an article at the beginning of the second line, reaching for that percussive rhythm that characterizes the poem—a rhythm emphasized by noisy consonants—c, p, d, g, c, c.

So: "cellar" is more particular and local and intimate than "winter." I've always had trouble *saying* "cellar" out loud; listeners may hear "seller." I decided to let the printed version assert itself, even though the spoken version might contain an ambiguity. In some poems, when the spoken version is ambiguous because of a homonym, I print it one way and say it another; here I could say "rootcellar" and print "cellar"—but "rootcellar" on the page would make the line too long.

The vessel. I always tend to think of this poem in terms of liquids. "Only if you empty the well will the water return to the well." But why a liquid? I don't know. I like the image—the analogy works—but in this poem I let the story tell itself rather than explaining it in an analogy—or writing an editorial about it.

JW The next draft, number four, shows the five-line stanzas. How did you decide on this form?

DH The form is improvised. Say, I found myself making a first stanza that did its job in five lines, with cadence and length of utterance that pleased me—and so I set out to follow the template that I arrived at. Sometimes it won't work—and I must go back and change the template.

JW You seem in this draft also to be searching for the right details, the objects he loads into his cart and carries to market. What was your primary concern at this stage?

DH I wanted details, the right details. I read about "birch brooms" in a book about colonial times. Some things I knew already. Then I must set the objects in the right order. Heaven knows the sounds of the words—sometimes their percussiveness, as with "flaxseed"—determine them *together* with their accuracy. I could have found seventy-five other things for him to put in the cart.

JW What guided you as you searched for the right details, the right objects for him to carry?

DH Probability and the sound of the word.

JW In the fifth draft, the second stanza seems to begin to take shape, though in the third stanza you've eliminated something you'd later include again: "and the bag that carried potatoes." The fourth stanza is close to the final version. This draft seems to include an interesting shift in your thinking, a movement away from the vessel idea toward something to suggest continuity and repetition. Was this a breakthrough?

DH I think that "continuity and repetition" was always there. They were the shape and attraction of the story to begin with, but the cutting away of other things—like the metaphor of a vessel—allowed this shape to show more clearly. Remove the feathers and you see the bird's shape.

I suppose I eliminated "the bag that carried potatoes" to keep to my stanza-shape. You will see what I eliminated, in the next draft, in order to bring the bag of potatoes *back*. When he sells not only the thing contained but also the container, I foreshadow the sale of the ox-cart after he emptied it.

JW The next draft is the first typewritten one. Does this signal that you've taken a poem to a certain stage of its development?

DH Yes, a typewritten draft. At this time in the history of my writing habits, when I arrived at a stage where the poem stopped moving around on me, I typed a draft. I never liked to type, and held off typing as long as I could, but then I needed to type it up in order to see it. (My handwriting never showed me the poem, as the poem came to finish itself.) The typed draft showed me the visual shape of the poem.

JW Here, again, you've eliminated the final stanza about the vessel, and in fact this draft ends where the final version would, although here the comma (as well as the partial typed stanza at the bottom of the page) indicates you're still searching for something more. At this point were you beginning to sense that you might combine the second and third stanzas?

DH I had been cutting down the final editorial comment even in the draft before this one. Here, I almost get the notion of ending it, as I finally did, with building the cart again . . . but not quite. I reckon I wanted at this time to end with something obviously—too obviously—beautiful.

I don't remember whether at this point I was thinking about combining the second and third stanzas.

JW In the seventh draft, you've put an *X* through stanzas two to four, even though your revisions within those stanzas seem to be moving rapidly toward the poem's final version. What did that *X* signify?

DH In the seventh draft, where I make the big *X*, I wrote a note to myself on the right-hand side of the page, virtually illegible: "Cut to two?" I think I had the notion that my listing was simply too heavy, too many objects, went on too long. . . . I wanted to cut down the numbers of things and let the story tell itself more quickly.

Note also that I cut out "my" four times and substituted the definite article—which I think springs the tone loose, maybe from the particular toward the general, or from the self-regarding toward the fabulous.

JW You've also included a new final stanza.

DH The last stanza of this seventh draft is the one hinted at in the typing at the bottom of the sixth draft. I suspect that we miss some scratch sheets of handwritten revision here.

JW In the eighth draft, you seem concerned mostly with the second and third stanzas. Each draft, in fact, seems to reveal that you focus on discrete challenges in a poem. Is this your usual way of working?

DH In the eighth draft I cut the second draft down in order to make the stanzas more *integral*, finishing cider in the second stanza. This cut allowed me to return "the bag that carried potatoes" to the third stanza.

I don't believe I *chose* to work on the one part of the poem at a time. I saw problems and possible solutions in a localized way, first here and then there.

JW The next draft seems to represent a significant leap forward: the note indicating your decision to use the third person, present tense. What made you decide to switch to the third person?

DH Sometimes I will look at the poem not during my work hours but later in the day. I don't want to work on it then, so I make notes for future work—thus the "he" and "but present tense" notes toward the top of the ninth draft. Later—probably the next morning after making the note at night—I followed my own suggestions.

Some of the details like "linen" had been there earlier in earlier drafts.

Typical: to put words in and take them out and put them back in again—as with the potato bag.

The switch to the third person resembled the switch from "my" to "the." Sometimes the proper tone for a poem *steps back*, making the subject something seen from a distance, as through the wrong end of a telescope. Local particulars diminish; general features become clear.

JW After experimenting in one draft [draft 9] with the past tense, you appear to have decided against it right away. Is this because the past tense undermines the perennial aspect of the narrative—that sense of repetition and continuity?

DH Exactly. The present tense should be luminous here, or even fabulous.

JW The next version shows continued work on the second and third stanzas. What was the hardest part about getting them right?

DH My problem in the order of details had nothing to do with meaning, nothing semantic in the sequence, but with the cadence and the voice of detail.

JW Apart from the slight revision, changing "scent" to "cry," you seem to have continued to leave the final stanza untouched. Did this represent an ambivalence about the ending?

DH It's interesting that later Howard Moss wanted me to turn "cry" back into "scent." By the time I was arguing with him, I didn't remember that I had ever thought of "scent." (I scorned his suggestion!) I wrote "cry" not only for noisy synaesthesia but for assonance with the first syllable of the last word.

I didn't feel ambivalent about that ending—later rejected. At the time, I thought it was the best thing in the poem! Watch out for what you think is best.

JW In the thirteenth draft, you exchange "linen" and "yarn," and except for the inclusion of the final stanza, the poem is virtually complete. Does your signature at the bottom of the poem indicate that you sensed the poem was nearly complete at this point?

DH In the thirteenth draft, I changed the positions of "linen" and "yarn" because—saying the poem aloud—I could *hold* the last three letters of "yarn," almost singing it.

The signature at the bottom means I was showing it to someone, or even thinking of sending it to a magazine.

JW The next draft is another clean draft—another break from the poem? If so, how long will you generally let a poem "cure" before returning to it? Or, more to the point, how long did this sit before you went back to it again?

DH It's a clean draft because I wanted to see it as finished. Every draft is a final draft, after a while. But I know from experience that I will probably keep on tinkering.

I first show my poems to my wife, Jane Kenyon. Then I mail them to friends. At some point—usually after my friends have given me verdicts—I type it up clean again and send it out to a magazine.

I don't know how long I waited on this—or if I waited very long at all. It interests and amuses me to realize that I have been lying about this poem for years. (When I talk about process, I always emphasize how long it takes me, how arduous the process is, and how much I love it—but often I admit that all poets lie about their processes, and add that therefore I must be lying too.) I've said for years that it took me two years to write this poem, and at least fifty or sixty drafts. Well, we have found something like nineteen drafts, and if anything is missing it's not *much*. I began writing the poem no earlier than September of 1975, my first year back in New Hampshire. Paul Fenton told me the story in the autumn, I'm certain, and apparently I mailed the poem to the *New Yorker* the next spring, May of 1976. So it took me eight months at the longest. Well, I did fiddle with it afterwards, partly at the *New Yorker*'s suggestion.

JW In the fifteenth draft, you decide to omit the final stanza, and you include some notes to yourself about the poem. "I'm pretty sure about omitting the last stanza—it's fidgety. And redundant." How hard was it to reach the point where you could let go of the idea of going beyond the previous stanza?

DH These are not my comments on the poem. These are Louis Simpson's, and as you can see he helped me a lot. Louis was right about the unnaturalness of "by ox head," and I should have made it "the ox's head" as he suggests, or (as I have it now) "his ox's head." Louis's comments were probably in the summer or early autumn of 1976—because I think he suggested omitting the last stanza *after* Howard Moss told me that there was something wrong with it. I mentioned Louis's suggestion to Moss in our correspondence.

JW The next [sixteenth] draft shows you trying to find the right rhythm for the last line. What guided you here?

DH Having decided to eliminate the final stanza, I didn't admire the concluding cadence of "to build the cart again," maybe because it's too solidly iambic trimeter. I needed something to provide a finality. The simple change of an infinitive into a participle seemed to do the trick.

JW At this point, when the poem was virtually complete, would you have set it aside for a while or sent it to the *New Yorker*? Or do you send things through an agent?

DH I send my poems out myself. My agent would do it for me, but I know the market better than he does, and I enjoy handling things myself. Frequently I send poems to the *New Yorker* before I send them elsewhere. Lots of people read a poem there; and they pay a bit more than other people do.

This may have been the draft that I sent the *New Yorker* when I made the final revision after they had bought the poem. As you can see from Howard Moss's letters to me, I sent him a draft of the poem in May of 1976. He was about to go on vacation and asked me to send the poem back again in September.

Which I did, for you see his letter of October 21. I must have asked him in my letter whether I should say "ox head" or "the ox's head." How did I ever lose the article, for *Kicking the Leaves*? I went through an article-destroying phase during the latter portions of work on that book. There are a lot of telegraphic phrases in there. Both Jane Kenyon and Galway Kinnell, I remember distinctly, warned me that I was sounding too damned much like Samuel F. B. Morse.

You will note Howard's "grave doubts" about the last line. Naturally enough he objected to the phrase I liked best in the poem—"cry of lilac." (Incidentally, I have found a place in another poem to say that "bees wake, roused by the cry of lilac." It's in "Daylilies on the Hill," which I've published in a magazine but not yet in a book.) Note how Howard, having taken the poem, now tries yelling and screaming to get me to change this last line.

Maybe it was about now that I received the note from Louis Simpson which we spoke about earlier. When I first read Louis's suggestion about omitting the last stanza, I thought it was ridiculous: "It's the best part, etc., etc." But Louis is a genius about narrative. He was absolutely right. When, in the original final stanza, I completed the circle, I insulted the reader; writing a circle-poem for grown-ups, you do not make the circle complete; you do something like the capital *C* and you leave it to the reader to make the circle whole by turning a *C* into an *O*. People don't literally feel insulted but bored: "I knew this was coming." However, when you write for five-year-olds you are allowed to complete the circle. In the children's book about the ox-cart man, a child can turn from the last page back to the first page and start it all over again.

As you can see, I argued fiercely with Howard about "cry" versus "scent." It seems fairly typical of the *New Yorker* that it would avoid the loud obviousness of synaesthesia and assonance in favor of something more tame and/or tepid like "scent." Of course I had originally written "scent" myself.

In his letter to me dated the tenth of November, taking the new solution, Howard actually goes into literary criticism in his first paragraph. Editors rarely do that.

JW The final *New Yorker* proof shows that you've decided to change "ox head" to "ox's head." Do the other marks on this version reflect conversations with editors? Someone appears to have been concerned as to whether "deerhide" is a word—"(not in Web)." Also the question of whether to hyphenate "Ox Cart" in the title, and whether to include a comma after "harness."

DH The *New Yorker* is writer-friendly. They make suggestions; they even implore you on bended knee to make changes—but finally they will let you do what you want to do.

I have found editorial suggestions useful from time to time over the years: Howard Moss, Alice Quinn, M. L. Rosenthal, Robert Pinsky, Mary Jo Salter.

JW The only other revision to this poem I'm aware of is the small one that occurred between the time the poem was collected in *Kicking the Leaves* and the time it was included in *Old and New Poems*: you revise "ox's head" to "his ox's head." Is it difficult, if not impossible, for you to reread any of your poems, years after they've been published, without wanting to make changes?

DH Yes, I keep wanting to tinker. In the margins of the book that I read from, when I do my poetry readings, I write continual small changes. Not long after *Kicking the Leaves* came out, I added "his" to my line about the ox's head. When I did *Old and New Poems* I was able to put this change into print.

JW The writing of this poem seems to recapitulate the challenge facing the ox-cart man: like his cart, the poem can only hold so much, and only what's absolutely essential. When you first heard the story of the ox-cart man, did it strike you immediately as, among other things, an analogy to writing poems, or was this a sense that developed as the poem did?

DH No, when I first heard the story it did not strike me as an analogy to writing poetry. Now I believe that it is—and maybe something inside me always knew. For years and years, I have told everybody—including myself—that when you write a poem you should bring everything to it that you know. I've quoted Galway Kinnell, who told me decades ago that he only respected poems to which the poet brought everything that had ever happened. You should never hold anything back. You should let everything go, and put everything that you know into the writing of every single poem. "Only if you empty the well will the water return to the well." I never thought of this analogy until after the poem was finished—and someone else suggested it.

JW I'm interested in how this idea of emptying the well relates to something you've addressed in your essay on two of your early teachers, Archibald MacLeish and Yvor Winters. In "Rocks and Whirlpools," you describe the condition of "busy laziness" that sometimes afflicts those who "put in their hours and with[hold] their spirits." How does the young writer who is concerned with craft and form, as well as with what Faulkner called "the eternal verities of the heart," distinguish between effective well-emptying and mere compulsiveness? This seems to me to be one of the hardest things to learn—how to get beyond just scratching at the surface, how to learn to make your revisions dig deeper.

DH Henry Moore quoted Rodin, advice an old craftsman gave him when Rodin was young; it was, more or less, "When something's not going right, don't keep making little changes in your model; drop it on the floor and see what it looks like then."

Well, in this one I could just keep picking at it. With other poems, I have often dropped them on the floor. Sometimes I begin over again with a new form of line or of stanza; sometimes I change narrative strategy, or point of view, or person, or the sex of the protagonist. Often I switch from history to fiction; or telling a lie sometimes liberates language and imagination.

JW You said in the *PR* interview that while the poem took you two years to write, the text for the children's book *Ox Cart Man* took only a couple of hours. Did you see the children's book as an opportunity (finally, after the rigorous process of paring down for the poem) to pursue the impulse you felt to go beyond the rebuilding of the cart?

DH In that interview I exaggerated; or maybe I *lied* . . . a little. Certainly the children's book was relatively easy—sometimes they take endless drafts—maybe because I had thought so much about the story.

I remember the occasion. My daughter was visiting—not a child, nineteen or twenty years old—but maybe her presence allowed me to think of the story as something for children. I had the sudden notion that if I took Paul's story and treated it differently (adding a whole family, which was there in Paul's version, and completing the circle), it might make a picture book. The solid shape of the circle was good for a kid's book, and for the mythic or archetypal nature of the story.

JW You once asked Ezra Pound whether he believed a poet's greatest quality was formal or a quality of thinking? Observing how you work, I wonder whether, at this point in your writing life, you see these qualities as distinct.

DH You're right. It is a *quality* of thinking—to think in formal terms, about wholeness of shape, about resolution, about marching to a particular tune. The tune is the thinker.

JW You've written about and discussed a number of older poets you had the opportunity to meet and get to know—Pound and Eliot, Dylan Thomas, Marianne Moore, Robert Frost. Am I wrong in thinking that this is a poem that perhaps Frost might have particularly admired?

DH I can't say that Frost would have liked it. After all, it's written in free verse, like playing tennis without a net.

JW In your *PR* interview with T. S. Eliot, you and he discussed the importance of common speech in poetry, and how common speech was being influenced by television. How do you think common speech has changed in the years since you spoke with Eliot, and what significance does that hold for poets?

DH Common speech changes. I have hope now that pockets of locality may resist the onslaught of the airwaves, and maybe ethnic enclaves, maybe the vitality of immigrant speech. Common speech will need to absorb Cambodian habits of thought, Russian, Haitian.

JW One of the most remarkable things about "Ox Cart Man," I think, is that it somehow manages to suggest a kind of traditional, old-fashioned, Yankee laconism using a language and syntax that seems to consist largely of contemporary common speech. "November cold" seems to me to be the only phrase that even remotely suggests an anachronistic syntax. Was this hard to pull off?

DH I suppose that "November cold" is a bit poetical. Maybe "November's cold" would improve it. Maybe I should make another note in the margin of my book.

The Ox Cart Man

In the fall of the year I count my potatoes for winter,
& put what I have left over in my cart.
The sheep's wool cut in the spring
Shingles I made in the evening
leather I tanned

I back my ox into the ox cart, & walk beside
a hundred miles to Portsmouth
and at market I sell potatoes, turnips, apples,
leather

when ~~I~~ my cart is empty I sell my cart
when my cart is gone I sell my ox
my ox and halter & the leather harness I stitched

then I walk home, my pockets full of the year's coin

and at home by the fire, as the night grows cold
I stitch leather for new harness
I cut planks to build my new cart
I teach the young ox new manners

and in spring I cut the sheep
and plant seed potatoes

however I have done this before I will do.
this again everything that I do is the product
of everything that I have done

and in March I tap the sugar ~~maple~~ trees,
and in April I shear the wool
from sheep who grow ~~their~~ their wool all over again,
and in May I plant ~~my~~ crops
while the bees wake up, ~~& fly to their old flowers.~~

~~smelling~~
~~dazzled with~~
~~overcome~~ by the scent ~~of roses~~
roused by ~~sweet~~ lilac.

~~sun's cold~~
~~day.~~

The Ox Cart Man

In the fall of the year
I count the potatoes brought in from the stubble field
I save ~~them~~ around potatoes a day for the winter family
in my ox cart I put the rest of the potatoes

in the ox cart I put wool sheared in the spring
I put cloth my wife wove
from the wool she spun, and shingles
I made in spring,
leather tanned ~~..~~ winter and summer,
carrots & cabbages ~~in~~ in barrels
I ~~..~~ hooped with metal ~~from~~ beat at my own forge

I walk beside my ox in front of my ox cart
a hundred miles to Portsmouth market
and I sell ~~[illegible]~~ my potatoes
and the barrel that carried potatoes,

aprons and nails, turnips, leather,

and when my cart is empty I sell my cart
and when my cart is taken I sell my ox,
~~and~~ his harness and ox bow,

and walk home, pockets full of the year's coin
for salt and ~~cotton~~ taxes,

and at home by fire's light, when nights grow cold,
I stitch new harness

for next year's ox,
~~from the hide of scraps of deer hide~~
I cut planks to build my next year's cart,
I teach manners to the ox of next year's journey,

after ~~cuttings~~ shearing wool in another spring
and planting the seed potatoes, knowing

I did this before, I will do it again,
and everything done is the product of everything done
and we empty the vessel, & set the vessel down,
knowing that it must fill.

Ox Cart Man

In October of the year,
I count potatoes dug from the brown field,
counting the seed, counting the cellar's ~~winter's~~ portion out,
~~and bag the rest~~
~~in bags on the cart's floor.~~
and bag the rest on the cart's floor.

Then I pack in
~~[illegible] them I stow~~ wool sheared from the sheep in April,
and cloth my wife wove from thread ~~wool~~ she spun,
~~and~~ shingles I carved ~~made~~ in winter,
leather tanned from the hides of deer and cattle,
apples, carrots, cabbages, honey in combs,
~~[illegible]~~ last year's cider in the vinegar barrel
hooped by own hand at the forge's fire.

I walk beside my ox, ten days' walk in the frost,
to Portsmouth market, and sell potatoes,
and the bag ~~sewn to~~ that carried them, ~~potatoes,~~ aprons & nails,
turnips, & smoked hams, bacon, ~~and~~ salt pork.

When my cart is empty I sell my cart.
When my cart is gone ~~hauled away~~ I sell my ox,
I sell his harness and yoke,
and walk home, my pockets full of the year's coins
for salt and taxes, for the Christmas orange.

At home by the fire's light, in November ~~when the nights~~ cold,
I stitch new harness
for the young ox in the barn.

I cut planks to ~~my~~ build ~~my~~ the ~~ox~~ cart again,
in the spring I shear new wool,
and plant my seed potatoes, always knowing

I did this before, I will do it again,
~~and everything new is the product of everything old,~~
~~and the new is the old very soon,~~
and we empty the vessel, and set the vessel down,
~~waiting for it to fill:~~

certain that it ~~will~~ must fill.

Ox Cart Man

In October of the year
I count potatoes dug from the brown field,
counting the seed, counting
the cellar's portion out,
and bag the rest on the cart's floor.

Then [in my cart] I pack ~~in~~ wool
sheared from the sheep in April, and cloth
my wife wove from thread she spun,
~~and~~ shingles I carved [all] winter,
leather tanned from the hides

of deer and cattle, [linen, flaxseed,] apples,
carrots, cabbages, honey in combs,
and last year's cider
in the vinegar barrel
hooped by my own hand at the forge's fire.

I walk by my ox, ten days
1. ~~walk in the frost~~ to Portsmouth market,
2. and sell potatoes [the potatoes,] / aprons, & birch brooms, /
3. and the bag that carried ~~them,~~ ~~aprons & nails,~~
4 ~~turnips,~~ smoked hams, ~~salt pork~~ goose feathers.
5 [turnips,]

When my cart is empty I sell my cart.
When my cart is gone I sell my ox,
harness and yoke,
and walk home, pockets full of the year's coins
for salt and taxes, for the Christmas orange.

And at home by fire's light, in November cold,
I stitch new harness
for ~~the young~~ next year's ox in the barn,
I carve his yoke, I cut planks
to build a cart again,

and in spring I shear new wool
~~and plant the seed potatoes, knowing~~
~~I did this before, I will do it again,~~
~~and~~ we empty the vessel, and set the ~~[illegible]~~ vessel down,
~~certain~~ that it must fill.
only ~~[illegible]~~

from sheep who grow it all over again,
and I plant ~~the~~ my seed potatoes, knowing

~~and in spring I plo~~

and in spring I shear new wool
from sheep who grow their wool all over again,
~~plant flax, plant seed~~
plant potatoes and flax, knowing
we empty the vessel, & set the vessel down,
only that it fill.

watching
the ~~empty~~ emptied vessel fill

Ox Cart Man

In October of the year
I count potatoes dug from the brown field,
counting the seed, counting
the cellar's portion out,
and bag the rest on the cart's floor.

I pack wool sheared in April,
spun yarn, honey in combs, ~~split &~~
~~shingles~~, leather tanned from deerhide,
and last year's cider
in the vinegar barrel

hooped by hand at the forge's fire.
I walk by ox head ten days
to Portsmouth Market, and sell potatoes,
flaxseed, ~~linen~~, birch brooms, maple sugar,
~~sugar~~, goose feathers.

When the cart is empty I sell the cart.
When the cart is gone I sell the ox,
harness & yoke,
and walk home, pockets full
of the year's coin for salt & taxes,

and at home by fire's light in November cold
stitch new harness
for next year's ox in the barn,
and carve ~~his~~ the yoke, and saw planks
to build the cart again,

~~He packed wool~~
~~sheared in April, and spun yarn,~~
~~shingles split all winter,~~
~~leather tanned from hides of deer,~~
~~linen, honey in combs,~~

He packed wool sheared in April,
spun yarn, honey in combs,
split shingles, leather tanned from deerhide,
and last year's cider
in the vinegar barrel

hooped by hand at the forge's fire.
He walked by ox head ten days
to Portsmouth Market, & sold potatoes,
~~and the to~~ flaxseed, birch brooms, maple
sugar, goose feathers.

Ox Cart Man

In October of the year
I count potatoes dug from the brown field,
counting the seed, counting
the cellar's portion out,
and bag the rest on the cart's floor.

Then in my cart I pack wool
sheered from the sheep in April, and cloth
my wife wove from thread she spun,
shingles I ~~carved~~ all winter, split /
leather tanned from the hides

of deer and cattle, linen, flaxseed, apples,
~~carrots,~~ cabbages, honey in combs,
and last year's cider
in the vinegar barrel
hooped by ~~my own~~ hand at the forge's fire.

I walk by ~~my~~ ox, ten days to Portsmouth Market,
and sell potatoes,
and the bag that carried the potatoes,
aprons, birch brooms,
shingles, ~~smoked hams,~~ turnips, goose feathers.

When my cart is empty I sell my cart.
When my cart is gone I sell my ox,
harness and yoke,
and walk home, pockets full of the year's coin
for salt and taxes, for the Christmas orange,

And at home by fire's light in November cold
I stitch new harness
for next year's ox in the barn,
I carve his yoke, I cut planks
to build a cart again,

~~and in April I sheer new wool~~
~~from sheep who grew their wool all over again,~~
~~plant potatoes, plant flax, knowing~~
~~we empty the vessel, and set the vessel down,~~
~~only that it fill.~~

maple sugar:

tap the trees busting with sap, and hear
the bees wake up, making sweetness again....

OX CART MAN

In October of the year
I count potatoes dug from the brown field,
counting the seed, counting
the cellar's portion out,
and bag the rest on the cart's floor.

~~[illegible]~~
I pack wool sheered
from ~~the~~ sheep in April, and cloth
~~my~~ wife wove from ~~thread she~~ spun,
shingles I split all winter,
leather tanned from the hides

of deer, linen, ~~flaxseed~~, ~~apples~~,
cabbages, honey in combs,
and last year's cider
in the vinegar barrel
hooped by hand at the forge's fire.

I walk by the ox's head, ten days
to Portsmouth Market, and sell potatoes,
and the bag that carried potatoes,
~~aprons~~, birch brooms,
maple sugar, ~~turnips~~, goose feathers.

When ~~my~~ cart is empty I sell ~~my~~ cart.
When ~~my~~ cart is gone I sell ~~my~~ ox,
harness and yoke,
and walk home, pockets full of the year's coin,
for salt and taxes, ~~for the Christmas orange~~,

and at home by fire's light in November cold
stitch new harness
for next year's ox in the barn,
and carve his yoke, and ~~cut~~ planks
to build a cart again,

and in March tap ~~the~~ sugar trees,
and in April sheer new wool
from sheep ~~who~~ that grew it all over again,
and in May plant ~~crops~~
~~while the~~ bees wake, roused by the ~~cry~~ of lilac.

OX CART MAN

In October of the year
I count potatoes dug from the brown field,
counting the seed, counting
the cellar's portion out,
and bag the rest on the cart's floor.

I pack wool sheered in April,
spun yarn, honey in combs, leather
tanned from deerhide,
and last year's cider
in the vinegar barrel

hooped by hand at the forge's fire.
I walk by ox head ten days
to Portsmouth Market, and sell potatoes,
and the bag that carried potatoes,
flaxseed, birch brooms, maple sugar,
goose feathers.

When the cart is empty I sell the cart.
When the cart is sold I sell the ox,
harness and yoke,
and walk home, pockets full
of the year's coin for salt and taxes,

and at home by fire's light in November cold
stitch new harness
for next year's ox in the barn,
and carve the yoke, and saw planks
to build the cart again,

and in March tap sugar trees
and in April sheer wool
from sheep that grew it all over again
and in May plant potatoes
as bees wake, roused by the scent of lilac.

OX CART MAN

In October of the year
I count potatoes dug from the brown field,
counting the seed, counting
the cellar's portion out
and bag the rest on the cart's floor.

I pack wool sheared in April,
spun yarn, honey in combs, leather
tanned from deerhide,
and last year's cider,in the vinegar barrel
hooped by hand at the forge's fire.

I walk by ox head ten days
to Portsmouth Market, and sell potatoes
and the bag that carried potatoes,
flaxseed, birch brooms, maple sugar,
goose feathers.

When the cart is empty I sell the cart.
When the cart is sold I sell the ox,
harness and yoke,
and walk home, pockets full
of the year's coin for salt and taxes,

and at home by fire's light in November cold
stitch new harness
for next year's ox in the barn,
and carve the yoke, and saw planks
to build the cart again

and in March tap sugar trees
and in April shear wool
from sheep that grew it all over again
and in May plant potatoes
as bees wake, roused by the scent of lilac.

OX CART MAN

In October of the year
I count potatoes dug from the brown field,
counting the seed, counting
the cellar's portion out
and bag the rest on the cart's floor.

I pack wool sheared in April,
spun yarn, honey in combs, leather
tanned from deerhide,
and last year's cider in the vinegar barrel
hooped by hand at the forge's fire.

I walk by ox head ten days
to Portsmouth Market, and sell potatoes
and the bag that carried potatoes,
flaxseed, birch brooms, maple sugar,
goose feathers.

When the cart is empty I sell the cart.
When the cart is sold I sell the ox,
harness and yoke,
and walk home, pockets full
of the year's coin for salt and taxes,

and at home by fire's light in November cold
stitch new harness
for next year's ox in the barn,
and carve the yoke, and saw planks
to build the cart again

and in March tap sugar trees
and in April shear wool
from sheep that grew it all over again
and in May plant potatoes
as bees wake, roused by the scent of lilac.

OX CART MAN

In October of the year
He counts potatoes dug from the brown field,
couàting the seed, counting
the cellar's portion out
and bag the rest on the car's floor.

He packs wool sheared in April,'
yarn, honey in combs, leahher
tanned from deerhide,
and last year's cider, in the vinegar barrel
hooped by hand at the forge's fire.

He walks by ox head ten days
to Portsmouth Market, and sells potatoes
and the bag that carried potatoes,
flaxseed, birch brooms, maple sugar,
goose feathers.

When the cart is empty he sells the cart.
When the cart is sold he sells the ox,
harness and yoke,
and walks home, pockets full
of the year's coin for salt and taxes,

and at home by fire's light in November cold
stitches new harness
for next year's ox in the barn,
and carves the yoke, and saws planks
to build the cart again

and in March taps sugar trees
and in April shears wool
from sheep that grew it all over again
and in May plants potatoes
as bees wake, roused by the scent of lilac.

OX CART MAN

In October of the year
He counts potatoes dug from the brown field,
counting the seed, counting
the cellar's portion out
and bags the rest on the cart's floor.

He packs wool sheared in April, [honey]
yarn, honey in combs, leather [yarn,]
tanned from deerhide,
and last year's cider, in the [a] vinegar barrel
hooped by hand at the forge's fire.

He walks by ox head ten days
to Portsmouth Market, and sells potatoes
and the bag that carried potatoes,
flaxseed, birch brooms, maple sugar, [goose]
goose feathers, [linen.]

When the cart is empty he sells the cart.
When the cart is sold he sells the ox,
harness and yoke,
and walks home, pockets full
of the year's coin for salt and taxes,

and at home by fire's light in November cold
stitches new harness
for next year's ox in the barn,
and carves the yoke, and saws planks
to build the cart again

and in March taps sugar trees
and in April shears wool
from sheep that grew it all over again
and in May plants potatoes
as bees wake, roused by the [redacted]t of lilac.
[cry]

OX CART MAN

In October of the year,
he counts potatoes dug from the brown field,
counting the seed, counting
the cellar's portion out,
and bags the rest on the cart's floor.

He packs wool sheared in April, honey
in combs, ~~yarn,~~ linen, leather
tanned from deerhide,
and vinegar in a barrel
hooped by hand at the forge's fire.

He walks by ox head, ten days
to Portsmouth Market, and sells potatoes,
and the bag that carried potatoes,
flaxseed, birch brooms, maple sugar, goose
feathers, ~~linen.~~ yarn.

When the cart is empty he sells the cart.
When the cart is sold he sells the ox,
harness and yoke, and walks
home, his pockets heavy
with the year's coin for salt and taxes,

and at home by fire's light in November cold
stitches new harness
for next year's ox in the barn,
and carves the yoke, and saws planks
to build the cart again,

and in March taps sugar trees,
and in April shears wool
from sheep that grew it all over again,
and in May plants potatoes
as bees wake, roused by the cry of lilac.

Donald Hall

OX CART MAN

In October of the year,
he counts potatoes dug from the brown field,
counting the seed, counting
the cellar's portion out,
and bags the rest on the cart's floor.

He packs wool sheared in April, honey
in combs, linen, leather
tanned from deerhide,
and vinegar in a barrel
hooped by hand at the forge's fire.

He walks by ox head, ten days
to Portsmouth Market, and sells potatoes,
and the bag that carried potatoes,
flaxseed, birch brooms, maple sugar, goose
feathers, yarn.

When the cart is empty he sells the cart.
When the cart is sold he sells the ox,
harness and yoke, and walks
home, his pockets heavy
with the year's coin for salt and taxes,

and at home by fire's light in November cold
stitches new harness
for next year's ox in the barn,
and carves the yoke, and saws planks
to build the cart again,

and in March taps sugar trees,
and in April shears wool
from sheep that grew it all over again,
and in May plants potatoes
as bees wake, roused by the cry of lilac.

OX CART MAN

In October of the year,
he counts potatoes dug from the brown field,
counting the seed, counting
the cellar's portion out,
and bags the rest on the cart's floor.

He packs wool sheared in April, honey
in combs, linen, leather
tanned from deerhide,
and vinegar in a barrel
hooped by hand at the forge's fire.

He walks <u>by ox head</u>, ten days
to Portsmouth Market, and sells potatoes,
and the bag that carried potatoes,
flaxseed, birch brooms, maple sugar, goose
feathers, yarn.

An odd phrase.
Is it better than
"by the ox's head"?

When the cart is empty he sells the cart.
When the cart is sold he sells the ox,
harness and yoke, and walks
home, his pockets heavy
with the year's coin for salt and taxes,

and at home by fire's light in November cold
stitches new harness
for next year's ox in the barn,
and carves the yoke, and saws planks
to build the cart again.

This strikes me as
the place to stop.

and in March taps sugar trees,
and in April shears wool
from sheep that grew it all over again,
and in May plants potatoes
as bees wake, roused by the cry of lilac.

omit

Very well finished. No big cracks
that I can see. I'm pretty sure
about omitting the last stanza—
it's fidgety. And redundant.

OX CART MAN

In October of the year,
he counts potatoes dug from the brown field,
counting the seed, counting
the cellar's portion out,
and bags the rest on the cart's floor.

He packs wool sheared in April, honey
in combs, linen, leather
tanned from deerhide,
and vinegar in a barrel
hooped by hand at the forge's fire.

He walks by ox head, ten days
to Portsmouth Market, and sells potatoes,
and the bag that carried potatoes,
flaxseed, birch brooms, maple sugar, goose
feathers, yarn.

When the cart is empty he sells the cart.
When the cart is sold he sells the ox,
harness and yoke, and walks
home, his pockets heavy
with the year's coin for salt and taxes,

and at home by fire's light in November cold
stitches new harness
for next year's ox in the barn,
and carves the yoke, and saws planks
~~to build the cart again,~~

~~and in March taps sugar trees,~~
~~and in April shears wool~~
~~from sheep that grew it all over again,~~
~~and in May plants potatoes~~
~~as bees wake, roused by the cry of lilac.~~

to make
build the new cart.

Build

~~building another cart~~

building the cart again.

building the new cart

OX CART MAN

In October of the year,
he counts potatoes dug from the brown field,
counting the seed, counting
the cellar's portion out,
and bags the rest on the cart's floor.

He packs wool sheared in April, honey
in combs, linen, leather
tanned from deerhide,
and vinegar in a barrel
hooped by hand at the forge's fire.

He walks by ox head, ten days
to Portsmouth Market, and sells potatoes,
and the bag that carried potatoes,
flaxseed, birch brooms, maple sugar, goose
feathers, yarn.

When the cart is empty he sells the cart.
When the cart is sold he sells the ox,
harness and yoke, and walks
home, his pockets heavy
with the year's coin for salt and taxes,

and at home by fire's light in November cold
stitches new harness
for next year's ox in the barn,
and carves the yoke, and saws planks
building the cart again.

G NY'r A-331—RRD 150

JAN. 21, 1977—M—HANDLE M—OC—PREFERABLY OCTOBER

OX CART MAN

In October of the year,
he counts potatoes dug from the brown field,
counting the seed, counting
the cellar's portion out,
and bags the rest on the cart's floor.

He packs wool sheared in April, honey
in combs, linen, leather
tanned from deerhide,
and vinegar in a barrel
hooped by hand at the forge's fire.

He walks by the ox's head ten days
to Portsmouth Market, and sells potatoes,
and the bag that carried potatoes,
flaxseed, birch brooms, maple sugar, goose
feathers, yarn.

When the cart is empty he sells the cart.
When the cart is sold he sells the ox,
harness and yoke, and walks
home, his pockets heavy
with the year's coin for salt and taxes,

and, at home by fire's light in November cold,
stitches new harness
for next year's ox in the barn,
and carves the yoke, and saws planks,
building the cart again.

—Donald Hall

OX CART MAN

In October of the year,
he counts potatoes dug from the brown field,
counting the seed, counting
the cellar's portion out,
and bags the rest on the cart's floor.

He packs wool sheared in April, honey
in combs, linen, leather
tanned from deerhide,
and vinegar in a barrel
hooped by hand at the forge's fire.

He walks by the ox's head ten days
to Portsmouth market, and sells potatoes,
and the bag that carried potatoes,
flaxseed, birch brooms, maple sugar, goose
feathers, yarn.

When the cart is empty he sells the cart.
When the cart is sold he sells the ox,
harness, and yoke, and walks
home, his pockets heavy
with the year's coin for salt and taxes,

and, at home by fire's light in November cold,
stitches new harness
for next year's ox in the barn,
and carves the yoke, and saws planks,
building the cart again.

—Donald Hall

Ox Cart Man

In October of the year,
he counts potatoes dug from the brown field,
counting the seed, counting
the cellar's portion out,
and bags the rest on the cart's floor.

He packs wool sheared in April, honey
in combs, linen, leather
tanned from deerhide,
and vinegar in a barrel
hooped by hand at the forge's fire.

He walks by ox's head, ten days
to Portsmouth Market, and sells potatoes,
and the bag that carried potatoes,
flaxseed, birch brooms, maple sugar, goose
feathers, yarn.

When the cart is empty he sells the cart.
When the cart is sold he sells the ox,
harness and yoke, and walks
home, his pockets heavy
with the year's coin for salt and taxes,

and at home by fire's light in November cold
stitches new harness
for next year's ox in the barn,
and carves the yoke, and saws planks
building the cart again.

THE
NEW YORKER
25 WEST 43RD STREET
NEW YORK, N. Y. 10036

EDITORIAL OFFICES
OXFORD 5-1414

May 29, 1976

TO OUR CONTRIBUTORS:

The poetry department will be closed from June 4th through September 6th. Only poems that are topical or scheduled for imminent book publication should be submitted during this period.

THE EDITORS

THE
NEW YORKER
25 WEST 43RD STREET
NEW YORK, N. Y. 10036

EDITORIAL OFFICES
OXFORD 5-1414

1 June 1976

Dear Donald,

We like OX CART MAN, but we're so jammed up at the moment, and so close to closing down that I wonder if we might ask you to re-submit it in September, if it's still available.

I hope you will, and thanks for sending it to us. In the meanwhile, I hope you have a good summer. You seem to be having a marvellous year.

Best wishes,

Howard

Howard

Mr. Donald Hall
Eagle Pond Farm
Danbury, New Hampshire 03230

THE
NEW YORKER
25 WEST 43RD STREET
NEW YORK, N. Y. 10036

EDITORIAL OFFICES
OXFORD 5-1414

21 October 1976

Dear Donald,

I'm happy to say we want to take OX-CART MAN, and I think "He walks by the ox's head" is clearer.

We have grave doubts about the last line, and have two suggestions. Either to end the poem with "and in May plants potatoes," completing the cycle. Or changing the word "cry" in the last line to "scent" or something like. That's what we object to most, I guess, the phrase "cry of lilac."

Could you let me know how you feel about this? And I'll hold off putting the poem through until I hear from you.

Thanks for sending this back. It was good and patient of you to wait. And I look forward to new poems.

Best wishes,

Howard
Howard

Mr. Donald Hall
Eagle Pond Farm
Danbury, New Hampshire 03230

THE
NEW YORKER
25 WEST 43RD STREET
NEW YORK, N. Y. 10036

EDITORIAL OFFICES
OXFORD 5-1414

10 November 1976

Dear Donald,

The more I think about it -- and the more I reread the poem -- it seems to me that Louis may be right: the poem should end with the penultimate stanza. It completes the cycle, suggests that the poem is about to start all over again, and seems a perfect place to end the poem. The three "and"s in the last stanza may be a clue to that; they introduce a coda consisting mainly of a catalogue of seasonal actions, but they are all implicit in the rebuilding of the cart. And so I'd be for -- if you would -- cutting the last stanza.

On the other hand, we'll print the last stanza if you like, and also "cry" in place of our suggested "scent." It's true it's pretty tame, but we felt "cry" was a little fancy. So there's an awful lot to be said on a lot of sides.

We'll go by your decision, and so, once more, I'll hold onto the ms. until I hear from you again. And thanks for your help.

Best wishes,

Howard

Mr. Donald Hall
Eagle Pond Farm
Danbury, New Hampshire 03230

THE
NEW YORKER
25 WEST 43RD STREET
NEW YORK, N. Y. 10036

EDITORIAL OFFICES
OXFORD 5-1414

8 March 1977

Dear Donald,

Here is the author's proof of OX CART MAN. We'd like to have it back, corrected and signed, at your convenience.

Thanks again for this poem, and we look forward to others.

Best wishes,

Howard

Howard

Mr. Donald Hall
Eagle Pond Farm
Danbury, New Hampshire 03230